Penguin Special

War and an Irish Town

Eamonn McCann was born in Derry in 1943 and was educated at local Catholic schools. He became involved in left wing politics after going to Queen's University, Belfast in 1961, where he was Chairman of the Labour Group and President of the Union Debating Society. He left Queen's in 1965 without a degree and worked in London, mainly on building sites, until February 1968 when he returned to Derry and became involved in local radical politics. He helped to organize the first civil rights march in Derry in October 1968. He was a Labour candidate in the February 1969 Stormont elections, and was selected as Labour candidate for the June 1970 Westminster election for Derry constituency. His nomination was rejected by the Northern Ireland Labour Party executive because he refused to give a commitment to non-violence. He stood as an Independent Socialist, polling 7,500 votes.

He is a member of the International Socialists and a regular contributor to *Socialist Worker*. At present he divides his time between Derry and London, and is active in revolutionary politics.

Eamonn McCann

War and
an Irish Town

Penguin Books

Penguin Books Ltd, Harmondsworth,
Middlesex, England
Penguin Books Inc., 7110 Ambassador Road,
Baltimore, Maryland 21207, U.S.A.
Penguin Books Australia Ltd, Ringwood,
Victoria, Australia
Penguin Books Canada Ltd, 41 Steelcase Road West,
Markham, Ontario, Canada

First published 1974
Copyright © Eamonn McCann, 1974

Made and printed in Great Britain by
C. Nicholls & Company Ltd
Set in Linotype Pilgrim

This book is a development and an extension of a number of articles I wrote in the *Irish Times* and in *International Socialism* in 1971. It is an attempt to examine events in Ireland in the last five years from a Marxist viewpoint and to draw some conclusions. I put the conclusions forward tentatively, as a basis for discussion. I welcome comment and criticism from socialists.

Many of the events I write about involve 'crimes', most of which are 'unsolved'. It is not possible to deal with such events in full. Some incidents I have thought it proper not to refer to at all.

I have to thank Mary Holland for her unceasing help and encouragement.

Jeff Bell allowed me to read and to use his excellent history of the Protestant working class in Ulster, *This We Will Maintain*.

This book is dedicated to the memory of:

Samuel Devenney   Gerald McKinney
William King   William Nash
Joe Coyle   William McKinney
Tommy Carlin   James Wray
Tommy McCool   John Young
Seamus Cusack   Patrick Doherty
Desmond Beattie   Gerald Donaghy
Gerry Doherty   Jackie Duddy
Colm Keenan   Hugh Gilmore
Kevin McElhinney   Michael Kelly
Bernard McGuigan   Michael McDaid

John Johnston
Hugh Heron
John Starrs
Seamus Bradley
Daniel Hegarty
Billy McGreanery
Eamonn Lafferty
Manus Deery
Michael Quigley
John McGuinness
Kathleen Thompson
Eugene McGillen
Bernadette McCool
Carol McCool
Damian Harkin

Gerry Gormley
Annette McGavigan
James Casey
John Brady
James Carr
Tony Diamond
James O'Hagan
Junior McDaid
Frank McCarron
Charles McCafferty
Michael McGrinley
Charles Moore
Bernard Kelly
Gordon Gallagher
Kathleen Feeney

I finished writing this book a few months ago. Nothing which has happened since seems to conflict with my general analysis.

On 20 November the Unionist, Alliance and SDLP groups in the Northern Ireland Assembly agreed to form an Executive. This triggered the loudest brouhaha heard in Ireland since the Irish Problem was settled once and for all in 1922.

The Annual Conference of Official Sinn Fein (23–25 November) pledged uncritical support for the 'socialist countries' – a reference to the Soviet Union plus satellites – and decided that, reality notwithstanding, members should continue to fight for 'civil rights'.

Stories on the front page of this morning's *Derry Journal* tell that talks on the formation of a Council of Ireland will begin next week, and that the local Provos claim responsibility for the killing of two soldiers on Rossville Street on Sunday night.

Eamonn McCann *Derry, 27 November 1973*

An event has taken place of a magnitude scarce if at all inferior in importance to that of the French Revolution. The Pope is dethroned and in exile. The circumstances relating to this great event are such as to satisfy my mind that there is a special Providence guiding the affairs of Europe at this moment, and turning everything to the great end of the emancipation of mankind from the yoke of religion and political superstition, under which they have so long groaned. Some months ago, in the career of his victories, Buonaparte accorded a peace, and a generous peace, to the Pope; it was signed at Tolentine ... Many people thought at the time, and I was one of the number, that it was unwise to let slip so favourable an opportunity to destroy for ever the Papal tyranny. One would have thought that so narrow an escape might have prevented the Pope from rashly embarking into a second contest with the Republic, holding, as he did, his every existence dependent on the breath of Buonaparte, who might with a single word have annihilated him. But Providence, for its own wise and great purposes, the happiness of man, and the complete establishment of civil and religious liberty, seems to have utterly taken away all sense and understanding from the Pope and his councils ... The Roman people, assembled in the Capitol, formally deposed the Pope and declared themselves free and independent ... Two or three days after this the Pope left Rome ... Thus terminated the temporal reign of the Popes after an existence of above 1,000 years ... The Pope, who has often at his will and pleasure disposed of crowns and monarchs, is himself deposed without effort or resistance ... He is now Prelate *in partibus*, his means are gone, his cardinals, his court, his wealth, all disappeared, and nothing remains but his keys. It is a sad downfall for the 'servant of the servants of God'. But I will scorn to insult the old gentleman in his misfortune : *Requiescat in pace*.

– Wolfe Tone, the Father of Irish Republicanism, 1 March 1798

8

Part 1

When I was a very small boy we used to sing at passing Protestants:

> Proddy, proddy dick
> Your ma can't knit
> And your da
> Won't go to bed
> Without a dummy tit.

We might meet Protestants on the way to school because our school was outside the Bogside. No Protestant lived in the Bogside. The Unionist Party had seen to that. Not that the absence of Protestant neighbours was regarded by us as any deprivation. We came very early to our politics. One learned, quite literally at one's mother's knee, that Christ died for the human race and Patrick Pearse for the Irish section of it. The lessons were taught with dogmatic authority and were seemingly regarded as being of equal significance. Pearse ranked high in the teeming pantheon of Irish martyrdom. There were others. They had all died in the fight to free Ireland from British rule, a fight which had paused in partial victory in 1922 when twenty-six of our thirty-two counties won their independence. It was our task to finish the job, to cleanse the remaining traces of foreign rule from the face of Ireland.

No one was explicit as to how this would be done. Some said that Catholics, because of their higher birth-rate, would one day outnumber Protestants in the Six Counties and that we could then vote ourselves democratically into an all-Ireland republic. Vague confidence was occasionally expressed that eventually the Protestants themselves would re-discover their Irish national heritage. And there were always those who said that sooner or later we were going to have to fight for it. We recognized that it was not an immediately attainable object, that it was not going to happen tomorrow, but no one ever doubted that someday, somehow, it would come, and at moments of greater patriotic fervour we sang of it; that Ireland, long a province, would be 'a nation once again'.

We learned of the United Irishmen, the Fenian Movement, the Easter rising; of Emmet hanged, and Tone who had cut his throat in his cell to cheat the English executioner; of Connolly who was wounded in the leg and could not stand up so they strapped him to a chair to be shot; snatches from Pearse's speech at the grave of O'Donovan Rossa: 'The fools, the fools, the fools, they have left us our Fenian dead . . .' There were men in the area who embodied the tradition – Paddy Shiels, Neil Gillespie, Sean Keenan, Old Republicans who had fought in the past and been jailed and whose suffering represented a continued contribution from our community to the age-old struggle. They were regarded with guilty pride by the great majority as living out too urgently the ideals to which, tacitly, we were all committed. When Paddy Shiels died everyone said that he was a 'Great Irishman'.

Frankie Meenan was of the same stamp and always resented the fact that he had to speak English to make himself understood in the area. He ran classes in Gaelic for local children in a disused billiards hall in Chamberlain Street. Rows of children, few of whom would ever progress beyond primary school, would sit reciting in unison, '*Ta me, Ta tu, Ta se, Ta si* – I am, you are, he is, she is', and wrestling with the intricacies of the vocative case. Women in the street would ask Frankie: 'How's he getting on at the Irish?', to which he always replied: 'Oh, coming on, coming on'. Few ever became fluent, but it was felt right to make the effort. Frankie probably paid for the hire of the hall himself. He bought about thirty hurling sticks once and on Saturday mornings would take a crowd of us up to a field behind the Rosemount School, distribute the sticks and try to teach us the national game. The instructions were shouted in Irish,'*Anois, Buail e, buail e!*' and '*Ach, amadan, bloody amadan*' (Now hit it, hit it! Fool, bloody fool!) when one missed the ball completely for the *n*th time. There were always those who, privately, affected amusement at Frankie's activities, but no one openly denied him respect.

The Irish lessons and the hurling classes ended when Frankie was arrested one night in 1957. It was during the IRA's border campaign. He was coming home when a police car stopped and he was asked his name. He could have said, 'Frankie Meenan' but, being what he was, he said, '*Prionsias O'Mianain, ta me ag dul abhaile*' (I am going home), for which piece of bilingual impertinence he was taken to Crumlin Road jail in Belfast and held without trial for seven months. No one came out to riot about it – there was no point. He was released for his father's funeral and in an outburst of humanitarianism the then Minister of Home Affairs, Brian Faulkner, did not order his rearrest. Some months later Frankie went to live in Dublin.

What people like Frankie Meenan and Sean Keenan sought was not to be sneered at, but at the polls votes went to the Nationalist Party, who had a more realistic approach. My political cradle was rocked by Mr Eddie McAteer, Nationalist MP for Foyle until February 1969, who has, I believe, come to rue the day. I sat on a high chair in his election headquarters copying names and addresses from the electoral register on to his polling cards. Beside every name on the register was either an orange or a green mark. One was pleased to turn over and discover a page with a preponderance of orange marks. Such pages were easily done. Orange marks denoted Protestants, and Mr McAteer did not send polling cards to Protestants.

Mr McAteer was a scion of Derry's premier Republican

family. His brother, Hugh, had been chief-of-staff of the IRA and in 1941 had led a fabled escape from Belfast prison. The family connection did Eddie no political harm. He had a way with hecklers. At an election meeting in Cable Street once, he faced opposition from a small group noisily urging a boycott of the Stormont Parliament. From the back of the flat-bed lorry which served as a platform Mr McAteer surveyed them sadly and said: 'There are times when I weep for Mother Ireland,' which he then proceeded to do. Real tears coursed down his cheeks and, reaching up for the corner of the Tricolour which fluttered over the platform, he *dried his eyes on the national flag*. He won that election, of course. The Nationalist Party always did.

In the fifties and early sixties the only organized opposition came from *ad hoc* trade-union groups, which would put forward one of their number as an 'Independent Labour' candidate. Mr Stephen McGonagle, local organizer for the Irish Transport and General Workers' Union, made a number of such sorties into politics. When he did it was said, and widely believed, that he was a communist. Red paint was splashed on the front of his house in the middle of the night. Some suspected that it would be a mortal sin to vote for him. Actually, Mr McGonagle never had a communist thought in his life and in later years has been praised by industrialists and government ministers for his eminently reasonable approach to labour relations. But at the time the suspicion was powerful enough to deprive him of whatever remote chance of success he might have had. On election days Mr McAteer's loudspeaker cars would tour the Bogside blaring that 'The Protestants in Belmont are all voting for McGonagle', which was enough to clinch the matter.

The fear that it was possibly sinful to vote against the Nationalist Party was quite real. The party was closely associated with the church. Its basic unit of organization was not the electoral ward but the parish. The local parish priest would, in most cases automatically, be chairman of the convention called to select a candidate. Mr McAteer was once opposed by a man who had been defeated for the nomination at a convention chaired by Monsignor O'Doherty, parish priest of the Waterside, and who had refused to accept the convention's decision, alleging that the vote was rigged. It was said of him that not only would it be a sin to vote for him but that he himself, by standing, was guilty of sacrilege. Nationalist candidates were not selected; they were anointed.

Religion and politics were bound up together, were regarded, indeed, as being in many ways the same thing. The oppression against which the political heroes of the past had fought was, we learned, primarily oppression of the church. Children would be taken by their parents to see Father Hegarty's Rock, outside Buncrana in Donegal, and told how Father Hegarty had dived from there into Lough Foyle to escape from the Redcoats, how the Redcoats had shouted to him that he would be guaranteed safe passage if he came back, how they had bayoneted him to death when, believing them, he had returned to the shore. It probably happened. We knew all about the Penal Days, when Catholics were not allowed to become lawyers or doctors or to own a horse worth more than five pounds, when every priest had a price on his head and people were burned to death for going to mass. Masses had to be said away deep in the hills, the people gathered around flat rocks, 'altar rocks', with sentries posted to watch for the Redcoats. During the Famine the English had offered food to anyone who would agree to change his religion, but through it all the people stayed faithful. The most rousing hymn in our repertoire was 'Faith of our Fathers':

> Faith of our Fathers, living still,
> In spite of dungeon, fire and sword.

An essential part of the Irish Freedom for which patriots had fought through the centuries was, we understood, the freedom to be Catholic. Priests themselves had often taken up the sword to lead the people in the fight. 'Father Murphy from old Kilcormack' who had 'spurred up the rock with a warning cry' in 1798 was among the most celebrated.

And it was not only in Ireland that the church was persecuted. We learned of the massacres of clergy during the Mexican Revolution, the slaughter of priests and nuns by the communists during the Spanish Civil War, the martyrdom of missionaries in Africa and Latin America and of the continuing persecution behind the Iron Curtain. Cardinal Mindszenty of Hungary and Archbishop Stepinac of Yugoslavia were local heroes. The Hungarian Rising of 1956 was seen clearly as an attempt by the Hungarian people to end oppression of the church. Collections were taken up at all masses. There were tales of the dreadful tortures used against priests in Red China. Communism was seen as an international movement fanatically seeking to destroy the church. That, one gathered, was what communism was *about*. The church was persecuted everywhere. The fact that it had survived was proof positive of its divine mission.

Some of this one learned at home, a lot of it at school. The church controlled our education. At infants' school we were taught by nuns, who were kindly and dedicated. One learned the prayers and the catechism answers by rote, how to salute a priest in the street, and what to do if one was ever introduced to a bishop. The three Rs were not neglected, but there was never any doubt about the priorities. After infants' school everything was geared towards passing the 11-plus.

The 1947 Education Act made a great difference to places like the Bogside. It created an educational obstacle-course which, if one could negotiate it, opened the way to grammar school and even university education – and Catholics had no handicap. Those who passed went to St Columb's College. Catholic Derry is steeped in the influence of St Columb's. Almost every Catholic teacher, Catholic doctor,

Catholic solicitor, Catholic architect, accountant and businessman in the city was schooled there. The headmaster of a local intermediate school has no one on his staff whom he himself did not teach when he worked at St Columb's. Before the introduction of state scholarships St Columb's was the preserve of the Catholic middle class and, until the school got used to it, Bogsiders who arrived were made aware that they were intruding. Priest in a maths class: 'Where do you come from?' 'Rossville Street.' 'Oh yes, that's where they wash once a month.'

St Columb's described itself as a 'junior seminary' and one of its main functions was to supply candidates for the priesthood. Its other aim was to turn out upstanding Catholic citizens. About half the teachers were priests. Only the priests were eligible to become principal or vice-principal. Some of the priests interpreted their role in an eccentric fashion. Father D. could come into class and pick on a pupil in the front row: 'Kearney, think of a number.' 'Two, Father.' Then, starting with the boy sitting next to Kearney and counting: 'McLucas one, Patton two. Come out here, Patton.' Patton was given a beating with a strap and told, 'Don't blame me. Blame Kearney: he chose your number.' In later years Father D. explained that this was designed 'to encourage respect for your betters'. Dr M.'s favourite technique for inculcating love of the Latin language was to invite a boy to kneel on a platform in front of the class with hands stretched out in front and the feet, behind, raised off the ground. This is a very difficult thing to do. The boy was then made to open his mouth and a chalk duster inserted into it. If he fell forward on to his hands or relaxed backward so that his feet touched the ground he would be beaten around the head. Thus balanced precariously on the fulcrum of his knees and emitting animal grunts he would be invited to agree by a nodding of the head that he was a rogue, a ne'er-do-well, a stupid oaf who ought to be out digging roads and not wasting teachers' time and taxpayers' money here in St Columb's. Outside class Dr M.

walked quietly and read his breviary. He was said to be an extremely clever and a very saintly man. Not all techniques were quite so sophisticated. Father F. might simply knock a boy unconscious and tell two of his class-mates to 'cart him outside. I'm not having him here, lying about in my class-room.' These were exceptions, but exceptions which were tolerated, in no way regarded as outrageous. Had lay teachers behaved so, there might have been protest from parents, but one did not question the activities of priests.

History lessons did not always rigidly follow the curriculum laid down by the Northern Ireland Ministry of Education. One teacher, admittedly regarded as something of an eccentric, was at pains to discredit English propaganda, such as that which suggested that Charles Stuart Parnell and Mrs Kitty O'Shea had been anything more than good friends. At the beginning of a new school year he would lead the class through the set text-book instructing them to tear out passages of fiction, such as those alleging that the Papal States had played a reactionary role during the Risorgimento. That done, lessons could begin.

Between a quarter and a fifth of the students at St Columb's were boarders. They were the sons of farmers and rural businessmen from Donegal and Counties Derry and Tyrone, and they were reckoned to be altogether more solid and sturdy than the tatty products of the Bogside who went to dances at night and consorted secretly with females. The boarders all played Gaelic football. Everyone was supposed to play but most day-boys dodged it. The priests most of whom came from the same milieu as the boarders, were fanatical about the game and scornful of those whose distasteful origins placed them outside its fraternity. Which is not to say that the boarders had a good time. They were not allowed to go outside the school grounds and spent much of their free time walking around the paths in the grounds, which were known as 'the walks'. They did not have a great deal of free time anyway: there were four hours of compulsory study each evening.

Recreational facilities consisted of two gravel football pitches and two handball alleys. There was no gymnasium. Until the middle-fifties, all newspapers were banned. It was a punishable offence to possess a comic-book of any description or any book which had not been obtained from the school library. One was not allowed to have a radio on the premises. In so far as it could be organized and enforced, nothing alien was allowed to penetrate the defensive walls of the school grounds, nothing which might disrupt the educative process designed, in the words of Archbishop John Charles McQuaid, 'so to train the child entrusted to us that supernatural habits may become more firmly and more deeply rooted in its soul'.

One was taught to respect the authority of the church in all things. 'Catholic Social Science' provided a framework for industrial relations, of which 'doing a fair day's work' was a vital component. 'Catholic Apologetics' armed us with the answers to demolish anti-Catholic arguments from atheists, Protestants or any other errant individual. 'Church History' detailed the struggles of the church from the time of Christ to the present and proved the apostolic succession of the Pope. We were warned against 'modern errors' and told that undoubtedly we would come up against these in the future. In the late fifties Mr Bertrand Russell and his writings and activities were the subject of especial execration.

By 'ordinary' educational standards St Columb's was quite a successful school, yearly notching up the average number of state exhibitions and university scholarships. But this, one was told repeatedly, was by no means the only or most important aspect of its work. In the end we had been involved in an intellectual package deal, and had been given a complete set of ideas, attitudes and pieces of knowledge and urged to understand that these were

17

adequate to equip one for any human situation in which it was proper ever to find oneself. One sensed that it was suspected that we were not properly grateful. In our own area St Columb's boys were seen in a different light. We were the first generation ever given the opportunity to climb out of our condition, and much was expected of us.

The church's insistence on controlling the education of Catholic children affected not only those directly at the receiving end. Through the parish Building Fund it involved the whole community. The price of opting out of the state system was that the church authorities had to find thirty-five per cent of the cost of school buildings. In a depressed community with a high birth-rate and a thirst for education this was a considerable problem. It was answered with sales-of-work, jumble sales, Christmas bazaars, lotteries, Sunday night concerts, silver collections on the third Sunday of each month, pantomimes, door-to-door collections, and much else besides. All these required volunteer workers with high motivation. For some, the parish Building Fund became not so much a spare-time activity as a way of life. The collection of money and articles for sale and the selling of tickets for weekly functions kept every household in almost daily contact with the church, provided the occasion for constant, repeated renewal of commitment to it.

The intellectual diet served by the church, the schools and the Nationalist Party was supplemented by the local paper, although not to the extent of providing any variation. Everyone in the area read the *Derry Journal*. The *Journal* appeared thrice weekly until 1958, when it became a bi-weekly, published on Tuesdays and Fridays. The harmonizing voices of the church and the Nationalist Party spoke to us from its editorial columns. These were couched in a curious, florid style which may be peculiar to Irish provincial newspapers. The word 'forsooth' was commonly employed to indicate emphasis. The *Journal* was, and is, bitterly anti-Unionist, passionately pro-Fianna Fail, reverently Catholic and hysterically anti-communist. It never wrote 'Northern Ireland', always ' "Northern" Ireland'; never 'Londonderry', always ' "London" derry'. Even the punctuation was patriotic.

On religious matters the *Journal* spoke in the authentic tones of hierarchic authority. On the birth-control controversy arising out of the Second Vatican Council it followed the line of the Irish bishops, firmly aligned itself with the 'traditionalists' and expressed itself in traditional language:

Viewed in the perspective of the nineteen hundred years since the Church's foundation her present trial is by no means the first nor the greatest either that has beset her mission on earth. Though often wounded and at times deeply so by these ordeals, she emerged and remained as indestructible and resilient as when each tribulation had passed in its turn. And so it will assuredly be by her inbuilt guarantee of divine protection and durability to the end of time. The latest issue upon which the present successor of St Peter and inheritor of his mandate has given his judgement by virtue of the Apostolic and teaching authority vested in that succession, and therefore in his so weighty responsibilities in the Church and before God for the guidance of the fold, concerns no less fundamental subject than the transmission of life itself. (August 1968)

Editorials along such lines were not at all uncommon. Attention was frequently drawn to 'the moral filth that pollutes the cinema and TV screens ... Too much filth is seeping through the wide meshes of the censorship net and there is surely need for additional safeguards' (5 March 1963). The Campaign for Nuclear Disarmament was said to be 'a menace to national security'(19 April 1963). Irreligious materialism was relentlessly exposed.

What a sorry disillusionment has succeeded such as the Wellsian dreams and glowing prophecies earlier in this century of the millennium, the earthly paradise that was to be the outcome of the marvels of the new scientific and technological age in which the genius of man would be all-sufficient unto itself. (21 June 1968)

Mr Frank P. McCauley, who taught history at St Columb's, contributed a popular weekly column under the pseudonym 'Onlooker' in which he expressed conventionally wise attitudes to the problems of the day. Mr McCauley may be the last man in Europe still fighting the French Revolution. Without doubt there are a few people dotted around Europe – clustered, perhaps, in the Iberian peninsula – who regret that the French Revolution actually happened. Mr McCauley however, may well be the last *combatant*, drawing attention to the fact that scarlet women pranced déshabillé across the altar of Notre Dame and hinting that lack of vigilance on the part of Derry Catholics could easily result in the same thing happening in St Eugene's at the top of William Street. He was a keen-eyed and indefatigable opponent of red subversion. In the early sixties, for example, he was one of the first to discern its hand in the fashion for 'satirical' humour on television and in magazines. He was quick to notice also that 'anything Jewish is exempt from raillery and skit' (8 January 1962). He was a very influential man.

The views of the Hierarchy, and of our local bishop in particular, were given wide publicity in the *Journal*. The Lenten Pastoral, the keynote address of every new church year, was always front-page news. Their content resembled so closely the *Journal* editorial statements that many believed (wrongly, I think) that they flowed from the same pen. Press filth

is so widespread that unless you are on your guard even the best can become contaminated . . . The Catholic Church is faced with an enemy – Communism – determined on its destruction and using every diabolical method to destroy its influence. Whether you are at home or abroad you must take your place in the Church's line of defence . . . If you are a member of an organization where Communists may be hiddenly but actively working it is your duty to attend the meetings of these organizations and see that power is not placed in the hands of those who are active, if surreptitious Communist agents . . . You only have to look at the evil in the world today, and hear every day of trades disputes, stoppages of work, young people in revolt, to realize that the Christian way of life is not being put into operation.

Politically the *Journal* was the voice of the Nationalist Party, the owning family being prominent members of the organization. The sayings of Mr McAteer were faithfully recorded. The unity of Ireland was advocated, predicted and foreshadowed. A *Journal* pamphlet on 'Ireland's Fascist City' caught the note exactly: 'Certain it is that this panoplied, Gilbertian monstrosity of a statelet will perish in God's good time' (F. Curran, 'Ireland's Fascist City', p.3). The Catholicism of the area was not challenged from within, and it did not commonly come into contact, much less conflict, with antipathetic forces from without. (Very few, for example, read the local Protestant paper, the *Londonderry Sentinel.*) Ordinarily there was thus little fierceness in our expression of religion. We were never taught to hate Protestants. Rather we were taught to accept that it was for the best that we did not know them. We resented them, of course, in a generalized way. We resented the stubborn loyalism which stood in the way of our joining the South. We resented the fact that they controlled the Corporation even though we were in a majority in the city. We resented the fact that they discriminated against us in the allocation of houses and jobs. We resented their parading in Derry every 12 August, with their bands and banners and their purple collarettes, jigging through the city centre to celebrate the Siege of Derry and bellow renewed fealty to the glorious, pious and immortal memory of William III. They used to march along the city walls which beetle over Bogside, the ones who had come from outside, from Belfast and Antrim, even Glasgow and Liverpool, leaning over the ramparts to look down at us. Some of them threw pennies. We told one another to 'just ignore them'.

We had our own processions, though on nothing like the same scale, to commemorate the Easter Rising and, sometimes, on St Patrick's Day. Ours did not go through the centre of the city. There was a rigid, unwritten law that Catholics could not march within the city walls. The walls had a mystical significance for Protestants. It was the successful defence of them against the Catholic army of King James in 1689 that they came to celebrate every year and the continued inviolability of the still-unsullied Protestant patch within was fiercely asserted.

We knew that those who marched on 12 August looked on us with a mixture of hostility and fear. Sometimes the younger ones would sing down from the walls:

> Slaughter, slaughter, holy water,
> Slaughter the Papists one by one.
> We will tear them asunder
> And make them lie under
> The Protestant boys who follow the drum

before joining their contingents as the parade formed up.

Their sense of superiority was based on more than illusion. They *were* privileged. The lessons about the oppression of Irish Catholics were not academic.

They had jobs, for a start. At the moment, the male unemployed rate in the Bogside is about one third, which is usual. There was plenty of work for women in the shirt factories. Young men would emigrate to England at the age of eighteen or nineteen. There was scarcely a family without some son away. Between 1951 and 1961, for example, 12.6 per cent of the population left Derry. Those who stayed signed the dole twice a week and stood around the corner in the evening cursing the government. Many afternoons were spent in the bookies', studying form before risking the last few shillings. The Bogside was a bookmaker's paradise. Gambling, much more than drink, was the area's addiction. There were many men in the Bogside who knew off by heart the names of every horse which won a big race in England and Ireland for the last twenty years. There were not a few who knew as well the names of the jockeys, trainers and owners and what came second and third. Not, of course, that such encyclopedic knowledge was ever a match for the bookies' odds.

It was accepted that the Unionists were responsible for unemployment. New industries which came to Northern Ireland were directed to the Protestant centres to the east. Antrim, Larne, Ballymena and Lisburn had unemployment figures which were derisory by Derry standards. The Unionist tactic, we believed, was designed to compel a disproportionate number of Catholics to leave Northern Ireland and thereby to preserve the Protestant majority. It was not the whole story, but it contained a kernel of hard fact which made it rational to believe that Derrymen were sentenced to unemployment for the crime of being Catholics. There was no swelling outrage about it. It was the way things had been for as long as anyone could remember, and no one could see quite how it would be changed. One remembers the recession in Britain in the early sixties when the unemployment figures for north-eastern England crept dangerously close to five per cent and Lord Hailsham donned a cloth cap and made a safari to Sunderland to assure the local populace that they had not been forgotten. There was some comment in the area, resigned rather than bitter, that such a situation in our city would be greeted as economic paradise.

Men who were working were grateful for the fact. There was a theory that industrialists who had 'brought work to the town' were benefactors and ought to be treated as such. Militant trade unionism was a luxury which most workers calculated they could not afford: too many strikes and the owners might just close down and put everyone back on the dole.

The housing situation too was very bad and enmeshed in the complexity of the local government structure. Only householders could vote at local government elections. To give a person a house, therefore, was to give him a vote, and the Unionist Party in Derry had to be very circumspect about the people to whom it gave votes. It would have been political suicide for it to have given Catholics houses and votes outside the South Ward where most Derry Catholics were corralled. So houses were built on a bleak hill, Creggan, overlooking the Bogside, and after 1946 it gradually expanded, the spillage from the Bogside flowing uphill.

The housing allocation system was possibly unique. The Corporation, with its gerrymandered Unionist majority, elected a Unionist-controlled housing sub-committee each session. The housing sub-committee would then vote to delegate all its powers of allocation to the mayor. The mayor, on his own, allocated the houses. He was not required to report to the sub-committee or to the Corporation. The operation was completely secret. There were no set criteria to guide him. The only way to get a Corporation house, therefore, was to convince the mayor that you *ought* to get one, and members of his local Orange lodge were obviously better placed than Bogsiders to do this. One of the most common sights in Derry Guildhall was that of a gaunt woman from our area down with her children pleading with the mayor in the corridor : 'Please, Mr Anderson, we have been on the list for fifteen years.'

Since Catholics, who were in an overwhelming majority on the housing waiting list, were not 'eligible' for the estates outside the South Ward, houses in these were, for Protestants, very easy to come by. Or so it seemed to us. When building land in the South Ward began to run short the Corporation was faced with the problem of either housing Catholics in other wards or not housing them at all. It opted for the latter.

The problem was aggravated by the fact that we were a very fertile people. In 1964 the birth-rate was 31.8 per thousand, which is to be compared with the sparse contemporaneous performances of Sardinia (22.9) and Sicily (22.2). The 1961 census revealed that the natural annual increase in the population of Derry was 21.2 per 1000, against 11.5 for Northern Ireland as a whole and 5.7 for England and Wales. The same census showed that two fifths of the residents of the South Ward were under fifteen years. Eighty per cent of births in the city were Catholic. The population 'pyramid' for the area resembled that of a tropical 'third world' rather than a Western metropolitan country. It corresponded to that for Britain in the middle of the nineteenth, not the twentieth, century.

While the Bogside bulged with people, iron law decreed that insufficient houses be built and prevented those which were built being allocated fairly. Ours was a teeming, crumbling area of ugly, tiny, terrace houses, mean streets where men stood in sullen groups at the corner while their wives went out to work and children skipped to songs of cheerful hatred:

> Oh, St Patrick's Day will be jolly and gay,
> And we will kick all the Protestants out of the way.
> If that won't do
> We'll cut them in two
> And send them to hell with their
> Red, white and blue.

There was no revolutionary ferment arising from it all. Expectations were little higher than the reality. As long as the state existed there would be discrimination, and as long as there was discrimination we would suffer unemployment and slum housing. Everyone knew that. Demands were made, of course, that discrimination be stopped, but more for the record than in real hope of result. Mr McAteer would get up in Stormont and allege that Catholics were being treated very badly. A Unionist minister would reply that this was a lie; it never happened; and even if it did it was no more than Catholics deserved since they were all disloyal subversives; and, what was more, if the situation was reversed Catholics would do the same thing to Protestants. The matter would rest. The fact that the resultant miseries could be looked on as a price to be paid for remaining true to the national ideal made them more easily acceptable. Any concentration on economic reform, as opposed to pursuit of a united Ireland, appeared, in the light of that, to be near to national apostasy, as Mr McGonagle had discovered to his cost. 'We don't want their jobs and houses,' shouted a perorating Nationalist businessman to a cheering audience of Bogsiders at one of Mr McAteer's eve-of-the-poll rallies. 'We-want-our-Freedom!'

Nationalist feeling in the area achieved one of its periodic climaxes in 1951, when Mr de Valera came from Dublin to declare open a week of Gaelic games and cultural activities. The kerbstones were painted green, white and orange, and flags and bunting hung everywhere. When he came up Rossville Street in an open car the crowds surged forward and almost swamped him, waving their arms, delirious, cheering, laughing, and jumping up on one another's shoulders to be sure to see him. Women craned precariously out of upstairs windows waving handkerchiefs, frantic, screaming 'Dev, Dev, Dev!' He who had fought in 1916, the last living leader of the single most glorious episode in all our history, was come here among us, and for a day at least all care was quite forgotten. Everybody said afterwards that it was the greatest day there had ever been in Derry. That was the measure of our Bogside innocence, that the old Fagin of the political pickpockets could, by his mere presence, excite such uncensorious fervour.

Part 2

...

Most accounts of the current trouble in Northern Ireland begin at 5 October 1968, which is as good a date to start from as any other. It was the day of the first civil rights march in Derry. Had all those who now claim to have marched that day actually done so, the carriageway would have collapsed. It was a small demonstration, perhaps four hundred strong – and a hundred of these were students from Belfast. Most of the rest were teenagers from the Bogside and Creggan. The march was trapped between two cordons of police in Duke Street and batoned into disarray.

The march had been organized by a loose group of radicals who had been trying for months, with some success, to create general political mayhem in the city. Those involved were drawn mainly from the local Labour Party and the James Connolly Republican Club. In March they and some others had organized themselves, if that is not too strong a word, into the Derry Housing Action Committee, which set out with the conscious intention of disrupting public life in the city to draw attention to the housing problem. The DHAC introduced itself to the public by breaking up the March meeting of Londonderry Corporation. We invaded the public gallery of the council chamber with banners and placards and demanded that we be allowed to participate in the meeting. The mayor naturally refused, and made it clear that he was not going to tolerate hooliganism in the chamber. From the Nationalist benches Alderman James Hegarty voiced the opinion that we were 'under the control of card-carrying members of the Communist Party'. Eventually the meeting had to be adjourned. The police were

27

called and we were ejected. There was wide publicity in the Irish papers. It was a very successful demonstration. We repeated it at the April and May meetings of the Corporation.

The Housing Action Committee had immediate internal problems. It started with about twenty members. It split twice during the first few months of its existence. One group broke away because it was 'too political', another because it was not political enough. Its first chairman, Matt O'Leary, resigned during the summer after a series of seemingly trivial rows. But through it all the Committee's campaign continued to gather momentum. Its strength was that, unlike the opposition groups which hitherto had had a monopoly of anti-Unionist politics in the city, the HAC gave people something to *do*, even if it was only kicking the mayor's car as he fled under police escort from another abandoned meeting of the Corporation, and thus it managed to siphon in behind it some of the gathering frustration of the Bogside and Creggan. And the decision to select the Corporation as the primary target and to set about the systematic disruption of its business was in itself a minor political masterstroke.

The gerrymandered Corporation was the living symbol in Derry of the anti-democratic exclusion of Catholics from power. The stated reason for our activities in the gallery was to highlight the housing situation, but they were generally regarded by Catholics as an attack on the whole political set-up; which, of course, they were. There were many in the Bogside who did not approve of our 'extremism' and were nervous of our 'communistic ideas' – but there were none who would defend the Corporation. In that sense it was the safest of safe targets. After the mayor abandoned his chair and adjourned one Corporation meeting, Finbar Doherty vaulted from the public gallery into the chamber, installed himself in the mayoral chair, declared himself First Citizen and issued a number of decrees. Finbar was a passionate Republican, much given to violent rhetoric. He was five feet tall, with double-lens glasses. It can be doubted whether more than a tiny percentage of the people would, given the chance, have actually voted for him as mayor, but there were very few in our area who failed to smile when they heard of the incident.

By early summer the group around the Housing Action Committee was beginning to be seen as a real challenge to the Nationalist Party in the Catholic working-class areas of the city. There was much muttering about communists and on Easter Sunday the bishop had abjured young people not to allow themselves 'to be led by the mob'. The campaign of disruption was also bringing to the surface differences within both the Labour and Republican movements in the city. The local Labour Party was a branch of the Northern Ireland Labour Party, an eminently respectable body based on a markedly timid trade-union bureaucracy. Its local leaders were sternly disapproving of members roughing up the mayor. One of the party's stalwart moderates, Mr Harry Doherty, warned a branch meeting around this time that 'I can detect left-wing ideas creeping into this party'. More than that, there was vigorous opposition to any liaison with Republicans. The Labour Party prided itself – publicly and often – on the fact that it bridged the sectarian barrier and had in its ranks both Protestant and Catholic workers. Protestants, it was said, would be frightened off by the mere mention of Republicanism. Mr Ivan Cooper – now a member of the SDLP but then the best-known Labour Party personality in the city – demanded the expulsion of any member who appeared on a platform with Republicans, 'especially with that fool Finbar Doherty'.

The situation within the local Republican movement was almost the exact obverse. Older members of the movement, exponents of 'pure' Republicanism, objected to cooperation with members of the 'partitionist' Labour Party. They were, anyway, angry at concentration on what seemed to them to be short-term bread-and-butter issues to the neglect of the 'national ideal'.

The issues were never fully resolved in either organization. The *ad hoc* alliance between the left of the Labour Party and the left of the Republican Club continued, and continued to be frowned on by both local party establishments. But the leftists involved carried out no clear political struggle within either organization. We could not, because what we shared was not a common programme but a general contempt for the type of politics which prevailed in the city.

The only attempt to codify our ideas was made in May, when a 'perspectives document' was prepared by Labour leftists:

The situation which confronts us is not promising. The great mass of the people continue, for historical reasons, to see religion, not class, as the basic divide in our society. This sectarian consciousness is reinforced, week in, week out, by local Tory newspapers. The machinations of Catholic and Protestant Tories such as McAteer, Glover, Anderson, and Hegarty are carefully calculated to maintain the *status quo*. The end result is a working class which is unresponsive to socialist ideas...

We must ask ourselves whether the Labour Party itself is adequate to the needs of this situation. We, like all branches of the Labour Party, have operated along conventional lines – putting our personalities and our policies before the people at elections, issuing intermittent statements on current events, attempting to recruit more members and to perfect the party machine. Most parties operate so...

People in Derry are worried about housing and jobs and the denial of civil rights. The question before us is: how best can the discontent arising from each issue be gathered together and directed against the root cause – i.e. the political and economic set-up?

One of the basic difficulties arises out of the present division of the working class along religious lines. Many Protestant workers in Derry feel that they are members of a vaguely privileged section of the population (as, in one sense, they are). As a result, despite the economic situation of the area, they are resistant to change. Many of the Catholic workers interpret the bulk of Governmental activity as being to some extent directed against them *as Catholics*. Thus, they are 'easy meat' for the adroit demagogy of the McAteers and Hegartys.

To dispel this confusion we will have to engage in patient grass-root organization on the concrete issues affecting the working class in its day to day life. This means participating actively in the developing tenants' movement in the city, attempting to reorganize the unemployed, participating *as a party* in such activities as protests against the banning of Republican Clubs, etc. *The party, in a phrase, should go to the people rather than attempt to attract the people towards it.*

Housing agitation provides a good example of what the party could be doing. While most people, as individuals, feel alienated from such remote institutions as the Housing Trust, they are actively worried about such questions as the awarding of rehabilitation grants, the operation of the Rent Rebate Scheme and the need for a faster rate of redevelopment. These are concrete and specific grievances all of which are *capable* of a relatively short-term solution. Around these it would be possible by door to door campaigning to build up an active housing movement in the city. . .

Similarly with the unemployment; we cannot hope immediately to make the Labour Party the focus of the desire for work. We can, however, assist the re-emergence of an unemployed action committee and thus heighten the general level of political militancy . . .

It can do this by declaring publicly its unequivocal support for the aims and activities of such organizations by co-ordinating and giving direction to its members who would be active in them: by attempting through the activity of its members gradually to politicize such struggles : by assuming a quasi-educational function in tracing the connection between the political system and bad housing, unemployment and the negation of democracy.

All this would require an act of political faith on the part of us all, from party leaders downward, faith in ourselves and in socialist ideals and ideology. *It would mean that we have no enemies, only arguments, on the left,* that we should have confidence in our politics and state them openly without regard to what Tory-influenced sections we might annoy : that we should wage at every level an uncompromising anti-Tory crusade.

Such a party would have a real hope of becoming, eventually, the natural repository for the aspirations of the discontented.

Insofar as we had a perspective, that was it. There were frequent discussions around the points in the document in various pubs and houses during the summer. These were attended by Johnnie White, Liam Cummins and Finbar Doherty from the Republican Club; Charlie Morrison, Dermie McClenaghan and myself from the Labour Party; Matt O'Leary of the Housing Action Committee; Eamonn Melaugh, a free-wheeling radical who had ten children and a bizarre vocabulary; and a few others. Little came of these discussions. There was always too much to do, because one of the results of our having made an initial impact was that people came in a constant stream with problems to be solved: people who wanted houses or wanted repairs done to houses, people who believed – correctly, almost always – that they were getting less than their full entitlement from Social Security, people who were in trouble with rent arrears. It seemed to them that the much publicized and more aggressive tactics we had brought to bear on the Corporation might avail them better than the official channels.

Indeed, up to then people did not use even the official channels for complaint. They knew that they were being treated badly and believed that there was little anyone could do to stop it. We began squatting people in empty houses, of which there were a considerable number in the area, in each case issuing statements that we would 'physically resist' any attempt to evict the family involved. Private landlords charging exorbitant rents were picketed. The local office of the Northern Ireland Housing Trust was subjected to a daily barrage of phone calls and personal visits about the cases of individual families on the housing list. We confronted landlords and officials with more aggression than they had ever met before. Dermie McClenaghan, on being told that the Housing Manageress was too busy to see him, said quietly (he always spoke quietly) that if she did not see him at once he would return with 'a gang of hooligans' and smash the office up. Electricity Department officials, come to cut off the supply from a Creggan woman who could not pay the bill, were, after a long argument during which a crowd gathered, told that the first man to put his foot over the threshold would be shot. In almost all such cases our tactics were successful. This was very satisfying, but it took a lot of time which meant that often we resembled a rather violent community welfare body rather than a group of revolutionaries. Any perspective of building a clear-minded political organization in opposition to the dominant tendencies within the Labour or Republican movements was forgotten in the frenetic round of breaking into empty houses, organizing pickets and encouraging individuals to stand up to the landlords and local bureaucrats. And, anyway, such activities seemed to be bearing some fruit. There was a feeling gathering in the area that, however unacceptable our political ideas might be, we were at least getting things done. This in turn encouraged us to believe vaguely that we must be making *some* political progress.

At the beginning of June Dermie McClenaghan discovered John Wilson. Mr Wilson was living with his wife and two children in a tiny caravan parked up a mucky lane in the Brandywell district. The caravan was an oven in the summer, an icebox in the winter. One of the children had tuberculosis. Mr Wilson had been told by the Corporation Housing Department that he had 'no chance' of a house. Mr Wilson's case was tailor-made. On 22 June, a Saturday, about ten of us manhandled the Wilsons' caravan on to Lecky Road, the main artery through the Bogside, and parked it broadside in the middle of the road, stopping all traffic. We distributed leaflets in the surrounding streets explaining that we intended to keep the caravan there for twenty-four hours as a protest against the Wilsons' living conditions and calling for support. We then phoned the police, the mayor and the newspapers, inviting each to come and see. The mayor did not come. We expected that the police would try to arrest us, or at least to move the caravan to the side of the road. But they merely looked and left.

We stood guard on the caravan all night, equipped with a loud-hailer with which we intended to try to rouse the district if the police made a move. But nothing happened. On the Sunday we hauled the caravan back to its original parking place. We had about two hundred supporters with us on the return journey. Reports of the incident were carried with some prominence in the Irish Sunday newspapers and on local radio and TV. We announced that next weekend we would repeat the performance, this time for forty-eight hours. During the next week we were visited by policemen who explained, almost apologetically, that if we went through with this they would 'have to take action', which greatly encouraged us. On the Wilson issue we now knew that if we were arrested we would have strong support in the area. The facts had been given wide publicity and no one could deny that a great injustice was being done. Few, therefore, could openly oppose vigorous protest against it. If we could force the police to act against us we could be certain of an upsurge of sympathy which would further weaken the Nationalist grip on the area.

We lugged the caravan on to the road again the following Saturday and waited up two nights for the police onslaught. But again nothing happened. We dragged it back to its laneway and resolved next week to take it into the city centre. Before the week was out the Wilsons had been guaranteed a house and ten of us had been summoned to appear in court for contravening the Road Traffic Act (N.I.), 1951. It was a perfect ending.

It had very publicly been made clear that outrageous tactics worked, that blocking roads worked better than an MP's intervention — if the latter worked at all. The court proceedings provided us with a platform; fines and suspended sentences conferred on us an aura of minor martyrdom. At the first meeting of the Housing Action Committee after the court hearing we really began to believe ourselves when we said that we had the Nationalist Party on the run.

On 3 July the mayor, Councillor William Beattie, was scheduled to declare open a new lower-deck carriageway across the River Foyle. The opening was to take the curious form of Councillor Beattie's ceremonially *walking* across the bridge. It was too good a chance to miss and, sure enough, as soon as he set off seven young men sat down in his path displaying placards, some of which bore the pardonably exaggerated legend 'Hitler–Franco–Beattie'. Finbar Doherty intervened and, as he was seized by plain-clothes detectives, burst into 'We shall overcome'. No one joined in. As yet they did not know the words. Two of the seven, Roddy Carlin and Neil O'Donnell, refused to sign bonds to keep the peace and instead went to jail for a month. The result was more press statements, more publicity and a further noticeable increase in what appeared to be our political support.

By this time our conscious, if unspoken, strategy was to provoke the police into over-reaction and thus spark off mass reaction against the authorities. We assumed that we would be in control of the reaction, that we were strong enough to channel it. The one certain way to ensure a head-on clash with the authorities was to organize a non-Unionist march through the city centre. We decided to march in commemoration of the centenary of the birth of James Connolly. A 'James Connolly Commemoration Committee' was called into being, with Finbar Doherty as chairman, and a route through the city centre was submitted to the RUC. The march, on 21 July, was to end with a rally in the Guildhall Square. Mr Gerry Fitt, Miss Betty Sinclair, leading communist and chairman of the Northern Ireland Civil Rights Association, and Connolly's son Roddy were invited to speak, along with three of our own number. When the order banning the march was served it found the

Committee in complete disarray. A dispute as to whether the Irish Tricolour should be carried at the head of the procession had reached deadlock. Some of the Republicans said that they would not march without it. To do so would be an insult to the memory of Connolly. For the same reason others said that they would not march with it. The march was abandoned in a welter of recrimination. The rally went ahead and was a significant success. About a thousand people attended. The Nationalist Party was strongly attacked. Mr Fitt said that he regretted the decision not to defy the ban. It was immediately suggested to him from the crowd that he should now lead the people through the city walls and into the outlawed Diamond. Mr Fitt did not answer the call. The *Derry Journal* said that Connolly's memory had been 'poorly served' by the event.

The Nationalist Party was now running very scared indeed. We made our regular appearance at the next meeting of the Corporation. In March we had come thirty strong. Now we overflowed the council chamber out into the foyer of the Guildhall building and into the street. Before the meeting was abandoned Alderman Hegarty declared in stirring fashion that he was renouncing the party pledge to cooperate with Unionist members. The public gallery reacted to this announcement with a mixture of applause and shouts of 'hypocrite', there being different levels of consciousness present. And others were coming round. In the foyer outside Ivan Cooper closed a speech by paying tribute to 'the great work being done by Finbar Doherty'. The police formed a cordon to allow the mayor to make a getaway. On leaving the Guildhall Eamonn Melaugh phoned the Civil Rights Association and invited them to come and hold a march in Derry.

The CRA had organized a march – the first civil rights march in Northern Ireland – from Coalisland to Dungannon in August to protest against discriminatory housing allocations in that area. About four thousand had marched, and it passed off peacefully despite being prevented by the

RUC from reaching its objective, Dungannon market square.

A delegation from the executive of the Civil Rights Association came to Derry to discuss the project with us. The CRA had no branch in Derry. At that point it had few branches anywhere. We met in a room above the Grandstand Bar in William Street. Melaugh, as the man who had thought of the idea, delivered a pep-talk before we went in to meet the delegation : 'Remember, our main purpose here is to keep our grubby proletarian grip on this jamboree.' It was good advice. It was immediately clear that the CRA knew nothing of Derry. We had resolved to press for a route which would take the march into the walled centre of the city and expected opposition to this from moderate members of the CRA. But there was none. No one in the CRA delegation understood that it was unheard of for a non-Unionist procession to enter that area. The route we proposed – from Duke Street in the Waterside, across Craigavon Bridge, through the city walls and into the Diamond – was accepted without question. The CRA proposed that all political organizations in the city – including the Unionist Party – should be invited to attend. We argued down the proposed invitation to the Unionists, but accepted that the Nationalists should be asked. We knew that the invitation would put them in a very embarrassing position. If they accepted they would be seen as coming in *behind* us – a demeaning position for the elected representatives of the people. If they refused we could denounce them as deserters. It was agreed that in the absence of a CRA branch a committee – to be called the Ad-hoc CR Committee – should be set up with one representative from each supporting organization to attend to local details. 5 October was selected as the date for the march because we thought, wrongly as it turned out, that Derry City Football Club was playing away that Saturday.

In the end only five organizations committed themselves far enough to nominate a representative onto the Ad-hoc

Committee. It consisted of Johnnie White (Republican Club), Eamonn Melaugh (Housing Action Committee), Finbar Doherty (James Connolly Society), Dermie McClenaghan (Labour Party Young Socialists), and Brendan Hinds (Labour Party). It was suspected that the James Connolly Society existed mainly in Finbar's mind. The Young Socialists was the Labour Party under another name. Brendan Hinds was a local shop-steward of intermittent militancy who called everyone 'kid' and had a penchant for talking in aphorisms, a characteristic which was subsequently to unsettle many a television interviewer's style. ('Mr Hinds, can you explain the background to these riots?' 'Idle hands throw stones, kid.')

The Ad-hoc Committee never functioned. It was not clear who was to convene it, and less clear what authority it had, if any, to make decisions without reference to the CRA in Belfast. By mid-September Eamonn Melaugh and I had taken effective control. We issued press statements daily, successively under the name of each of the five supporting organizations, calling for 'a massive turn-out', 'a gigantic demonstration', and so on. We churned out leaflets on a duplicator owned by the Derry Canine Club, the chairman of which had a son in the Labour Party, went flyposting at night, and made placards. None of the placards demanded 'civil rights'. We were anxious to assert socialist ideas, whether or not the CRA approved. We used slogans such as 'Class war, not Creed war', 'Orange and Green Tories Out', 'Working Class Unite and Fight!' The intention was to draw a clear line between ourselves and the Nationalist Party, to prevent pan-Catholic unity. We understood in general terms that the Nationalist Party, if we did not clearly differentiate ourselves from it, might be able to assume control of whatever movement arose out of 5 October, and no movement with the Nationalist Party at or near its head could hope ever to cross the sectarian divide.

During the previous months we had managed to make

contact with some Protestants from the Fountain, a small working-class area which abutted the Bogside. They too had their housing problems, mostly concerned with hold-ups in a redevelopment scheme, and a few of them had approached us suggesting that we devote some of our agitations to their cases. This we had done, heartened that our non-sectarian intentions had been accepted. We knew that none of our Protestant contacts was going to march on 5 October – that would have been too much to expect – but we had real hope that the socialist movement we were going to build after, and partly as a result of, the march would engage Protestant support.

We had no doubt that 5 October was going to be a very significant day. (After the meeting at which the CRA had accepted our route Melaugh had remarked: 'Well, that's it. Stormont is finished.') For six months we had been making steady and seemingly inexorable progress. We began as a small, disparate group and by simple direct action tactics we had month by month accumulated support. Despite all splits, confusions and inefficiencies everything that we did seemed to turn out right. Now we were in control of an event which was seriously perturbing the government and exciting concerned editorials in the Belfast papers.

There seemed no reason to suppose that 5 October would not be our most significant advance to date. There were one or two problems. The CRA was a liberal body with no pretensions to revolutionary politics. But then we were paying little attention to them. Their sponsorship of the march was nominal. We had no common political organization. But this had proved no real drawback in the last six months. Indeed the absence of organization, the fact that we rarely sought formal approval of our actions from the Labour Party, the Republican Club or anyone else, appeared to have been a positive advantage. The decision to block a road with John Wilson's caravan, for example, had been taken in the name of the HAC at a street corner by Matt

O'Leary, Dermie McClenaghan and me within a few hours of Mr Wilson's contacting Dermie. And that had worked out very well.

Under the Public Order Act two people had to sign a document notifying the police of the route of the march, thus assuming legal responsibility for it. The CRA, in pursuit of respectability, approached Councillor James Doherty, businessman and chairman of the Nationalist Party, and John Hume, a factory manager who was prominent in the Credit Union Movement. Both refused pointblank. Two members of the CRA itself signed instead.

A week before 5 October the march had still not been banned. In an effort to force the issue Melaugh and I issued a statement saying that the march would go on 'despite any undemocratic ban which might be imposed'. It was 3 October before the government rose to the bait and orders prohibiting the march, signed by Home Affairs Minister William Craig, were delivered in the late afternoon to Melaugh, Johnnie White, Finbar Doherty and me. The ostensible reason for the ban was that the Apprentice Boys had given notice of a march over the same route at the same time. We phoned the CRA and Mr McAteer. The CRA said that they would meet that night. Mr McAteer advised us to postpone the march for a week.

A CRA delegation came to Derry on the Friday night. At a meeting in the City Hotel they announced that the march was cancelled. In anticipation of this Hinds and McClenaghan were already touring the Bogside and Creggan with a loudspeaker car holding off-the-cuff street-corner meetings appealing to people to 'come out tomorrow and show your contempt for the law'. For two hours the CRA representatives explained to us that it was their march, it was they who had formally notified the police, and that they, therefore, were the only people with authority to decide whether or not it should go ahead. We explained that we were marching anyway. It was some time before the Belfast delegation grasped the central point that they had no means of stopping us marching. Their opposition collapsed when one of their number, Frank Gogarty, broke ranks and announced that 'if the Derry people are marching I'm marching with them'.

We expected about five thousand people to turn out. There had, after all, been four thousand at Dungannon. Our calculation all along had been that a ban would encourage thousands of outraged citizens who would not otherwise have marched to come and demonstrate their disgust. Gerry Fitt arrived from Blackpool, where the Labour Party conference was in session, bringing three Tribunite MPs with him as 'observers'. Our loudspeaker van toured the streets from early morning with Hinds at the mike informing the populace that 'when you gotta go, you gotta go and we gotta go today'. Police reinforcements poured into the city, and there were rumours that there were 'dozens' of Alsatian dogs in the Waterside police station.

Commentators afterwards were unanimous that the imposition of a ban had indeed doubled the number of marchers. If this is so, then without the ban the turn-out would have been pathetic indeed. About four hundred people formed up in ranks in Duke Street. About two hundred stood on the pavement and looked on. It was a very disappointing crowd. People may have been deterred not by the ban but by the expectation of violence. And our somewhat melodramatic advance publicity had probably done little to reassure them. The march would proceed, we had said, 'come hell or high water', and the overwhelming majority of people in the Bogside and Creggan were not yet ready for either. Moreover, the whole route of our march lay outside the Catholic ghetto. We were to learn in time that when organizing a march towards confrontation it is essential to begin in 'home' territory and march out, so that there is somewhere for people to stream back to if this proves necessary.

On the day, however, numbers soon became irrelevant. Our route was blocked by a cordon of police and tenders drawn up across the road about three hundred yards from the starting point. We marched into the police cordon but failed to force a way through. Gerry Fitt's head was bloodied by the first baton blow of the day. We noticed that another police cordon had moved in from the rear and cut us off from behind. There were no exits from Duke Street in the stretch between the two cordons. So we were trapped. The crowd milled around for a few minutes, no one knowing quite what to do. Then a chair was produced and Miss Betty Sinclair got up and made a speech. She somewhat prematurely congratulated the crowd on its good behaviour and advised everyone to go home peacefully. Mr McAteer and Mr Cooper spoke along similar lines. Austin Currie, Nationalist MP for East Tyrone, was much less explicit about peace. I made a speech which was later to be characterized by the magistrates' court as 'incitement to riot'. It was an unruly meeting. Our loudspeaker had been seized by the police and it was difficult to make ourselves heard. Some of the crowd were demanding action. 'There must be no violence,' shouted Miss Sinclair, to a barrage of disagreement. But the decision as to whether there would be violence was soon taken from our hands.

The two police cordons moved simultaneously on the crowd. Men, women and children were clubbed to the ground. People were fleeing down the street from the front cordon and up the street from the rear cordon, crashing into one another, stumbling over one another, huddling in doorways, some screaming. District Inspector Ross McGimpsie, chief of the local police (now promoted), moved in behind his men and laid about him with gusto. Most people ran the gauntlet of batons and reached Craigavon Bridge, at the head of Duke Street. A water cannon – the first we had ever seen – appeared and hosed them across the bridge. The rest of the crowd went back down Duke Street, crouched and heads covered for protection from the police, ran through side streets and made a roundabout way back home. About a hundred had to go to hospital for treatment.

In the evening the lounge of the City Hotel looked like a casualty clearing station, all bandaged heads and arms in slings. In a corner Miss Sinclair was loudly denouncing the 'hooligans and anarchists' who had provoked the police and 'ruined our reputation'. Later there was sporadic fighting at the edges of the Bogside which lasted until early morning. Police cars were stoned, shop windows smashed and a flimsy, token barricade was erected in Rossville Street. A few petrol bombs were thrown. By the next morning, after the television newsreels and the newspaper pictures, a howl of elemental rage was unleashed across Northern Ireland, and it was clear that things were never going to be the same again. We had indeed set out to make the police over-react. But we hadn't expected the animal brutality of the R U C.

The Bogside was deluged with journalists. Some spent their time trying to identify a local Danny the Red. (The May events in France were fresh in the memory.) Others wandered into the area and asked to be introduced to someone who had been discriminated against. A lady journalist from the *Daily Mail* came to my front door asking for the name and address of an articulate, Catholic, unemployed slum-dweller she could talk to. Derry was big news. The prime minister, Captain Terence O'Neill, delivered a liberal homily appealing for moderation and restraint. Mr Craig praised the police for their tactful handling of the affair. Eamonn Melaugh, Finbar Doherty and I were arrested on Sunday afternoon and charged with contravention of the Public Order Act.

We had a mass movement, but no organization. The Housing Action Committee was obviously inadequate in the new situation. We called a meeting of 'the local organizers' for Tuesday night in the City Hotel. The index of our political and organizational chaos was that, having called

43

the meeting, we were not at all certain who would have the right to attend. At the time that did not seem very important. We would as always muddle through. All seemed to be going according to plan – insofar as there was a plan. At a stroke we had shaken the government, fatally undermined the Nationalist Party in the city and made Derry world news. Who needed organization? Who needed theory? About fifteen people attended, the 'regulars' plus Ivan Cooper and a few members of the Labour Party and the Republican Club who had not until then played a very prominent part. It was agreed that we should march again the next Saturday over roughly the same route. We forecast a turn-out of ten thousand people. Ivan Cooper and Johnnie White agreed to sign the document notifying the police of our intention.

Another meeting was called in the City Hotel for Wednesday night. It was not, and still is not, clear who had organized it. But word got around during the afternoon that 'all interested parties' were meeting to 'consider the situation'. In the nature of things there was no mechanism whereby our loose group could convene itself and arrive at a joint attitude to this. Some of us met in the foyer of the City Hotel in the evening and decided to attend the gathering, see who was there and perhaps participate in the meeting. We agreed, too, that nothing the gathering decided could be binding on us. In the room upstairs there were about a hundred and twenty people. The Catholic business community, the clergy, the professions, trade-union officialdom and the Nationalist Party were well represented. In the event I took the chair, flanked by McClenaghan and Johnnie White, and told the meeting that we, the organizers of the march, would be interested in what they had to say. Various speakers congratulated us on the marvellous work we had done over the past few months. A few expressed their regrets, apologies etc. that they had not 'been as active in the past as I would have liked'. All urged that we now all work together. Finally it was proposed that the meeting elect a number of people who, together with the original organizers, would constitute a new committee. I explained that the meeting could elect anything it wished as long as it understood that the 'original organizers', as they had come to be called, would make up their own minds what status, if any, to accord those elected. Eleven people were elected from the floor and the meeting closed.

There followed immediately a short, bitter row between myself and the four other 'original organizers' who were present. I argued that we should immediately walk out, leaving the eleven persons just 'elected' to their own devices. 'Without us they have no credibility. Why should we give it to them?'

White, McClenaghan, Hinds and Melaugh countered that we should join with these eleven, reasoning that since we held the initiative we would be able to force the pace, drag some of them along in our wake and force the others quickly to resign. (Finbar Doherty, who had not heard that the meeting was taking place, was absent.) In a fit of either pique or principle I then stomped out and denounced the persons elected at the meeting as 'middle-aged, middle-class and middle of the road'. The other four stayed behind and joined in a meeting of the new, expanded body.

The organization called itself the Citizens Action Committee. It immediately elected five officers. They were: chairman, Ivan Cooper; vice-chairman, John Hume; secretary, Michael Canavan, owner of a chain of bookmaker's shops, a pub and a salmon-processing factory; treasurer, Councillor James Doherty; press officer, Campbell Austin, Liberal-Unionist and owner of the biggest department store in the city. It was a far cry from the *ad hoc* committee of five days previously. The Committee's first action was to call off the march scheduled for the following Saturday.

The Committee arranged a sit-down in Guildhall Square for 19 October. Campbell Austin resigned in protest. About five thousand people came on a wet day and sat down in the square to hear speeches. The emotional and political keynote was set by Paddy Doherty, a tough-minded and rigorously honest right-winger, when he asked the crowd, rather in the manner of a retreat priest inviting the congregation to renounce the devil:

'Are you, the people of this city, irresponsible?'
'No' thundered the fervent reply.
'Are you, the people of this city, communists?'
'No!'
'Are you, the people of this city, under the influence of any political organization?'
'No!'
'Will there be bloodshed in this city tonight?'
'No!'
'Thank God!'

A local solicitor, Claude Wilton, the usually unpaid advocate of every Bogsider in trouble, appealed to us to 'Forget the past and live together for the future. I ask you to treat every person fairly and give employment fairly, provided always that you have your fundamental rights.' John Hume conducted the singing of 'We shall overcome'. All joined in the chorus.

It was that kind of meeting. The Citizens Action Committee declared at the outset that it was a 'non-political' body. It renounced violence. Its watchword was 'Anti-Unionist unity'. No speech from its platforms was complete without a declaration of pacifist intent and an appeal for 'the unity of all our people'. Unity was impressively demonstrated when fifteen thousand people assembled in Duke Street on 16 November to try again to march to the city centre. Craig had now banned all demonstrations within the city walls. The march faced a police cordon on Craigavon Bridge, and hundreds of stewards held back the younger and more aggressive elements who wanted to fight their way through. After a thirty-minute stand-off which threatened at any moment to erupt into the biggest riot seen in Derry in living memory, the crowd surged around the police cordon, which, perhaps with some foresight, was so positioned as to leave open an alternative route into the city centre, and made its way to the Diamond. The meeting was held in the outlawed area. This was considered a famous victory and it established the CAC as the unchallengeable leaders of anti-Unionism in Derry.

The CAC's sudden strength did not lie in its having committed the Catholic masses to a new political programme. Its strength was that in a sense it had no programme. Certainly it made specific demands – universal franchise in local government elections, an end to gerrymandering, laws against discrimination and so on. But there was nothing in this that the Nationalist Party had not, in its own way, been campaigning for for decades, nothing with which the Republican movement, the Labour Party, the Liberal Party and even a section of the Unionists did not agree. The CAC's strength was that it struck an attitude which perfectly matched the mood of the Catholic masses in the aftermath of 5 October. John Hume was its personification: reasonable, respectable, righteous, solid, non-violent and determined. The average Bogsider wanted to do something about 5 October; he could go out and march behind Hume, confident that he would not be led into violence, in no way nervous about the political ideas of the men at the front of the procession and certain that he was, by his presence, making a contribution to the struggle. The CAC did not challenge the consciousness of the Catholic masses. It up-dated the expression of it, injected new life into it and made it relevant to a changed situation. And the tiny miracle which sealed their success in doing this was that they had contrived to contain within their ambit most of those who had, until 5 October, been leading a struggle designed specifically to destroy that consciousness.

Revolutionaries and reformers can unite only when the revolutionary agrees, temporarily at least, to suspend those items in his programme with which the reformer disagrees.

There is no reciprocation. The revolutionary will *agree* with the reformer's demands; his basic objection will be that they do not go far enough.

So for the time being a fractious alliance held together. And it seemed to be getting some results. The civil rights demonstrations which took place throughout Northern Ireland, but most frequently and dramatically in Derry, in the weeks after 5 October forced concessions from the Unionists. On 8 November a specially requisitioned meeting of the Corporation accepted a Nationalist motion setting up a three-man committee to allocate houses. Alderman Hegarty and two Unionists were elected to the committee. Shortly afterwards O'Neill announced a five-point package of reforms. These involved a plan to abolish Derry Corporation, universal franchise, and a promise that sections of the Special Powers Act would be 'put into cold storage' (but not so cold as to prevent rapid re-heating when the occasion arose).

Had such measures been announced in Stormont three months previously they would have been hailed as a dramatic advance. Now they were far too little far too late. What they did was to confirm to the Catholic masses that the power which they were beginning to feel was real. When on 16 November fifteen thousand people stood in a mass on Craigavon Bridge confronting the police they felt, being there in those numbers, real power in their grasp. That was a heady thing to happen to people from the Bogside, something which no cabinet minister could ever understand.

There was a civil rights march in Armagh on 30 November. The Rev. Ian Paisley called a counter-demonstration. With hundreds of followers, most of them armed with sticks and clubs, he occupied the centre of the city, the march's objective, from early morning. The march had not been banned, but the RUC blocked its path and prevented the two sides coming into contact. There was no clash, but the gruesome possibilities were not missed by many people.

Dr Paisley protested loud and long about the weakness of O'Neill in the face of the rebel threat. Mr Craig repeatedly asserted his conviction that IRA men and Trotsky-ites were masterminding the Catholics. The CRA, the CAC and the Nationalist Party demanded that the government charge Paisley and sack Craig. Tension grew. Then on 9 December Captain O'Neill apparently had the biggest success of his career. He made a dramatic prime-ministerial broadcast immediately after the news on local television. It was ten minutes of emotional clichés delivered in the whining nasal drawl which is, apparently, his natural voice. He ended by asking 'What kind of Ulster do you want?' and appealing to 'men of goodwill to come together'.

Immediately afterwards he sacked Craig from the government. This was generally regarded as a very courageous thing for Captain O'Neill to do. In his own terms it may well have been. The civil rights movement welcomed it triumphantly, and glowing tribute was paid to the principled liberalism of the prime minister. Both the CRA and the CAC called 'a truce' – that is they promised not to organize any marches in the immediate future. O'Neill's broadcast was printed and reprinted in the press and generally touted as the keynote address of a new era. The majority of people in the Bogside, and in the Catholic community in Northern Ireland generally, believed at this point that the trouble was *over*. For a brief period we had gone marching mad. Reforms were on the way and, with the Unionist hard-liners 'routed' (*Derry Journal*), there was no reason why there should not be 'steady progress' (*Irish News*) towards a 'society where all men live in dignity' (John Hume).

Actually, what the Catholics had been given was a sense of achievement. It was a new experience, and for the moment it sufficed. Meanwhile, an 'I'm backing O'Neill' campaign was launched. The *Belfast Telegraph* printed forms bearing this legend with spaces for people to sign their names. The forms were taken round factories and distributed outside churches. At least one member of the CAC signed. Car stickers, even, were printed. The Parliamentary Unionist Party supported the sacking of Craig by twenty-eight votes to none with four abstentions. 'His departure from the meeting, crestfallen and alone, was symbolic in itself,' crowed the *Derry Journal*. Clergymen, trade-union leaders and prominent academics publicly pledged their support for the 'O'Neill policy'. A casual visitor to Northern Ireland might have wondered who it was, apart from William Craig and Ian Paisley, who had ever been against reform. 'His appeal met with an instant and voluminous response that soon amounted to a tide of support from the Protestant community,' continued the *Journal*. 'From the churches, the academics and the professional and commercial classes to a multitude of ordinary Unionists came striking testimony that Captain O'Neill could count on their backing for a policy of conciliation and reform.' In a poll conducted by the Dublin-based *Sunday Independent*, which has an almost exclusively Catholic readership, Captain O'Neill was elected 'Man of the Year' by an overwhelming majority.

The 'truce' was broken when the People's Democracy announced that it was marching from Belfast to Derry, starting on 1 January. The PD had been formed by the students at Queen's University, Belfast, who had been in Derry on 5 October. It was a loose organization without formal membership and with an incoherent ideology comprising middle-class liberalism, Aldermaston pacifism and a Sorbonne-inspired belief in spontaneity. At its core was a small group of determined left-wingers who had been in close liaison with the Labour left in Derry before and after 5 October, most of whom retained simultaneous membership of the Northern Ireland Labour Party. The march was condemned by the Nationalist Party. Mr McAteer said that the 'public are browned off with marches' and that it was 'bad weather' for such activity. The attitude of the Catholic establishment was summed up by Frank McCarroll, owner of the *Journal*. 'Let the truce stand. The difference between what they [the civil rights movement] demanded and what the government offered was certainly not sufficient to justify any risk of chaos in the streets.' Neither the CRA nor the CAC would support the march, but neither felt sure enough of its ground to condemn it outright.

About eighty people, Queen's students and half a dozen supporters from Derry, set off from Belfast City Hall at nine in the morning of 1 January. Dr Paisley's right-hand man, Major Ronald Bunting, came with a Union Jack and a group of supporters to give it a barracking send-off. The march was a horrific seventy-three-mile trek which dredged to the surface all the accumulated political filth of fifty Unionist years. Every few miles groups of Unionist extremists blocked the route. Invariably the police diverted the march rather than open the road, so that much of the time it wound a circuitous way through country lanes from stopping place to stopping place. It was frequently stoned from the fields and attacked by groups of men with clubs. There was no police protection. Senior RUC officers consorted openly with leaders of the opposing groups. On the final day of the march, at Burntollet Bridge a few miles outside Derry, a force of some hundreds, marshalled by members of the B Specials and watched passively by our 'escort' of more than a hundred police, attacked with nailed clubs, stones and bicycle chains. Of the eighty who had set out fewer than thirty arrived in Derry uninjured. But they had gathered hundreds of supporters behind them on the way and were met in Guildhall Square by angry thousands who were in no mood for talk of truce. Emotion swelled as bloodstained marchers mounted a platform and described their experiences. Rioting broke out and continued for some hours.

The scene of the battle shifted from the city centre to Fahan Street, Rossville Street and William Street as the police tried to drive us into the Bogside. It died out in late evening when, having succeeded in moving us back into our own area, the police made no real attempt actually to come in after us. The area was peaceful and deserted at 2 a.m. when a mob of policemen came from the city centre through Butcher Gate and surged down Fahan Street into St Columb's Wells and Lecky Road, shouting and singing:

> Hey, hey we're the monkees,
> And we're going to monkey around
> Till we see your blood flowing
> All along the ground.

They broke in windows with their batons, kicked doors and shouted to the people to 'come out and fight, you Fenian bastards'. Anyone who did come to his or her door was grabbed and beaten up. The only phone in St Columb's Wells is in No. 37, McMenamins'. Roused from his bed and seeing the mob rampaging around the street Johnny McMenamin lifted the receiver and dialled 999. He had been put through to Victoria RUC Barracks before realization dawned on him that this was ridiculous. The police stayed for about an hour, roaming up and down the Wells and Lecky Road, shouting, singing, throwing stones through any upstairs windows at which a face appeared. When they had gone, people crept out to clear up the damage, tend to those who had been beaten up and comfort hysterical neighbours. Lord Cameron in his restrained report on these events recorded 'with regret that our investigations have led us to the unhesitating conclusion that on the night of 4th/5th January a number of policemen were guilty of misconduct which involved assault and battery, malicious damage to property in streets in the predominantly Catholic Bogside area, giving reasonable cause for apprehension of personal injury among other innocent inhabitants, and the use of provocative sectarian and political slogans'.

By mid-morning the streets were filled with people discussing and arguing about what we should do. Hundreds of teenagers had armed themselves with sticks and iron bars and were of the opinion that we should march on Victoria Barracks and take revenge. At the corner of Wellington Street Gerry Fitt was saying that 'it's time to get the guns out'. Calmer counsels prevailed, and in the early afternoon the women of the area went in a body and told District Inspector McGimpsie that the RUC would not be allowed back into the area until those responsible for the attack on Bogside were named and disciplined. Vigilante squads organized themselves immediately afterwards. The Foyle Harps Hall in Brandywell and the Rossville Hall in Bogside were opened as recruitment and organizing centres. Vinny Coyle, an enormous man well known in the area, the violence of whose language and demeanour belied a genuinely peaceful nature, emerged as the energetic commandant of vigilantes. Barricades were erected across the three or four main entrances to the Bogside. By nightfall vigilante patrols complete with official armbands and carrying clubs were patrolling the streets. It was half-expected that the police would come. The atmosphere was exciting.

John 'Caker' Casey, who by dint of his dab hand with a paint brush was recognized as an expert wall-sloganeer, fetched out the tools of his trade and in a moment of inspiration wrote 'You are now entering Free Derry' on a gable-end in St Columb's Street. In the middle of the night someone arrived with a radio transmitter. It was installed in an eighth-storey flat in Rossville Street with the aerial on the roof. We began broadcasting, describing ourselves as 'Radio Free Derry, the Voice of Liberation'.

The only people more appalled than the government by the situation were the leaders of the CAC. They had never intended *barricades*. But blood was up and there was nothing they could do about it. By chance the radio transmitter had been presented to Dermie McClenaghan and me. We used it to make propaganda encouraging the people to keep the barricades up and the police out and to 'join your vigilante patrols'. We were perhaps erratic. On one occasion Tommy McDermott, who believed in the revolutionary potential of underground music, was left alone with the transmitter, an opportunity which he used to treat the populace to two hours of the Incredible String Band interspersed with whispered injunctions to 'love one another and keep cool'. But for the most part we played rebel songs, and White, McClenaghan, Melaugh and I and some others delivered regular harangues. Reception was good, the listening audience vast.

The police made no real attempt to enter the area. The barricades remained for five days, by which time the enormous implications of what was happening had seeped through. Keeping the barricades up indefinitely meant, in effect, to opt out of the state, and seemed to require some permanent institution separate from and opposed to the police to control the area. This had not been thought of. And rioting was one thing, but the police sooner or later were going to try to re-enter, and to keep them out would require fighting some sort of set-piece battle. That was another thing altogether. For a start, the police had guns and, Mr Fitt notwithstanding, we had not. Radio Free Derry nightly bombarded the area with pleas to 'keep up the resistance'. We failed to swing the population round completely to this point of view, which possibly was not a bad thing because at the time we had neither the organization nor the means to put such resistance into effect. By the end of the week nervousness and uncertainty had replaced the excitement of Sunday night. The CAC had kept on the sidelines. Late on Friday night Hume, Cooper, Canavan and a few others descended on the area and with a series of perfectly pitched and brilliantly timed speeches convinced the vigilantes that the barricades ought to be dismantled. They were gone by the morning. Any attempt to re-erect them would have been a frontal challenge to the CAC, and the revolutionary disc-jockeys of Radio Free Derry were in no position to do that, most of them, after all, being members of that body.

There was rioting in Newry on 11 January and sporadic trouble in other areas. In Derry unemployed teenagers, of whom there were and are no small number, took to the casual stoning of any police car which came into view. Dr Paisley continued to stomp the country telling Protestants that 'O'Neill must go'. Mr Craig was appealing to the rank and file of the Unionist Party. Captain O'Neill was being given almost weekly votes of confidence by various executive organs of the party, each of which was immediately interpreted by commentators as further evidence of the good sense and moderation of the Protestant people and the isolation of Craig and Paisley. In February Captain O'Neill put the matter to the test when he dissolved Parliament and called an election. He put up 'O'Neill Unionists' in constituencies where the local organization had selected a pro-Craig candidate. It was said that Captain O'Neill's team was 'very impressive'. It included the Duke of Westminster, the son of Lord Carson and the husband of Lady Moira Hamilton. They were slaughtered. For some reason it took months for press commentators, the British government and some other interested observers to realize this.

The announcement of the election threw civil rights organizations into some disarray. The PD, after some soul-searching about the corrupting influence of parliamentary politics, put up nine candidates, all of whom, in the end, polled well. The most common sight in the lounge of the City Hotel in Derry was that of leaders of the CAC who had hitherto been dogmatic about the 'non-political' nature of their activities circling one another, dagger in hand, wondering into which back it might most profitably be plunged. Ivan Cooper sought and accepted the Labour nomination for the rural area of mid-Derry, discovered quickly that the Labour tag was not popular in the constituency, resigned from the party and won easily as an

Independent. Hume stood for the Foyle constituency, which includes the Bogside, against Eddie McAteer. I stood against the two of them as an official Labour candidate, with some tacit Republican support. We rejected the party manifesto and wrote one of our own. The election agent ran away with the deposit (one hundred and fifty borrowed pounds) the night before nomination day. He had taken a taxi to Norfolk to see his girl-friend. We lost another deposit when the result was announced. Mr Hume won handsomely.

After the election things went from bad to worse for moderates of all hues. It had been hoped that the decision of the people expressed through the ballot box would be accepted by everyone in the proper democratic spirit and that politics would, as a result, return to the chamber at Stormont. The problem was that it was by no means clear what the people had, in fact, decided, and in such a situation all tendencies retain their hopes. O'Neill was still prime minister but most of his critics in the Parliamentary Unionist Party had won their way back to Stormont. Dr Paisley had run him close in Bannside and could justifiably feel that his star was still rising. The unexpected performance of the PD against both 'liberal' Unionist and Nationalist candidates showed that Catholic working-class resistance to the blandishments of O'Neill was stronger and deeper than had generally been supposed.

Rioting started again in Derry within a few weeks. It was on a small scale at first, teenagers stoning police cars at the edge of the Bogside. It built up and, on 19 April, erupted into the bloodiest violence the city had seen to date, with youths from the Bogside using stones and petrol bombs to hold the police off. The police burst into a house in William Street and, probably out of frustration, beat up everyone present. The man of the house, Sammy Devenney, was subsequently to die from his injuries. A policeman cornered in Hamilton Street drew his gun and fired two shots. No one was hit but the point was well taken. Afterwards the talk was of the next time and there were some who said that we ought to be prepared. No one doubted that there would be a next time. There was rioting on and after 12 July when the Protestants celebrated the result of the Battle of the Boyne.

The Derry riots were a minor affair, but around Unity Flats in Belfast and in Dungannon there were fierce clashes between Catholics and Orange marchers, with the RUC intervening on the Protestant side.

O'Neill had resigned in April and taken himself off, ennobled, to the boardroom of a merchant bank in the City of London, where he is believed still to be. He was replaced by Major James Chichester-Clark, a bumbling squire from the Maghera district. Chichester-Clark – or 'Chi-Chi', as he came to be called after an exotic animal in the London Zoo – announced that he believed in being 'fair'. Mr Hume, Mr Cooper, the CRA and other leaders of moderate Catholic opinion counselled their supporters to give him a chance. But in the Bogside and elsewhere the rioting classes were not impressed. The unemployed youth of areas like the Bogside had, at the outset of the civil rights campaign, been regarded as marching fodder. Energetic and instinctively aggressive, they could be counted on to turn out for sit-downs, marches, pickets or any other protest activity which was organized. It was they who had turned out on 5 October. It was their impatience which had then impelled the CAC into more activity, and more militant activity, than its leading members would have wished. It was their energy and aggression which had powered the civil rights campaign through its first frenetic months. In the end it was they, not the RUC, who frightened organizations like the CAC off the streets. The CAC died in Derry after the riots of 19 April. It was difficult after that to organize a demonstration which did not end in riot, and the CAC was not about to assume such responsibility. But by ending demonstrations the moderates took away from the youth any channel for expression *other* than riot. The rage and frustration which lay just beneath the surface of life in the

Bogside could no longer be contained within the thin shell of the CAC's timid respectability. The 'hooligans' had taken over, and the stage was set for a decisive clash between them and the forces of the state. Everyone knew it would come on 12 August, when the Apprentice Boys were scheduled to march past the Bogside in their annual celebration of the Relief of Derry in 1689.

At the end of July the Republican Club announced that they had formed a 'Derry Citizens Defence Association', to protect the area against attack on the Twelfth. They invited all other organizations in the area to nominate two representatives to sit with them on this body. There was some annoyance that the Republicans, before inviting the co-operation of any other group, had parcelled out the leading positions among themselves. Sean Keenan was chairman, Johnnie White secretary, Johnnie McAllister treasurer. But most political groups in the area accepted the Republican initiative, reasoning that something decisive was going to happen on the Twelfth and it was as well to lay title to some of the action in advance.

The matter was clinched by what appeared to be a joint assault by the RUC and Orange demonstrators on Unity Flats in Belfast on 2 August. One man was beaten to death and many others were injured. Reports of this sent a *frisson* through the area. Obviously something similar might happen in Derry on the Twelfth. We had better be prepared. The CAC met, nominated two people to sit on the DCDA and quietly went out of existence. At the time no one noticed.

The stated purpose of the DCDA was to try to preserve the peace and, as soon as this failed, to organize the defence of the area. Maps were procured and we counted out the forty-one entrances to the area. Materials for making barricades were stored adjacent to each. Enthusiasm was high. The 12 August procession was regarded as a calculated annual insult to the Derry Catholics. There was a surge of resentment and much bitter muttering every year. But this time, after all we had come through in the last nine months, the attitude was very different. This year at last they were going to be shown that things had changed drastically. And if they dared to attack ... The first barricades went up on the night of the 11th in anticipation.

On the Twelfth stewards made a token effort to prevent the march from being stoned as it passed the end of William Street. Mr Hume, Mr Cooper and some others were at the front appealing for calm. Some of the stones tended to fall short and Mr Cooper was felled. As the volume of stone-throwing increased a mixed force of RUC and supporters of the Apprentice Boys made a charge into the area, which was the signal for the real hostilities to begin. The battle lasted for about forty-eight hours. Barricades went up all around the area, open-air petrol-bomb factories were established, dumpers hijacked from a building site were used to carry stones to the front. Teenagers went on to the roof of the block of High Flats which dominates Rossville Street, the main entrance to the Bogside, and began lobbing petrol bombs at the police below. This was a brilliant tactical move and afterwards there was no shortage of people claiming to have thought of it first. As long as the lads stayed up there and as long as we managed to keep them supplied with petrol bombs there was no way – short of shooting them off the roof – that the police could get past the High Flats. Every time they tried it rained petrol bombs.

The DCDA set up headquarters in Paddy Doherty's house in Westland Street. Throughout the battle all doors in the area were open. Tea and sandwiches were constantly available on the pavement. The police started using tear gas after a few hours, which nonplussed us momentarily. A call to the offices of the *Red Mole* in London – they seemed the most appropriate people – produced an antidote involving vinegar and a series of instructions for lessening the effects. Soon there were buckets of water and vinegar stationed all over the battle zone. As an alternative, Molly Barr was dispensing free Vaseline from her shop under the High Flats.

Four walkie-talkie radio sets were taken from a television crew. One was installed in Doherty's house and the other three used to report back on the state of play in the battle. Our possession of those instruments was later to be adduced as evidence of the massive, subversive conspiracy behind the fighting. When the batteries ran out after a few hours the sets were given back to their owners. On the evening of the 13th Mr Jack Lynch appeared on television and said that he could 'not stand idly by'. Irish troops were to be moved to the border. This put new heart into the fight. News that 'the Free State soldiers are coming' spread rapidly. Three first-aid stations, manned by local doctors, nurses and the Knights of Malta, were treating those overcome by the gas or injured by missiles thrown by the police. The radio transmitter, now operating from Eamonn Melaugh's house in Creggan, was pumping out Republican music and exhortations to 'keep the murderers out. Don't weaken now. Make every stone and petrol bomb count.' The police were making charge after charge up Rossville Street.

Phone-calls were made to contacts in other areas begging them to get people on to the streets and draw off some of the police from Derry. We appealed through Telefis Eireann for 'every able-bodied man in Ireland who believes in freedom' to come to Derry and help us. 'We need you, we'll feed you.' In the main battle area, Rossville Street, the fighting was being led by Bernadette Devlin, who had seemingly developed an immunity to tear gas and kept telling people, implausibly, that 'it's O.K. once you get a taste of it'.

On the morning of the 14th we heard reports of fighting in Belfast, Coalisland, Dungannon, Armagh and other places; we took this as encouragement. Other people were coming to our aid. The Tricolour and the Starry Plough were hoisted over the High Flats. Two people were shot and wounded by the police in Great James Street. A duplicated leaflet entitled 'Barricade Bulletin' appeared: 'The enemy is weakening. They have been on their feet two nights. One more push.' The tear gas came in even greater quantities until it filled the air like smog. People were running through it, crouching, eyes closed, to hurl a petrol bomb at the police lines and then stagger back. In William Street, a group breaking into Harrison's garage to steal petrol was stopped by a priest who told them it was wrong. 'But Father, we need the petrol.' 'Well,' said the priest dubiously, 'as long as you don't take any more than you really need.' And thus absolved in advance, they went at it with a will.

By three in the afternoon the police had been dislodged from their footholds at the bottom of Rossville Street and the battle lines, after two days, were being pushed back inexorably out of the Bogside and towards the commercial area of the city. Then, looking through the haze of gas, past the police lines, we saw the Specials moving into Waterloo Place. They were about to be thrown into the battle. Undoubtedly they would use guns. The possibility that there was going to be a massacre struck hundreds of people simultaneously. 'Have we guns?' people shouted to one another, hoping that someone would know, inching forward, more slowly now, as the police retreated, suddenly fearful of what was about to happen. We were about half way down William Street when the word came that British soldiers were marching across the bridge.

The Specials disappeared, the police pulled out quite suddenly and the troops, armed with sub-machine-guns, stood in a line across the mouth of William Street. Their appearance was clear proof that we had won the battle, that the RUC was beaten. That was welcomed. But there was confusion as to what the proper attitude to the soldiers might be. It was not in our history to make British soldiers welcome. A meeting started outside the High Flats in Rossville Street. (In every riot in Northern Ireland there is a man

with a megaphone waiting for the meeting to start.) Bernadette Devlin, her voice croaking, urged 'Don't make them
welcome. They have not come here to help us', and went
on a bit about British imperialism, Cyprus and Aden. It did
not go down very well. The fight had been against the RUC,
to 'defend the area'. The RUC was beaten; the soldiers had
prevented the Specials coming in and had not attempted to
encroach on the area. They had deployed themselves
around the edges. And, anyway, everyone was exhausted,
clothes torn and faces begrimed, their eyes burning from
the tear gas. It was victory enough for the time being.

Paddy Doherty struck the right note: 'We have done
well. We can rest on our laurels for a bit. Let us see how all
this works out before we rush into anything we might regret.' With Ray Burnett, a Scottish member of the International Socialists who had been hitch-hiking around
Ireland and been given a lift into the middle of a riot, I
drafted a leaflet which by seven o'clock was being distributed as 'Barricade Bulletin No. 2'. 'This is a great defeat
for the Unionist government. But it is not yet a victory for
us.' People were not in the mood for political analysis and
it didn't have much effect.

Later we were able to listen to the news from other
areas. The Specials had killed a man called Gallagher in
Armagh. Belfast was desperate. Police, Specials and Protestant extremists had wreaked what appeared to be a mini-
pogrom on Catholic areas. Tracer bullets had been used on
blocks of flats. Whole streets of houses had been burned out
and there were refugees living in school halls. There were
some dead: And it went on the next day, burning and
shooting. It sounded very different from Derry, inconceiv-
ably horrific. But by the afternoon of the fifteenth soldiers
were deployed in all the troubled areas and it seemed that
the situation had stabilized.

The Defence Association had had no effective existence
during the actual fighting. When the radio sets had been in

operation and reports from various fronts coming into the headquarters, some, particularly those in the headquarters listening to the reports, had been encouraged to believe that this amounted to organization. But really there was no organization involved, and none needed. Those bearing the brunt of the fighting were the stone-throwers and petrol-bombers of weekends past and they did not need instruction on what to do and would not have been amenable to it had it been offered. When the fighting ended, however, and the army made no move to come into the area there was an immediate need for a body which could claim to speak for the people. The Defence Committee fitted the bill. It began to get bigger. On the Twelfth it had had perhaps eighteen or twenty members. No one was quite sure, since the qualifications for membership had never been set out clearly and the meetings, up to then, had been fairly informal. When the fighting ceased representatives of various groups – tenants' associations, street committees and so on – were accepted as members.

Individuals became members simply by taking jobs which had to be done. For example, one man was independently arranging accommodation for the fifty or so volunteers who had answered our call to 'every able-bodied man in Ireland who believes in freedom', and on that account he became billeting officer. He did a very efficient and unrewarding job for the next three months. Later the 'Outsiders' demanded a say for themselves on the Committee, and Sean Matgamna, now editor of the British weekly *Workers' Fight*, became a member. In the end we were forty-four strong. Most of these were not members of any political organization and it was some weeks before the relative strength of the different factions on the committee became clear.

Within twenty-four hours of their appearance the army asked for a meeting. A delegation went to Victoria Barracks on the Strand Road, and met Brigadier Lang and Colonel

Millman. It had been decided beforehand that we would tell the army that we intended to hold the area until the police were disarmed and the Specials, the Special Powers Act and Stormont abolished, and that no soldier would be permitted to come through our barricades. We had not discussed what we would do if the army decided to come on in regardless. But the issue did not arise. The Brigadier assured us that they had no intention of coming in without our agreement. He was a tall man of plausible appearance and Sandhurst accent. He said that the army had come to see that justice was done, that he knew of the injustices of the past, that things would be different now and that he hoped for a friendly relationship with us. He quite understood that we might have certain things in the area which we wished now to move out and, to facilitate this, there would be no check on vehicles on one of the roads to the Republic for the next twenty-four hours. We thought he was talking of our radio transmitter, which shows that at that point we were almost as naïve as the army.

In the immediate aftermath of the fighting relations between the army and most of the people of the area were very good. At Butcher Gate, William Street and other army positions at the edge of the Bogside women squabbled about whose turn it was to take the soldiers their tea. Army relations with the youth of the area, however, were to deteriorate very quickly. From the outset there were two opposing interpretations to be put on the fact that the army had encircled us. One was that they were protecting us from attack, the other that they were containing us, both to prevent us attacking anyone else (for example the police barracks) and to control who and what came and went: it suited 'moderates' to argue the former, 'extremists' to argue the latter. The youth, both by instinct and by experience, tended towards extremity. Within a week of the army's appearance the first minor conflicts occurred. The police were still patrolling in the centre of the city and our young people would go out looking for them. On the first

Saturday night of the army's presence a group of about fifty stoned a police patrol in Foyle Street. A company of soldiers intervened and stood between the two sides. The stoning continued, the stones being lobbed over the army lines. Brigadier Lang came to take personal control of the situation. Standing about three yards from him a young man threw a half-brick which struck a constable and knocked him to the ground. The Brigadier grabbed the culprit by the neck, shouting apologetically, 'I *have* to arrest him, he's hit that policeman.' The young man's comrades surged around the Brigadier screaming for his release. 'If you don't release him,' I told the Brigadier, 'there's going to be terrible trouble.' 'See that he does not do it again, then,' said the Brigadier, after a pause to look around to survey the situation, and released his hold on his prisoner. Thus victorious, the crowd went home, cheering. Some time later a Protestant man, William King, died from a heart attack after being kicked near the city centre by a gang from the Bogside while soldiers stood a few yards away, making no move to intervene. The soldiers had no instructions to cover such situations.

On the Defence Committee the political lines were emerging, hazily at first, then, as the Committee was forced to make decisions, more and more clearly. Almost all important decisions concerned the barricades: when and in what circumstances we would take them down. Attitudes to this were naturally determined by the degree to which one was willing to accept the army. Mindful of our experience of the Citizens Action Committee, the left decided to act as an organized faction on the committee and also to maintain a separate existence. We had, we discovered, fifteen out of the forty-four committee members with us. We held a meeting of the faction before each meeting of the committee, to discuss the business which was to come up and decide on a joint attitude. Most members of the faction were in the Labour Party or the Republican Club, although there were other Republicans and Labourites on the committee who were not members of the faction. Outside the Defence Committee we had a fairly informal and nameless group operating out of Dermie McClenaghan's house in Wellington Street. Dermie had sent his mother out of the town 'for your own safety', which meant that we had the house to ourselves. An assortment of people congregated here each day, our Labour-Republican group, two members of the People's Democracy from Belfast, some of the 'Outsiders' and Tom Picton, a six-foot-six-inch *Life* photographer of radical sympathies who introduced us to the concept of the permanent stew. He had a huge cauldron of potatoes, chunks of meat and vegetables simmering over a low gas on Mrs McClenaghan's cooker. Every morning he would throw in some more ingredients, so that it never ran out. Food was thus available at all hours of the day and night. Some people slept in McClenaghan's in sleeping bags and on the sitting-room couch, others would drift in during the day. We had a duplicator installed in one of the bedrooms and produced a 'Barricade Bulletin' every second day. This consisted of news snippets, anti-army propaganda (Cyprus, Aden, Ireland in the twenties and so on), attacks on the Wilson government and some rudimentary analysis of the situation. Sarah Wilson, a member of the London Poster Workshop Group, appeared complete with silkscreen. We found her a hall to work in, and, helped by a team of children, she produced a series of striking and effective posters which soon festooned the area.

We held public meetings every few days. At these we constantly reiterated the four demands originally put forward by the Defence Committee and exhorted the people to stand fast until they were conceded. All this was designed to prevent a repetition of our experience with the CAC. We anticipated that the Defence Association would compromise and wanted to ensure that when this happened there was some left-wing focus available which could be presented as a possible alternative.

For weeks we were fairly happy about the way things

were going. Our public meetings were well attended and enthusiastic. Our bulletins were accepted and read eagerly. It appeared that our faction represented a considerable body of opinion, that we were a force to be reckoned with – and no longer trapped within a 'moderate' alliance. When our references to the necessity to 'smash the rotten capitalist system' were applauded we took it as evidence that 'revolutionary consciousness' was on the increase.

But what the people were applauding was not so much what we said but the way we said it. We were great ones for violence of the tongue. We were forever 'giving notice that . . .'; giving notice to the government, the police, even 'the world at large', that we would or, more frequently, would not accept such and such a proposition. The police were always 'the uniformed thugs of the RUC'. British imperialism took a lot of stick. We never got down to defining with any precision what British imperialism was. We implied that it was the thing the Bogside had been fighting against for the past year and that we, the left-wingers, were more against it than anybody else. References to 'Adolf Craig' were always good for a cheer. Most of our meetings were held in the afternoons from the top of a barricade at the bottom of Westland Street. People from nearby streets, hearing the amplified voices, would gather around.

The Defence Association met almost daily, either in Paddy Doherty's house or in a disused bookmaker's shop which adjoined it. Not all discussion centred on matters of great moment. There were a host of day-to-day problems which had to be dealt with. People living on the fringe of or just outside the area and who felt threatened would want to move in. They would either be squatted in a vacant house or arrangements would be made to have men available to protect them if the necessity arose. Petty crime had to be investigated. A 'police force' was set up, and it dealt competently with what little crime there was. 'Punishment', more often than not, consisted of a stern lecture from Sean Keenan about the need for solidarity within the area, which seemed to work quite well. A vigilante corps to patrol the area at night was enrolled. It was divided into three sections, operating from halls in the Creggan, Bogside and Brandywell areas. Each hall had its own catering officer whose job it was to ensure that tea, soup and sandwiches were available as each patrol finished its two-hour duty and that the cigarettes were fairly distributed. (The cigarettes caused a lot of trouble and more than one meeting of the committee was dominated by minute investigation of alleged irregularities. Outraged by a report that Creggan was on twenty cigarettes a night while his men made do with ten, Bobby Toland, an aggressive young man with long hair who had somehow emerged as chief of the Bogside vigilantes, declared UDI one evening and barred members of the Defence Committee from his headquarters in the West End Hall. He was bought off with an extra alloca- tion.) Dignitaries came to 'see for themselves'. Lord Hail- sham came to assure us that his party was sensitive to the need for reform and that 'we never knew about the things which were going on here'. From the Republic came a pro- cession of politicians, from cabinet ministers to aspirant county councillors, each to be photographed in front of a barricade, preferably shaking hands with someone who could positively be identified as 'one of the Bogside de- fenders'. Tribunite MPs gave daring clenched fist salutes before leaving. The most notable visitor was James Calla- ghan, who, as Home Secretary, had responsibility for Northern Ireland at Westminster.

Mr Callaghan came at the end of August. In honour of the visit the Defence Committee had Caker Casey's 'Free Derry' slogan professionally re-done. The gable was painted white and a sign writer employed to do the lettering. There were many of us who preferred Caker's version.

Mr Callaghan's welcome in the Bogside was afterwards described by pressmen in terms ranging from 'enthusiastic' to 'ecstatic'. It was very noisy, very emotional, and a little confused. The left faction had argued successfully in the committee that, consistent with our policy of not permitting the forces of 'law and order' to enter the area, Mr Callaghan should not be allowed to bring any escort with him. The left had also decided that we would mount some sort of demonstration to make it clear that there were those in the area who did not place complete trust in him or in the Labour administration. Fairly typically, by the time Mr Callaghan arrived we had not decided what form this demonstration should take and it never happened. The vigilantes were mobilized to escort Mr Callaghan but when he appeared they, and he, were swept along by a surging crowd of thousands up Rossville Street and into Lecky Road. Mr Callaghan took refuge in a local house, where four members of the Defence Committee – Sean Keenan, Paddy Doherty, Michael Canavan and I – went to talk to him. We formally reiterated our demands: disband the Specials; disarm the police; repeal the Special Powers Act; abolish Stormont. We told him that the barricades would stay up until they were granted. Mr Callaghan said that, quite frankly, the demands were unreasonable. A committee under Lord Hunt had already been set up to look at the whole question of policing Northern Ireland. 'New structures' would now have to be created to give all sections of the community a 'sense of belonging'. We told him about the unemployment problem and he said that, yes, it was very serious, unemployment was always serious and that, indeed, he and his colleagues would have to see what could be done about it. Sean Keenan said that Mr Callaghan could see we were all reasonable people. Mr Callaghan agreed that indeed we were. He went upstairs and addressed the crowd outside from an open window.

It had been said, he began, that the London government was impartial. This was not true. The government was firmly on the side of justice. There was loud cheering. Mr Callaghan left and went to the Protestant Fountain area, where, it was reported, he had a distinctly more subdued welcome.

At the first meeting of the Defence Committee after Callaghan's visit it was proposed that the barricades be taken down. The left faction resisted this fiercely, arguing that none of the demands just put to Callaghan had been met. No vote was taken, but it was obvious that Callaghan had greatly impressed some of the leading moderates and that they were prepared to trust him and the Labour government to produce an acceptable solution. The 'demands' were, anyway, no longer being taken very seriously. They had been drawn up in the chaotic emotional atmosphere of 14 August. No one now really believed that Stormont was going to be abolished forthwith, and the majority on the Defence Committee was dealing in the realm of immediate possibilities.

Callaghan had not just impressed members of the Defence Committee; he had been very popular with the people as a whole, not because of any personal qualities but because, if the arrival of the British Army symbolized our physical victory over the RUC, Callaghan's appearance symbolized the political defeat of the Unionist Party. They were no longer calling the shots. The boss himself had arrived to put them in their place, and their discomfiture, of which his surly reception in the Fountain was seen as an example, was pleasant to behold. Things were going our way. (Callaghan's account of his visit to Derry, in his book *A House Divided*, suggests that he was completely unaware of this feeling.) But if things were going our way, if the British government was here in person to shackle the Unionist Party, there was no need any longer to maintain the militancy of recent weeks. While the elation of the battle had lingered on, revolutionary rhetoric at the bottom of Westland Street had been quite congenial. Now, increasingly, it seemed merely strident.

The left faction went to work churning out 'Barricade Bulletins' and posters and holding more street-corner meetings. But we were trying to turn back the tide. To the majority of people the barricades had had a simple function – to prevent hostile forces coming in to attack the area. The hostile forces had been defeated. So why not take the barricades down? It was a logical argument. We countered with the slightly dubious ploy of linking our barricades to those in Belfast, arguing that it would be a 'betrayal of Belfast' for us unilaterally to dismantle our defences. This had a powerful emotional appeal. The Catholic ghettoes in Belfast had suffered immeasurably more than we. The suggestion that we should keep our barricades up as a symbol of solidarity with them was well-nigh unanswerable. The argument did, however, have one enormous weakness. It would disappear as soon as the Belfast barricades came down, and we had no knowledge of, much less control over, what was happening in Belfast. Indeed contrary to Unionist paranoia about a well-coordinated plot to subvert the state it emerged at one point that no one on the Derry Defence Committee knew who the officers on the Belfast Defence Committee were. With the decisive support of the Catholic hierarchy the army talked the Belfast barricades down by mid-September, when an army Land Rover went through the Falls with Dr Philbin, the local bishop, perched incongruously in his robes in the passenger seat. Shortly afterwards a mass meeting at the Free Derry Corner – as the area around Casey's gable had come to be called – voted to breach the main barricade in Rossville Street.

After the manic days of August depression was slowly setting in. Vigilante patrols fell off. What was the point of tramping round the area all night? Nothing ever happened. If no one was going to attack, where was the need for defence? The issue was sealed on 9 October, when Lord Hunt's committee reported and Callaghan arrived back in Northern Ireland with Sir Arthur Young, the new Chief of Police. Hunt had recommended the disarming of the RUC and the abolition of the B Specials. It was, by any estimation, a victory for the Catholics. Any lingering doubt was removed on the night of 10–11 October, when the army in Belfast smashed a riot on the Protestant Shankill Road. The Hunt Report had driven the Protestants raging mad. It had castigated and disarmed their police force and abolished their B Specials and, by extension, humiliated their whole community. They came out now in their thousands and flung themselves down the Shankill to vent their wrath and frustration on Unity Flats. A policeman who stood in their way was shot dead. The army moved in and battered its way up the Shankill with bloodthirsty enthusiasm. In the shooting two Protestants were killed and a dozen wounded. Many others were beaten or kicked unconscious. Who in the Bogside could doubt now that at long last law and order were being administered impartially?

Callaghan brought Young into the area and introduced him to a cheering crowd. 'This is Sir Arthur Young. He's going to look after you.' 'Oh no,' said Sir Arthur, all London bobby and affability, 'they are going to look after me.' There were more cheers.

That ended the second phase of Free Derry. Military policemen came in, unarmed, to patrol the area, preparatory to a reformed RUC taking over. For a few weeks previously, after the dismantling of the Belfast barricades, the left faction had more or less given up any attempt to hold back the inevitable. We were occupied with other things.

From the beginning of September, Republicans and some members of the Labour Party had been learning to use guns. A Republican training officer had come up from Cork, and in a tiny house in the Brandywell district people who had perhaps joined the Labour Party a year or two ago out of admiration for the political principles of Harold Wilson (this is possible) learned how to dismantle and reassemble the Thompson and the Sten and how to make a Mills bomb. We went across the border into the Donegal hills for practice shoot-outs. It was exciting at the time and enabled one to feel that, despite the depressing trend of events in the area, one was involved in a *real* revolution. But after the Hunt report and the reaction to it this activity too lost its urgency. Only the hooligans – and the heroes of the High Flats were rapidly being relegated again to that status – retained the fire for conflict. The Republicans were having their own problems, as the conflicting opinions which were shortly to split the movement hardened on both sides.

The next six months were, by Northern Ireland standards, quiet. Military police patrolled the area. They were very friendly and fairly popular. People accepted them, chatted to them, invited them in for a cup of tea. And as the barricades tumbled the politicians re-emerged, blinking in the sunlight. Attention was shifted away from Rossville Street and the Falls Road to the more salubrious arena at Stormont. The attention of the British press seemed to shift altogether, with the exception of some dewy-eyed photo-features in the tabloids depicting the warm human relationship which had built up between the troops and the Catholics. The Ulster troubles, it appeared, were over, and Cabinet ministers turned with relief to the more pressing and electorally more important problems of the state of the pound, industrial relations and what to do about Ian Smith. But in Rossville Street and the Falls Road and a hundred other dusty streets in Derry and Belfast, things were different. Reforms had filtered through on to the statute book. An Ombudsman had been appointed. Derry Corporation had been abolished and replaced by a Development Commission. A points system for the allocation of houses was in operation. Moderate Unionists could, and often did, point proudly to this record of progress. None of it, however, made any difference to the clumps of unemployed teenagers who stood, fists dug deep into their pockets, around William Street in the evenings. Briefly elevated into folk-hero status in the heady days of August, praised and patronized by local leaders for their expertise with the stone and the petrol bomb, they had now been dragged back down into the anonymous depression which had hitherto been their constant condition. For them at least, nothing had changed and they were bitterly cynical about the talk of a reformed future. 'We'll get nothing out of it. The Orangemen are still in power.' Occasionally they would stone the soldiers. It was small-scale stuff.

On the last Sunday in March 1970, Easter Sunday, there were two Republican parades, one Official, one Provisional, in commemoration of the 1916 Rising. The movement had finally split in January. In Derry, initially at least, most of the younger Republicans had opted for the Official wing. Rioting broke out near the city centre as the Officials' commemoration ceremony broke up. It was by later standards a fairly minor affray but it was significant enough to draw forth a chorus of condemnation from Mr Hume, local priests and other leaders of moderate opinion. Much was made of the fact that such behaviour tended to make more difficult the full implementation of the reforms. Scorn was the hooligans' mildest response to this reasoning. It could not be gainsaid, however, that the overwhelming majority of the people of the area continued to be sternly disapproving of conflict with the army. The soldiers were still seen as protectors, as 'Disgusted', 'Derryman', 'Pro Bono Publico' and other prolific writers made clear in the letter columns of the *Derry Journal*.

On Easter Tuesday the Orange marching season began. It sparked off rioting in the Ballymurphy estate in Belfast. On television the Bogside saw the army deluge the estate with CS gas. The rioting went on sporadically for three days. Once again hooliganism was roundly condemned on all sides. There were further riots in Belfast at the beginning of June. The army, learning quickly, announced that it had acquired new transparent shields, the better to see the rioters. They were reputedly manufactured from the material used in the windows of American space craft.

74

They were unbreakable. And rubber-bullet guns were demonstrated for the first time on the television news.

On Friday 26 June Bernadette Devlin finally lost her appeal against a six-month jail sentence for riotous behaviour in Derry the previous August. The police agreed that she should surrender at Victoria Barracks in Derry that evening. A 'farewell' meeting was arranged for Free Derry corner. On her way to the meeting from Belfast her car was stopped about five miles outside Derry. She was arrested and taken to Armagh Prison. When word of this reached the waiting crowd it erupted in rage. The 'defence of the area' in August 1969 had already passed into local folklore. It was a noble episode in which we had all participated when, after decades of second-class citizenship, we had finally risen and asserted in a manner which made the world take notice that we were not going to stand for it any more. The jailing of Miss Devlin was a challenge to the area to stand by that estimation of its own action.

Not everyone answered the challenge. Miss Devlin may have been a heroine to the hooligans, but ardour tended slightly to dim as one ascended the age-scale. She had, it was well recognized, got 'communistic ideas' and her talent for instant rhetoric about the joys of revolution unnerved the cautious. Local upholders of the 'traditional values' may have thought that six months in Armagh would do her, and them, no harm at all. But it would have been a private thought. For a day or two it was not possible publicly to execrate rebellion.

The hooligans, for the first time since August, had some sort of mandate for riot, and they were joined by some who had not flung a stone in anger for almost eleven months. It lasted over the weekend. The first perspex shield appeared, edging around the corner of William Street and Abbey Street. A brick hit it and it broke. The first rubber bullets, fired according to regulations to bounce off the ground before hitting their target, were fielded and fought over and kept as souvenirs. Gas containers crashed and petrol bombs flared through the swirling CS haze. All day Saturday and through Sunday afternoon the 1969 scenario, with the army in the RUC role, was acted out, the fighting surging back and forth around the mouth of Rossville Street. On mid-afternoon on Sunday, supporters of Mr Hume called a meeting of 'prominent people' in one of Michael Canavan's bookmaker shops to try and find a peace formula. It was suggested that a deputation should go to the military authorities and ask them to withdraw their soldiers from around the area. Sean Keenan, the best-known figure in the embryo Provisional organization, refused to be part of the delegation. Sean said that what we had to do was to prepare to defend ourselves. 'Against whom?' he was asked. Against the British army. Most of those present were incredulous. 'But the army is here to *defend* us.' Outside, the fighting went on. A delegation did go to Victoria Barracks and spoke to the army commander and Frank Lagan, the local police chief. A curious agreement was reached – that if attacks on the troops stopped immediately the RUC would not attempt to patrol the area for a fortnight. Lagan was visibly depressed by the terms. 'We had been doing so well. People were beginning to accept us.'

The fighting died away on Sunday night, not as a result of the agreement, which meant little to those in the forefront of the battle, but out of general exhaustion. And once again, the news from Belfast was very bad. Orange parades had triggered further fighting in Ardoyne, Ballymurphy and East Belfast. In East Belfast a Protestant crowd had tried to storm the small Catholic enclave around St Matthew's church. Armed men had defended it. Four Protestants and one Catholic had been killed. Three Protestants were killed in shooting in Ardoyne. Reports were, as always, confused, with the Catholics, the Protestants and the army giving different versions of, and drawing different conclusions from, each incident. But the central point was clear enough – that in Belfast it was shaping up like a shooting war, the

Catholics were vastly outnumbered and the marching season was not nearly over. The controversies which occupied hours of parliamentary time and acres of newsprint – about which side threw the first stone or whether the soldiers, when the fighting started, had acted impartially – were of little interest to the rioters and potential rioters of the Bogside and Creggan. What was of importance was that the Orange parades, these noisy, never-ending celebrations of institutionalized Catholic inferiority, were, apparently, being shepherded around Belfast past hemmed-in Catholic ghettoes by British soldiers. It was enough to make anger rise in even the most moderate Catholic observer. And the Falls curfew followed immediately. On 3 July, a Friday, when nerves were still frayed from the bloodletting of the previous weekend, an army search party found guns in a house in Balkan Street in the Lower Falls. The search party was stoned as it withdrew and the inevitable riot developed. Hundreds of rounds of CS were fired until the whole area choked on it. Then, at ten in the evening, the army imposed a curfew and did not lift it until Sunday. The soldiers moved in to enforce it, firing over a thousand rounds from their SLRs and killing three men. The people were penned in their houses. The soldiers went on a house-to-house search for arms, smashing in doors, ripping up floorboards. No one was allowed out on the Saturday. Then pressmen and Unionist leaders, including Captain John Brooke, were taken on a tour of the subjugated area in Land Rovers. Having gassed and battered the people into submission and made them cower in their kitchens, they came then with this effete squire from the back end of Fermanagh – he who, on an ordinary day, wouldn't dare set foot in the Falls – gave him an escort as he lorded it over the people and brought British press photographers with them to record the scene for their readers. I watched it and listened to accounts of it on television in a house in Beechwood Street in the Bogside. The woman of the house is mild-mannered to an extreme. Clenching her fists and crying with impotent rage, she stuttered: 'The bastards, the rotten, lousy, English bastards.'

The Falls curfew did not totally alienate the Catholics from the army. There were many who believed that, despite all, the presence of the army was still some sort of defence against extremist Protestant attack. It was said that the army had been misled by Unionist politicians, that this did not really represent army policy, that only a Scottish regiment had been involved, English regiments were different. People believed what they wanted. But the hooligans knew. The only difference between the army and the RUC was that the army was better at it.

A fortnight before the curfew the Tories had won the British General Election, and it was argued by some that this accounted for the more stringent army tactics. In the Londonderry constituency Mr McAteer and I had stood against Robin Chichester-Clark, brother of the then Northern Ireland prime minister, now a Tory front-bench spokesman. Mr McAteer stood as a 'Unity' candidate, with Mr Hume, rather bizarrely, as his election agent. (Mr Hume's decision to act as Mr McAteer's election agent had been described by Mr McAteer as 'Mr Hume's finest hour'.) I stood as an Independent Socialist, the Northern Ireland Labour Party having come to the conclusion that I had 'too violent an image' to qualify for their endorsement. Our election workers in Derry City were drawn mainly from the 'hooligan element'. They worked their proverbial hearts out, though none of them in truth was entirely convinced that any election was worth worrying about. In the countryside, local Republicans, press-ganged by Johnnie White, manned the booths. Mr Chichester-Clark got 39,000 votes. Mr McAteer and Mr Hume got 27,000. We got 7,500. The result made little difference to what was happening.

The area was raising a sudden generation of kamikaze children whose sport it was to hurtle down Rossville Street, stones in hand, to take on the British army. The Saturday riot became a regular thing. It was known as 'the matinee'. People did their shopping in the morning so as to get home before the riot started. 'Come on,' women shopping in the city centre would say to one another around lunch-time, 'let's get back into the area. The trouble will be starting soon.' The hooligans would gather at the bottom of William Street in the early afternoon and throw stones down the Strand Road towards Victoria Barracks. Eventually armoured personnel carriers would trundle out. The rioters would withdraw up William Street to the Rossville Street corner. The APCs would follow, being stoned all the way. The army would first use rubber bullets, then gas. Then they would send in the snatch squad. The rioters would scatter and, being nimble on their feet, very few were ever caught. The snatch squad would withdraw, the rioters would regroup and battle would continue. There were few variations from Saturday to Saturday.

Whatever they now thought about the army, many local residents were still vehemently opposed to this type of activity week after week. Few issues of the *Journal* went to press without another statement from Mr Hume reiterating his belief in the efficacy of 'peaceful methods'. The same message boomed from the pulpits on Sunday. Commentators reported – and they may have been right – that only a minority of Catholics actively supported violence. Occasionally someone – usually a woman who lived around William Street or Rossville Street – would come out into the middle of a riot, box the hooligans' ears and tell them to get the hell out of it and let people live in peace. But for all that the hooligans were the sons and daughters of the area, and however much their activities may have been regretted or condemned there could be no question of any section of the people backing the army *against* them. 'Hooligans you can call them, Father,' asserted a woman to the priest in the grounds of the Cathedral after mass one Sunday, 'and hooligans some of them certainly are; but they are our hooligans.' Moreover, stoning the soldiers may not have been producing desired results, but then neither were the 'peaceful methods' of the politicians. Gradually the ground was slipping from beneath the feet of the moderates.

If the riots in Derry in 1970 were only semi-serious, the situation in Belfast was grim. On 31 July Danny O'Hagan had been shot dead by the army in the New Lodge Road. The army said he was a petrol bomber. Local people flatly denied it. *The Times*, appeasing all sides, described him as 'an *assistant* petrol bomber'. REMEMBER O'HAGAN was painted in foot-high letters on gable ends in Bogside. There was shooting in Belfast almost every week after that, and one fact emerged starkly from it all – that when the army was involved it was always against the Catholics.

Since 1969 there had been a feeling in Derry, based not entirely on demagogic appeals, that it was somehow up to us to stand by the Catholic ghettoes in Belfast. We were much more advantageously positioned than they. We had had things much easier, and not just in the past two years. The fear in Belfast was that the isolated Catholic communities might be swamped and devastated by the surrounding Unionist population. It was a very real fear. It had, after all, happened before. That could not happen in Derry where, in any sectarian conflict, we could win. We were aware that the holocaust in Belfast in August 1969 had been precipitated by people coming on the streets in solidarity with us in Derry and that they had suffered mightily as a result. We had done nothing during the Falls curfew. At the time ideas floated around, that we should march and sit down outside Victoria Barracks, that we should somehow create an incident which would stretch the army and perhaps draw them away from the Falls. No one imagined such a demonstration would have changed the course of curfew significantly, but there was a feeling that we ought surely to have done *something*. By rioting at the edge of the Bogside, the thinking went, we were now showing the people in the Catholic ghettoes of Belfast that we were still with them, that their admirable intransigence in a much more dangerous situation was finding an echo here in Derry. 'Up the Falls' was a favourite slogan as the hooligans charged down Rossville Street. The name plate at Moore Street in the Brandywell district had been removed and 'Hooker Street' painted in its place. Hooker Street is in Ardoyne in Belfast. It was a tribute.

Even had there been no other factor involved what was happening in Derry magistrates' court in this period would eventually have swung a solid section of public opinion behind the hooligans. The Criminal Justice (Temporary Provisions) Act was passed in July 1970. It laid down mandatory sentences of six months for disorderly behaviour. It was not opposed by any Catholic member of the Stormont Parliament, after Mr Fitt, Mr Hume and the others had negotiated a deal with the Unionist Party, whereby an act outlawing incitement to religious hatred was passed at the same time. Only Ian Paisley fought against the package.

The act meant in effect that anyone found guilty of being 'in a riot situation' *had* to be sentenced to jail. Very few rioters were caught red-handed : they were too quick and too experienced for that. The army resorted to picking up suspects days afterwards around the centre of the city or at the Unemployment Exchange in the Strand Road. The irony of that was not missed. 'The only place you can be certain of finding a Derry rioter is at the dole.' In a typical case three or four soldiers would appear in court and positively identify a youth picked up in these circumstances as having thrown stones at them a week or two weeks ago. It was inherently improbable that they could be so certain, and some 'identifications' were ludicrous – soldiers asserting that they 'had no doubt at all' about the identity of a youth glimpsed in the darkness throwing a stone from fifty yards a fortnight previously. The defendant would produce three or four witnesses to say that he had been nowhere near the scene of the riot; and in almost all cases the defence witnesses were telling the truth. For what the army was doing was picking up likely-looking individuals more or less at random, and by no means all long-haired, unemployed Bogside teenagers were involved in every single riot. The fact that a particular defendant had almost certainly been involved in other riots on other dates did nothing to lessen the sense of injustice. Magistrates almost invariably accepted the army evidence, frequently remarking that 'there seems no reason why these soldiers should come into court and perjure themselves'. Defendants, once found guilty, were automatically jailed. This combination of telescopic-eyed soldiers and myopic magistrates injected a weekly booster shot of bitterness into the Bogside and Creggan. After some months of this there were a number of acquittals. One of the most common 'weaknesses' of defence cases was that, in the nature of things, defence witnesses were drawn from the defendants' peer group. They would tend to be other teenagers who would say that they were with the lad in question in a different place when the offence was committed. The bench paid scant attention to such people and the counsel for the prosecution – usually Mr E. H. Babington, a man with a passion for law and order, whose voice when he questioned working-class people had a built-in sneer – would manage easily to confuse them. In a few cases, eventually this was countered by finding 'respectable' and more articulate people – teachers, for example – to supply the alibi. We out-perjured them. But one ought not to have been brought to such a pass. Every case was logged in the minds of the people.

All the while Mr Hume, Mr Cooper and other local 'moderate' leaders were striving desperately to redirect attention and activity towards the 'proper' parliamentary channels. Occasionally they would appear in the middle of a riot, counselling peace, offering to make representations, appealing to the army to withdraw to barracks, promising to ask Parliamentary questions. But by the beginning of 1971 they were being told by fifteen-year-olds to 'fuck off'.

It was explained in press and parliament – and no doubt accepted by the overwhelming majority of people in Britain – that the riots were fomented by the IRA. Unionist members of parliament explained at Westminster that areas like the Bogside, Ardoyne, the Falls and the New Lodge Road were in the grip of a 'reign of terror', that half the people were being manipulated and the other half intimidated. British papers, from the *Mirror* to *The Times*, carried lurid reports of men in black berets skulking in the background, organizing the deployment of child-rioters. Church leaders and moderate Catholic politicians also referred darkly to 'sinister elements' who were 'leading the youth astray'. 'Onlooker' in the *Journal* was very strong on this subject. In fact neither wing of the Republican movement was, on balance, in favour of rioting. What each wanted to do in its own way was to get organized. There *was* a split in the Catholic ghettoes between those for and those against violence. But at this time it had little to do with the IRA or other 'sinister elements'. By and large it was a question of age.

However, notwithstanding the absence of organized Republican involvement in the rioting, Republican sentiment was growing, and most strongly among the rioting elements. In 1969 it had been perfectly possible to see the struggle as one 'to defend the area' and, more generally, to end oppression by the Unionists at Stormont. But now it was the British army whom one had to fight, it was they who acted as the instruments of oppression, who wielded the Special Powers Act against us. The struggle 'against injustice' became, in practice, a struggle against British forces – a pattern of play which matched perfectly the old Republican idea of the way things really were – and people were almost relieved gradually to discover that the guiltily discarded tradition on which the community was founded was, after all, meaningful and immediately relevant. 'We Shall Overcome' and 'We shall not be moved' gave way to 'The Soldier's Song' and 'Kevin Barry'.

The local left's main activity was designed to recruit the hooligans into a socialist organization. This was made no easier by the fact that we had no common organization of our own. In 1970 we made three attempts to set up a Socialist Republican Youth movement independent of all other organizations. Each had a similar pattern. By distributing leaflets or merely by passing the word around we would call a meeting of young people in the Labour Party hall in Magazine Street. The meetings were fairly chaotic, the audiences having little respect for standing orders. We would explain that the purpose of the organization was to play a part in the struggle against British imperialism. We had become a degree more specific about imperialism. We explained that there was much more to it than the soldiers in the street; it meant the big businesses which dominated the economy of Ireland, North and South; that to defeat it involved building a movement which could take on and defeat the agents of imperialism, Green as well as Orange; that this could not be done by pelting soldiers in Rossville Street with stones, admirable though the spirit behind that activity might be. Johnnie White would outline the course and failure of the IRA's 1956-62 campaign: how they had failed because they had not understood the need for politics as well as military activity; how we must now learn the lessons of that failure and create a movement of the working class. The older people in the area were incapable of doing this; they were hidebound by the past; it was up to the youth to take the initiative. It was, in retrospect, all sound stuff. But what the hooligans wanted now more than anything else was action. Building a thirty-two-county movement based on the working class sounded a very long-term project. The imperialists were down at the street corner. At every meeting someone would ask sooner or later when the guns were going to be handed out. Johnnie would explain again about guns and politics. 'A man with a gun and no politics is a gangster.' But it cut little ice. With one of our organizations – a stupidly named 'Young Hooligans Association' – we progressed far enough to elect a committee, have badges printed and organize a trip to Belfast so that our group could meet its counterparts from Ballymurphy. It was a good day out. Regiments were compared. But that too, collapsed, after about six weeks, which for us was a record. (The rise and fall of three revolutionary youth organizations set up by the same people in one city in twelve months may be another record.)

As we entered 1971 events in Belfast were spiralling out of control by any available force towards all-out urban warfare. Guns were being used regularly. A few bombs went off. Clashes between the troops and the Catholics were progressively bloodier, and each left another increment of bitterness in its wake. The British press had stopped carrying the news. Most reports from Northern Ireland were, by now, straightforward propaganda exercises based mainly on army press handouts.

In the Bogside people saw the soldiers, during and after a riot, come rampaging into the area beating up rioters, bystanders or anyone else they could lay their hands on, firing rubber bullets, now sometimes stiffened by the insertion of torch batteries, at point-blank range, making random arrests and perjuring the victims to jail. They experienced the offensive arrogance of soldiers on patrol, the constant barrage of insult and sneer and invitations to come on and 'have a go'. And in the papers the next morning they read of Tommy's endless patience in the face of provocation, his gentlemanly demeanour in most difficult circumstances, his superhuman restraint and matchless discipline ('No other army in the world would, for so long . . .' etc.). 'The rioters' were reported in a different vein – cowardly, vicious, depraved, lusting for blood. The hand of the IRA was discerned in every incident, the reasoning seeming to be that, since the army at all times behaved impeccably and since a reform programme designed to institute 'social justice' had been enacted, the trouble could not be based on any legitimate grievance, and that therefore there *must* be some subversive body ordering or fooling or intimidating people into violence. Once that was established there was no necessity to investigate the background to any particular incident. Many a dispatch from Derry was written in the bar of the City Hotel after a quick call to the army PRO and phoned through from the foyer. There were those who got danger money for this exercise. And press lies made their own contribution to the gathering crisis. As the inhabitants of areas like the Bogside read the popular dailies and realized that the news bore no relation to the facts as they had seen and experienced them, that there was in progress a sustained and apparently coordinated campaign to distort the truth about what was happening in and to the community, the sense of isolation grew, the tendency to look inwards, to rely on ourselves alone because there was no one else who could be trusted, was daily reinforced. If the army's increasingly indiscriminate violence was the major reason for the turn towards the gun, Fleet Street played a minor, but not insignificant, part in the same process.

The continuing inability of the left throughout 1970 and early 1971 to channel the aggression of the youth left the field open for the Provisionals, who, unlike us, had a perfectly coherent and stunningly simple answer to the crisis – smash Stormont and unite Ireland. But at the time, notwithstanding press accounts of a massively-financed, well-organized army, the Provisionals had neither the organizational nor the military capacity really to take hold of the situation in the ghettoes. They were making progress in the more intense situation in Belfast. But in Derry up to the middle of 1971 the best-known figures publicly associated with them were not young activists, but Sean Keenan and Neil Gillespie, veteran Republicans who were identified with the political rather than the military side of things. They were remembered for action in times past and were widely respected even by those who disagreed fundamentally with them. Neither fitted the image of the archetypal

IRA man. In the spring of 1971 the Provisional IRA in Derry for practical purposes did not yet exist.

It had begun to exist in Belfast. On 6 February the first Provisional was killed in action. James Saunders, a staff captain, was shot dead in the Crumlin Road. The same night Gunner Robert Curtis of the Royal Artillery was shot dead in the New Lodge Road. It was one apiece, and the war was on. Saunders and Barney Watt, another Catholic who had been killed by the army on the same night, were given Republican funerals. It was the Provos' first public show of strength and it was very impressive. Hundreds of young men marched in ranks, feet stamping, behind the tricolour-draped coffins. A volley was fired over Saunders' grave. Thereafter, in Belfast the gun, rather than the stone or the petrol bomb, became the favourite weapon of those resisting the army presence. The turn to the gun was encouraged by the fact that the army was increasingly using lead in preference to rubber bullets against 'ordinary' rioters. It was not alleged, for example, that Watt had been armed. He had been in the vicinity of a riot and that had been enough. Every arms search – and army tactics on these occasions were of the type sometimes described by the press as 'no-nonsense' – was adding to the bitterness and hostility. The supply of recruits into the IRA – especially into the more military-minded Provisional IRA – was increasing, and the supply of guns was beginning to keep pace.

In Derry, as always, the atmosphere was more relaxed, and the set-pieces at 'Aggro Corner' – the junction of Rossville Street and William Street – were still the order of the day. But events in Belfast were having their effect. It seemed clear that what was happening there was that the British army, acting for the Unionist government, was taking on the Catholic community and attempting to beat it into submission, just as the RUC and the B Specials used to do; and that the difference this time was that sections of the Catholics, most noticeably the Provisional IRA, were fighting back. Labour Party, and to a lesser extent Official Republican, propaganda increasingly seemed quite academic. Labour Party membership in Derry was dwindling fast – the local party had cut its links with the parent organization in Belfast, which was marching steadily rightwards in step with the army, whose activities it persisted in describing as 'peace-keeping'.

Brendan Hinds, Charlie Morrison and other trade unionists of the party, demoralized by the burgeoning sectarianism all around them and our inability to do anything to stop it, dropped out of activity. Dermie McClenaghan, too, seemed to weary of it, of the fact that somehow it had all become completely detached from the day-to-day bread-and-butter issues on which we had based ourselves two years ago.

I was spending about half the time in London, and the burden of party activity fell on Willie Breslin, a local teacher with a passion for issuing press statements, and Kathy Harkin, a housewife whose ability to type at fifty words a minute had for years made her the willing dogsbody of every radical organization in the city. Willie plugged away doggedly attacking the Catholic middle class and appealing for working-class unity against 'the common enemy'. But to no avail. Every day produced new evidence that the Catholics were being attacked *as Catholics* and that the Protestant working class was enthusiastically in favour of this – indeed, thought that the army was not nearly aggressive enough. We no longer had any contact with the Fountain. 'Workers' unity' as a slogan seemed not just academic but positively perverse. The most prominent of the younger members of the party – Seamus O'Kane, Tommy McCourt, Micky Doherty and others – were moving towards the Officials, who, having abandoned the attempt to create an independent youth movement and alarmed that the Provos were beginning to pick up members, had embarked on a recruitment campaign. O'Kane and the others resisted all invitations to join, doubting the Officials' commitment to class politics, but they could see that quite soon in Derry too there might be a shooting war and that one could not remain uninvolved. Joint training sessions over the border in the Donegal hills were resumed. Willie disapproved of this activity, and the Labour members involved, while retaining formal membership of the organization, effectively dropped out. The Labour premises in Magazine Street were given up. The party could no longer afford them, and anyway they were too big for the numbers now coming to meetings.

Almost every day now something happened to stiffen the intransigence of Catholic attitudes. Disparities in the sentences handed down by the courts became grotesque. A Protestant dealer in illegal guns got a suspended sentence. Catholic pickets went to jail. Catholic areas were subjected to daily army searches; Protestant areas went untouched. People were being beaten up quite casually by army patrols in Catholic areas at night. And Faulkner became Prime Minister. Chichester-Clark had been toppled by right-wing pressure after three off-duty Scottish soldiers were killed in unexplained circumstances on 10 March. Faulkner was probably the man in the Unionist hierarchy most heartily detested by Catholics (and still is). He had a well-earned reputation for being completely untrustworthy – 'political astuteness', it was called – and hopes were expressed at Westminster that he might be the man to resolve the situation. There was never any possibility of this happening. 'He's got more faces than the Guildhall clock,' said Seamus O'Kane, which just about summed up Catholic reaction to his election.

With Faulkner at the helm and the 1971 marching season under way, relations between the army and the Bogside went into a tailspin. The final rupture came on 8 July, when Seamus Cusack and Desmond Beattie were shot dead. The army said that Cusack had been carrying a rifle and that Beattie had been about to throw a nail-bomb. These were lies. They were the first people killed by the army in Derry, and their deaths had a big effect.

The Provos and the army had been shooting at one another in Derry for some weeks, the local Provisional organization having by now acquired the capacity to emulate its comrades in Belfast. It can be doubted whether initially there was mass support for this escalation. People are frightened by gunfire. But after the killing of Cusack and Beattie, support rocketed. The next Sunday, the Provisionals held their first mass rally in the area. Speakers made a straightforward appeal to 'Join the IRA'. Afterwards, applicants for membership formed a queue. If the army was going to shoot us down unarmed, if they were going to lie about it afterwards, if the press was going to print the lies as fact, and if cabinet ministers in London were going to lie in their teeth in the Commons to cover up, there was only one answer.

Hume, Cooper and their colleagues, now formed into the Social Democratic and Labour Party, held a meeting in Hume's house in West End Park while the Provo rally was in progress, came out and threatened to withdraw from Stormont if the Westminster government did not set up an official inquiry into the shootings. This was a half-despairing attempt to prevent leadership of the Catholic masses passing into the hands of those who advocated taking on the army. All along the SDLP had been fighting to convince their constituents of the efficacy of 'parliamentary methods'. They realized that if they could not do that they would be swamped by the rising tide of Catholic anger. On 22 June they had seized on an offer by Faulkner to set up three 'Parliamentary Committees', two of which were to be chaired by Opposition members, to examine new legislation, and they tried manfully to represent this as a major breakthrough. It was Faulkner's 'best hour', said Paddy Devlin. 'It should be made clear to all people today who say that no change has taken place that this is simply not true,' said Hume, with more than a touch of desperation. 'There *have* been changes in this community.' When he walked through the Bogside a few days later John found out what his constituents, who had had more than a little experience of reform in the last three years, thought of the 'changes'. 'You'll never get anywhere, Johnnie, by doing the Stormont crawl.' It was in an effort to recover this lost ground that the SDLP now made their threat to leave Stormont. And despite any misgivings or second thoughts which they might have had, they were forced to go through with it. There was to be no public inquiry.

They reaped no immediate benefit from this display of militancy. Political battles were now to be fought on the street, and the weapons were the Thompson and the Sten rather than the private notice question or the point of order. July was a very violent month. The Provos began to blow Belfast to bits and there was shooting in both Belfast and Derry almost every night. The Officials, who up to now had been unconvinced that the time was right for a full-scale campaign, weighed in. If they had not, they would have been totally eclipsed by the Provos. The Unionists called for 'sterner action', 'more vigorous measures', more soldiers and other such recipes for peace. From their right wing and their grass roots with increasing insistence came the demand for the all-purpose panacea of Orangeism – internment. And on Monday 9 August they got it.

Internment was a calculated humiliation which Unionist governments had, since the inception of the state, regularly visited upon our community. In the twenties, the thirties, the forties, and the fifties, the RUC had come storming into our areas at night, dragged our people from their beds and taken them off to camps and prison-ships, where they were often held for years; no charge, no trial, nothing. There was not a family in the area which had not had a relative or a neighbour interned. Now it was happening again.

Sean Keenan was interned, of course. When the Special Branch draw up an internment list in Derry they write down Sean's name and then ask: 'Who else?' He had been interned in the prison-ship *Argenta* in Belfast Lough in the forties. He had been interned in Crumlin Road jail in the fifties. On 9 August they came for him again. He would have gone quietly, being used to it, knowing the drill. About twenty others were picked up with him.

The 'justification' for the introduction of internment was based on the supposition that a 'tiny minority' of blood-thirsty gangsters was 'holding the community to ransom'; if these were plucked out of the situation everything would fall back into its normal, peaceful pattern. There must have been many, in British government circles especially, who believed that indeed this is what would happen. Faulkner had assured them that this was the case, and, after all, there was independent confirmation from the press, which for many months had been describing in detail how IRA men were bribing children to riot, intimidating the 'decent' Catholics (who were in a great majority), terrorizing prospective jurors and witnesses, and so on. Remove 'the men of violence' and everything else would follow. They soon found out how wrong they were.

The days when the Bogside allowed itself to be kicked around like this were long gone. As the noise of the internment operation wakened the area at four in the morning, people poured into the streets. The resistance prevented the army completing its swoop. As a result Derry lost fewer people, proportionately, than any comparable area in the North. Not that that lessened the reaction. By dawn the area was hysterical with hatred. In Brandywell, Bogside and Creggan there were street-corner meetings in progress. Local people told of their experiences: how the soldiers had dragged Peter Collins down the stairs by the hair of his head; how they didn't even give Micky Montgomery time to dress, just kicked him into the Land Rover in his underclothes; how they had come for John Carlin of Anne Street and, not finding him there, had taken instead his father, who was over sixty, and fired a rubber bullet into his stomach from point-blank range and then threw him into a truck. And Johnnie White, and Liam Cummins, and Micky McNaught and Liam McDaid and the others.

For the next few days there were so many people wishing to play an active role in resisting the army that it was almost impossible for the IRA to use guns. The streets were overflowing. At Iniscarn Road in Creggan women and girls linked arms singing 'The Men who died at Upton for Sinn Fein' and blocked the path of an army platoon, while, about two hundred yards away in Central Drive, in full view of both sides of this confrontation, hundreds of youths fought a pitched stones-versus-CS battle, with another platoon. The girls cheered wildly whenever a stone felled a soldier. The soldiers, more disciplined, refrained from similarly acknowledging a success for their side. There was a sit-down in Marlborough Road, a Catholic middle-class street at the edge of Creggan, most of whose inhabitants would not hitherto have been seen dead at a demo. Obstructive behaviour, ranging from standing in a crowd refusing to allow soldiers to pass to petrol-bomb attacks on army vehicles, was to be observed all round the area. The passive resistance came to an end when the army hosed a crowd sitting down in Lone Moor Road with purple dye and arrested a number of people, including John Hume and Ivan Cooper.

Belfast, meanwhile, seemed to have gone berserk. On the news we heard that there were gunfights raging in the Falls, the Markets, Ardoyne, Andersonstown and New Lodge Road. There were many dead. Protestant crowds had joined in the fighting, backing the army up. Whole streets were burning and thousands of refugees began to flee to the South. The twenty-four hours after internment were the bloodiest Northern Ireland had known for decades. There was in the area a profound lack of interest in the spectacle of British liberalism wrestling with its conscience, and winning, in the editorial columns of the *Guardian*.

Faulkner was on radio the next day explaining that the operation had been a great success, that its purpose had been, not, after all, to pick the gunmen up, rather to 'flush the gunmen out'. And, indeed, he was able to point to quite a few flushed-out gunmen. They had been flushed out on to every Catholic street in Belfast, where they were shooting at the British army.

The internment operation had caught the left in the area in a state of no more than usual disorganization. By the afternoon we had at least made contact with one another. This efficiency was due in part to the fact that the Official leadership had sent Malachy McGurran, an affable and un-dogmatic veteran of the 1956–62 campaign, to take over as full-time political organizer in the Derry area. We took over a vacant shop in Meenan Square near Free Derry Corner, established it as our headquarters and worked out a common approach to the situation. As well as the Officials and their Labour collaborators, there were a few members of the People's Democracy, who had got out of Belfast just ahead of the army. We decided to go for a one-day indus-trial strike, a rent-and-rates strike, to put pressure on all anti-Unionists to resign from official positions and to an-nounce that until every man was released neither the police nor the army would be allowed into the area.

Strikes – industrial or rent-and-rates – had been near and dear to local left-wing hearts for a long time. We had called for strikes against RUC brutality in January and April 1969 and against the army on a number of occasions since, but they had never got off the ground. Now the mood was right, and the rent strike was on as soon as it was called. We printed thousands of window stickers saying RENT STRIKE HERE and distributed them around the area. These worked marvellously to persuade the few recalcitrant individuals. No one wanted their house to be the only one in the street with no sticker up. There was some over-enthusiasm on the part of the youngsters whom we used to distribute them. 'It's up to you, Missus, which you have in your window, this sticker or a brick.' This gave rise to allegations that the strike's effectiveness was based on intimidation.

But in truth ninety-five per cent of people in areas like the Bogside were on rent strike from the moment it was mooted. The one-day industrial strike took place the Monday after the internment operation and, again with no need for much persuasion, it was solid among Catholic workers.

The fact the people did what we, the left, demanded encouraged us to believe that they did it because we demanded it. It was the August 1969 delusion in a new setting. If the Plymouth Brethren had parked a soap-box at the bottom of Wellington Street and called for a rent strike they would have got it. The people were avid for action and it just so happened that we were first in the field suggesting what action they should take. The demand that the army and the police be kept out of the area was ridiculous. It was like making a demand that the sun rise tomorrow morning with a view to claiming responsibility for its eventual appearance.

In the next few months the area became used to the sight and the sound of guns, until a teenager walking along Lecky Road with a machine-gun would cause no *frisson* of excitement, rather speculation as to what target he might be preparing to hit.

Sympathy for his targets tended to diminish, even on the part of the many people who still did not really approve of gunplay. I arrived home one morning at two a.m. and told my father, the mildest man I ever met, that the lads had just got a soldier at Bligh's Lane. 'Ach,' he said, 'it won't do him a damn bit of harm,' and went on reading.

The army made few attempts to come in. Occasionally, for reasons best known to their tactical experts but quite unclear to anyone else, they would thrust a couple of hundred yards into the area, and stand there long enough to draw fire, before pulling out. Perhaps they were testing the water. On one such occasion they took up position at the top of a laneway near Westland Street. It was mid-morning and in the laneway a woman was buying bread from a bread van at her back door. Round the corner bounced a teenage Provisional with an M1 carbine. He loosed off half a dozen shots up the lane at the soldiers. This obviously put the woman and the breadman in some danger. 'Get out of it, you wee bugger,' she shouted, enraged. 'Can you not wait till the breadman's finished serving the bread?'

Within a month of internment almost all the Labour Party members who had been working with the Officials joined the latter. The Officials at the same time lost some people to the Provisionals. Shedding members on the right and recruiting on the left, the effect of the upsurge of militancy on the Officials was thus to move their centre of gravity sharply to the left, significantly to the left of the leadership in Dublin who were even now advocating the 'democratization of Stormont' as the next 'stage' in the revolution. This had little effect on the course of local politics in the next few months, since political debate was drowned out by the rattle of gunfire and the sound of Provo bombs. The overwhelming majority of the people in the area were impatient of the war of words now being waged in the columns of the local press between the Provos and the Officials. The point was to keep the army out of the area and bring the Unionist government, the never-ending source of all our grievances, to an end. The only difference to be discerned between the two organizations was that the Provos believed in bombing 'economic' targets whereas the Officials wanted to concentrate on the military. The Official leadership also insisted that their campaign was 'defensive' and not 'offensive', a distinction too nice for anyone involved in the situation to understand. As one member of the Officials' local staff put it: 'Shooting soldiers is shooting soldiers.' To most people there did not seem a big enough difference to justify the bi-weekly bursts of mutual denunciation in the *Journal*. Most households contributed indiscriminately to the weekly collection of both organizations. (Each offered the same wage to full-time volunteers – five pounds a week and no deductions.) Both had closed their books to new recruits, being unable to handle the numbers waiting to join. More than one ex-hooligan went from one wing to the other and back again asking to be let in and being told to 'come back in a few weeks and we will see what we can do'.

The antagonism of the area towards British authority received a further boost when word filtered out of the torture techniques being used to make internees talk. Apart from run-of-the-mill beatings-up, which everyone assumed would happen, the Special Branch had kept men hooded and spread-eagled against walls for hours on end, given them no food but bread and water, and played 'white noise' into their ears. The combination, it was said, would reduce strong men to gibbering idiots who would babble all they knew. The thought of that happening to people from our streets contributed greatly to the rising fury. (Lord Parker was to report the following March that all this had in fact happened but that it did not constitute cruelty since the perpetrators did not 'take pleasure' in their work . . .)

Meanwhile British commentators were searching for new words of execration to describe the I R A. They reached for *Roget's Thesaurus* after 9 November when a group of women seized Marta Doherty, a local girl who was about to marry a British soldier, and tarred and feathered her. This was a case in point. Within hours Miss Doherty was the best-known bride in Britain. Local photographer Larry Doherty captured a striking picture of her, head sheared, tied to a lamp-post and covered in tar. It appeared on the front page of every British paper and was scanned by the news cameras of BBC and ITV. At Westminster, Lord Balniel's elegant upper lip trembled with emotion as he expressed his shock/horror/detestation. It was related in tones of disgust that not one person in the large crowd watching had intervened to help her and that few people in the area seemed properly outraged by the incident. 'What kind of people are they,' it was asked, 'who can allow such a thing to happen in their midst?'

They were, of course, and are, ordinary, decent working-class people who happened to have to see and judge the incident in a context which newspaper editors and Tory politicians could not appreciate, even in the unlikely event of their wishing to. Less than a week before Miss Doherty's experience Mrs Elizabeth Groves was standing in her kitchen in a house in the Andersonstown estate. She had a Republican song playing on her gramophone. A soldier standing in her garden aimed his riot gun through the open window and blasted a rubber bullet at her face. It tore both her eyes out. There were no pictures of the blind Mrs Groves in the British papers or television, no cheep of protest from the liberal papers, no murmur of concern in Parliament. Mrs Kathleen Thompson, a mother of six, of Kildrum Gardens in the Creggan estate, was standing in her back garden around the same time. Kildrum Gardens stands on the brow of a steep hill in Creggan overlooking an army post in the Foyle Road. A soldier, bored perhaps by the lack of action, aimed up and shot her dead. There was no official reaction. Her death was largely unreported. It was with things like that that the people of our area compared and contrasted what was done to Marta Doherty. It was in that context that they judged the hullabaloo which followed. There was, as it happened, a great number of people in the area who did not approve of what was done to Miss Doherty. But in the circumstances they could not reasonably be expected to take a very strong line on the matter. Just as no one – even those who continued to disapprove of them – could be expected to take a strong line against IRA activities.

The shootings war continued unabated. Many of the battles took place around 'Fort Essex' army post, which lay between Bligh's Lane and Eastway, on the hill between Bogside and the Creggan estate. There were two hundred soldiers in it guarding a policeman. The policeman was there because in late 1970 Dr Paisley and Mr Craig were making political capital out of the fact that the area was almost completely unpoliced and insisting that the government do something about it. In a fit of something less than genius Major Chichester-Clark decided to open a police station in the heart of the area. A prefabricated hut was erected in the middle of some factory buildings. The perimeter was surrounded by barbed wire, sandbag emplacements were built, and two companies deployed. No one ever tried to go in to inquire about dog licences or stolen bicycles or to complain about the noise of the neighbours. The policeman never came out. After a time there were those who suspected that there was no policeman in there; just a hut with 'Police' written on it being guarded by two hundred soldiers. Mythical or not, three of the soldiers died to defend his presence.

Both Officials and Provisionals were patrolling the area in hijacked cars. For the most part they were fairly punctilious about not taking vehicles from private individuals. 'Company' and hired cars, though, were fair game. Taking them did not injure any individual and, as an added advantage, they were as a rule almost new. After a few months the local branch of the biggest car-hire firm in the world agreed to supply each wing with a free car – changed each week – in return for safe passage for the rest of its fleet. It was an equitable arrangement. Each battalion was responsible for hijacking its own cars and there was, at rank and file level, occasional over-enthusiasm, such as a unit deciding to hijack a new vehicle on the grounds that its current model had a puncture.

The Provisionals established headquarters in a house in Stanleys Walk, with separate district headquarters in Creggan and Brandywell. The Officials operated from an HQ in Creggan, using the Meenan Square shop for coordinating activities in the Bogside itself. Not all callers were on military business. People would come seeking advice, or with minor complaints – on the type of business which in Britain would naturally be taken to the welfare office or to a department of the local council. Provisional supporters would go to the Provisionals, Official supporters to the Officials. Neutralists had a choice.

Petty crime was handled by the Free Derry Police, which was independent of both IRAs. Tony O'Doherty, who had temporarily given up a career as an international footballer because, as far as one could judge, he preferred being at home in Creggan doing something constructive, emerged as police chief. His personal popularity had a lot to do with the fact that after a few weeks there *was* no petty crime. Shop owners in Creggan reported that for the first time since they had set up in business they could lock up at night with an easy mind. The police were obsessional about speed limits and many motorized visitors left the area outraged by an on-the-spot fine.

The barricades cut across the bus-routes through the area. One of the services was abandoned completely; the other, the Creggan service, had to thread a circuitous route through the few barricades which had been breached to permit access. The local authority was noticeably unwilling to send men into the area to carry out normal maintenance. Alternative arrangements were made. Street lights, for example, would be looked after by someone who had emerged as a particular street's handyman. Playgrounds – not that there were many of them – were maintained by the people living near by. Upkeep of the Creggan football field had somehow become a police matter and was supervised by Tony O'Doherty. It all worked quite well.

At the beginning of December the Northern Resistance Movement – a recently formed united front supported by the Provisionals and the People's Democracy – announced that if the internees were not released by Christmas they would organize a series of protest marches in defiance of a ban which had been in operation for some months. The first march took place up the M1 motorway on Christmas Day. The NRM's intiative forced the Civil Rights Association, which was supported by the Official leadership, to take to the streets also. In the first four weeks of January the NRM and the CRA held a total of nine 'illegal' marches in different parts of Northern Ireland, some of them ending in medium-sized riots when the army moved in. The CRA march in Derry on 30 January 1972 was one of this series.

When the shooting started that day the first reaction, after fear, was bewilderment. *Why* were they shooting? At Free Derry Corner where most people had gathered for the meeting the crowd flung themselves to the ground as the crack-crack of the self-loading rifles came from the bottom of Rossville Street. Looking up one could see the last few stragglers coming running panic-stricken, bounding over the barricade outside the High Flats, three of them stiffening suddenly and crumpling to the ground. One ought to have realized at the time that what was happening was that they were being killed. An hour and a half later no one knew for certain how many were dead. Some said three, some five. From McCafferty's house in Beechwood Street Bernadette Devlin phoned Altnagelvin Hospital and asked for the names of the casualties. About twenty people crowded around her into the hallway as she prepared to write them down. The pushing and shoving stopped as she just kept on writing.

Later in a shop in Creggan Martin McGuinness, the Provisionals' OC, proposed and an Official seconded a call for national strike until after the funerals. The Official Command Staff voted to drop the fiction that they were on a 'defensive' campaign. The next morning there were groups of people standing around in Rossville Street, staring at the spots where it had happened. Everyone knew them now, the names of the dead. They could recite them as readily as a football fanatic rhymes off the names of his favourite team. And they knew how each one died, from the telling and the retelling of it: how Jack Duddy had been just behind Father Daly in the car park of the High Flats laughing to see a priest running when the bullet got him; how Pat Doherty had been lying out in the open moaning 'I don't want to die on my own', and Barney McGuigan, a big quiet man, had gone out to him waving a white handkerchief and was shot in the base of the skull; how John Young had been dragging himself, wounded, in the shelter of the barricade across Rossville Street towards the door of the flats, people screaming down at him from the windows, pleading 'Come on, lad, come on, come on, you're nearly there,' but he didn't make it. And all the others. Bloody Sunday upset us considerably. A few weeks later the Officials planted a bomb outside the officers' mess of the Para headquarters in Aldershot. Unfortunately it killed six innocent people. Had it killed a dozen British soldiers there would have been dancing in the streets in Derry.

After Bloody Sunday the most powerful feeling in the area was the desire for revenge. Since the deaths of Cusack and Beattie and the introduction of internment there had been mass support for the IRA, but it had been tempered with a vague uneasiness about the morality of killing people. 'Moderate' elements such as Hume and his supporters and the local priests could do nothing to alter the course of events, but at least they were accorded a hearing. Now few listened to anything that they said. People made a holiday in their hearts at the news of a dead soldier. The feeling was made all the more fierce by the reaction of the British establishment. There was more outrage expressed in the British House of Commons when Bernadette Devlin didn't hit Reginald Maudling half hard enough than there was at our people being killed to keep Brian Faulkner in office. The strata that had traditionally wielded decisive influence in the area were now more powerless than ever. Members of Parliament sucked down to armed teenagers at the street corner and tried to buy friendship with offers of gelignite.

But for all the solidity of the area's opposition to the forces of outside law and order there was no plausible representative organization within it. There were attempts to create one. The Officials, inspired by their national leadership's attachment to some abstract idea of 'mass democracy', tried to set up a network of street committees. The plan was that the residents of each street would elect a committee and that these committees would in turn elect a 'coordinating committee' which would govern the area. Considerable time and energy were spent organizing street meetings and encouraging people to elect committees. They never really got off the ground and no coordinating body was ever formed. The Officials did not make it clear whether the street committees were to operate as mini tenants' associations, with responsibility for ensuring that lighting was adequate and the streets kept clear of rubbish, the things at present being handled on an *ad-hoc* basis; or whether they were to be part of a quasi-revolutionary structure; or both. They did not make it clear because they themselves were confused on the point. The Provisionals rejected the idea of street committees on the ground that they were an Official plot to initiate 'Moscow-style communism'. No one, not even the Provisionals themselves, took this allegation very seriously. What they meant was that they were not going to support any project thought up by the Officials. For much the same reason the Officials rejected the Provos' plan for a 'Free Derry Council' to be elected by proportional representation with political groups offering slates of candidates. The SDLP was against any new elected body on the questionable grounds that Mr Hume was still the 'elected representative' of the area, and that there was no need for any other. After a time the Provos, with some tacit Nationalist Party support (it seemed to have resurrected itself for the purpose), did manage to call a 'Free Derry Council' into existence but too late for it to establish its *bona fides* as the sole authentic voice of the people or to play any meaningful role.

The inability of the area to produce a single representative body was a reflection of the fact that there was no general political agreement. Everyone was in favour of keeping the barricades up and the army out. No one wanted

Stormont's writ to run again. But beyond that there was no clear consensus. Beyond that indeed there seems in retrospect to have been amazingly little discussion. The results of this became clear on 24 March, when the British government, realizing that Bloody Sunday, far from terrorizing the Catholics off the streets, had made them yet more determinedly intransigent, suspended Stormont and instituted direct rule from Westminster. The instinctive reaction of the people of the area was unrestrained joy. Stormont had for decades been the focus of all our resentments. Now it was gone. Only the Official leadership tried to argue that this was not a victory; that it was in fact a defeat. But most people dismissed this attitude as a curious aberration and suspected that in their heart of hearts the Officials, too, were delighted. Everyone realized that with the suspension of Stormont Northern Ireland was up for grabs. But to the crucial question which this raised – with what did we want the Stormont system replaced? – there was no easy or generally accepted answer. This resulted in a degree of confusion about what we ought to do now, a confusion which William Whitelaw, the new Tory Secretary of State for Northern Ireland, was not slow to recognize and use.

After direct rule the parliamentary politicians re-emerged, just as they had done in 1969, with dusted-off statements about 'peaceful progress to a just society'. For the previous seven months they had fought hard to make themselves relevant. Gerry Fitt had twisted and turned and tied himself in knots in an effort to reach some compromise on internment which might be acceptable to his constituents in West Belfast. In December he had planned to use his appearance on a three-hour BBC investigation of the 'Northern Ireland Problem' to suggest that if internees were charged with specific offences in the courts he and his party might return to 'normal' politics. However, his script was leaked and the reaction to it convinced him that this would not be a politic thing to say. Other of his parliamentary colleagues, reasoned that if you can't beat them and won't join them you might still skirt around the fringes making friendly noises at them. Some of these noises extended to offering overt support to anything that the Officials might propose, though exactly what this might mean was at no point made clear to the general public. The SDLP leaders, with the possible exception of Paddy Devlin of Falls, who often seemed big and aggressive enough to make up for any five lightweights, had wanted to sell out, but found themselves in a fairly unusual position for a social-democratic group in that they could not find a way to arrange the sale. Market conditions got better after direct rule.

The church, too, began flexing its political muscles. Most priests had all along held to the idea that killing people, including soldiers, was an offence against the law of God, and this was expressed in some sermons after specific IRA successes. But often it was tempered by a balancing condemnation of the British army and an expression of understanding that, of course, the violence had its roots in real injustice. The church had not yet launched the type of fierce, coordinated, openly-political campaign of which it was shortly to show it was capable.

The Provo bombing campaign was having some distinctly counter-productive effects. It was in the nature of the campaign that civilians were put at risk, and in Belfast there were a number of bloody tragedies, each of which was grist to the mill of the British propaganda machine. In the Catholic areas there was a widespread feeling of simple human horror. It was this horror, allied to the belief that with the suspension of Stormont we had already won a significant victory, which triggered a movement for 'peace'. This made its first newsworthy appearance when a group of women in Andersonstown tried to hold a meeting to appeal for a bi-lateral truce. They were supported by the local clergy. They were unfortunate, however, in some of their other supporters. The wife of Tory MP Nigel Fisher flew in from England and announced that she was 'here to do all that she could to help the women of Andersonstown in their search for peace', which had an impact on the women's movement something like a punch in the solar plexus. Other millstones such as the middle-class 'Women Together' organization insisted on tying themselves around the neck of the Andersonstown peace-seekers and succeeded very quickly in pulling them under. However, the fact that they had made an appearance at all was not without significance. There was public opposition to the IRA from within.

Reaction to the bombing campaign in Derry was more muted; not least because the Derry Provos, under Martin McGuinness, had managed to bomb the city centre until it looked as if it had been hit from the air without causing any civilian casualties. Local attitudes to the bombing had always been fairly equivocal. Few could deny the force of the Officials' constantly reiterated point that the people who suffered most by the destruction of business premises were the workers who lost their jobs. The owners, after all, would in due course get full compensation. It could not be gainsaid, either, that the bombing was pushing the Protestant masses even further to the right, and that was to be regretted. As against that, every bomb planted was a minor victory in the endless battle of wits against the security forces. Every blast, whether one approved of it or not, was a dramatic demonstration of the fact that we, who had been scorned for so long, could now strike out in an unmistakable fashion and make the establishment scream. A few hours after the Provos had blown the inside out of the Guildhall a supporter of Mr Hume remarked, 'Of course I don't agree with this bombing at all, but I must admit the Guildhall's looking well.'

In Derry it was not the Provo bombing campaign but the Officials' shooting of a Creggan teenager, home on leave from the British army, which gave Catholic Tories the op-opportunity to come storming out to oppose the IRA.

Nineteen-year-old Ranger Best, stationed in Germany, had foolhardily decided to spend his leave at home. As he wandered about the area renewing contacts with old friends he was twice warned by Official units to get out 'for your own good'. But he did not. So he was picked up by an Official Patrol and taken 'for questioning' to the shop in Meenan Park. Once there, he was doomed. The man who presided over the 'trial' explained afterwards: 'Once we had him there was nothing we could do *but* execute him. Our military orders after Bloody Sunday were to kill every British soldier we could. They didn't say anything about local soldiers. He was a British soldier and that is all there was to it.' Best was driven with a hood over his head to a piece of waste ground near William Street, told to get out and to walk straight ahead. After he had taken a few steps he was shot in the back of the skull. His body was found early next morning.

Had Best been an 'ordinary' soldier there would have followed a ritual, and largely disregarded, condemnation from the clergy and perhaps a statement from Mr Hume to the effect that this was not the proper way to proceed; but the majority of the people of the area would have considered it an act of war, maybe something which they were less passionately in favour of pursuing than they had been a few months previously, but an act of war nonetheless. But Best was not, of course, an ordinary soldier. He was a local lad, the son of solid and inoffensive parents who lived in a council house in Creggan, and his killing outraged that very feeling of communal solidarity which the last three years had created and which was absolutely essential to the maintenance of Free Derry. 'If he had stayed in Germany he would have been safe enough,' complained a local housewife the day after his death. 'He was killed because he came home to see his mother.' It was a line of argument which struck deep chords, not least in the hearts of local mothers.

The day after his death four hundred women marched to

the Official headquarters in Meenan Square. Two members of the organization, neither of whom had been present at the 'trial' or execution of Best, were unfortunate enough to be manning the premises at the time. Their encounter with the protesters was bruising. The British media seized on the issue with unconcealed glee. 'Women call on IRA to get out' was smeared across the front pages. The five women who had led the march were accorded the handy reference-title: 'the Derry Peace Women' and quickly became the darlings of the Tory press. The church, too, quickly showed its talent for seizing the time and called a 'peace meeting' in the school hall in Creggan. Sharing the platform with local priests were a member of the local police committee, Mr John Maultsaid, Mr Frank McCauley ('Onlooker'), Tom Doherty, a former Nationalist councillor, and some others of like ilk. Their message was clear: 'Things have gone too far. It is time to call a halt.' Most of the audience of two thousand agreed. Johnnie White mounted the platform and asked for the mike to explain the Officials' position. The chairman, the parish priest of Creggan, Father Martin Rooney, refused, telling him that 'You are not wanted. You are an alien influence', after which the meeting broke up in some confusion. What was quite clear was that for the first time in many months the people of the area were, sometimes literally, fighting among themselves, a luxury no embattled community can afford.

The bishop turned out for Ranger Best's funeral, flanked by twenty-five priests. (Two days previously fifteen-year-old Manus Deery had been buried. He had been shot for no particular reason by an army sniper from the city walls as he was on his way home from a fish and chip shop with the family supper. He got the standard two priests.) For the next week it seemed that no edition of the BBC's 'World at One' and no front page of any newspaper was complete without quotes from a local priest or a 'peace woman' explaining that the IRA was no more than a tiny minority within the area and that the majority of peace-loving people were in the process of evicting them. Father Hugh O'Neill, administrator of St Eugene's Cathedral, was particularly prominent. Father O'Neill had once accused me of being the Devil; that is, not of being an agent of the Devil but of *being* the Devil, Satan himself in human form. He was on surer theological ground now, asserting that the IRA had no respect for the law of man or God. 'They are finished – it's the end of the road for the IRA. Those Officials are not the IRA at all. They are communists pretending to be the IRA. The people have rejected them.' Father O'Neill also alleged that there were North Koreans in the area up to no good, a revelation which resulted in a confrontation between a *Daily Express* reporter and a waiter from the Rice Bowl restaurant from which the waiter, quite possibly, has not yet recovered. At mass the following Sunday the church pursued the attack. The pulpits became for the day political platforms from which a coordinated series of anti-IRA – anti-Official IRA in particular – speeches were delivered.

The killing of Best and the reaction to it detonated a number of minor political explosions both locally and nationally. The fact that the clergy had openly entered the political lists against them forced the local Officials to define more clearly than they had ever dared before their attitude to the church and to its role in politics. Hitherto their attitude had been not so much ill defined as undefined. They were members of an organization which, at national level, claimed to be Marxist or 'moving towards Marxism'. The local group, since its absorption of the Labour Party left after internment, had moved sharply to the left of the leadership's position and was probably the least 'Catholic' Republican group in the country. Since August 1971, however, there had been neither the occasion nor, it appeared, the necessity to express this in action. The 'defence of the area' was the task at hand; the enemy was the British army. The Officials fought alongside the Provos to keep the army out and the occasional questioning of the means of doing this by the church and the SDLP was not urgent enough to demand answer. For its part the church was unable in the same period to denounce the Officials as forthrightly as it would have liked. But now, as the church and the middle classes roused Catholic wrath against them, and as Father O'Neill argued that the killing of a local Catholic was a direct product of their 'alien ideology', the Officials had either to cut and run or to fight back. To their credit, they did the latter, producing perhaps the fiercest class-oriented, anti-church polemic ever to issue from within our community. 'We are not a Catholic organization. We never said that we were. If there is anyone in this community who has been giving us support in the belief that we are some sort of militant, Catholic, Nationalist organization, let them withdraw their support now. We are nothing of the sort. We are out to build a revolutionary socialist party of the Irish working class.'

It was, in Derry, fairly daring stuff and its authors expected that it would receive a fairly hostile reception when it was distributed in the *Starry Plough* ('Derry's own Republican paper') around the Creggan and the Bogside; but the reaction was more complex. The church's open entry into politics had deprived it of the total inviolability normally conferred on it by its 'spiritual' role. Those who wished to 'stand by the IRA' *had* to oppose the clergy on this issue. If the role of the IRA was being openly questioned for the first time in ten months, the role of the church was under similar scrutiny for the first time in fifty years. That too, in its own contradictory way, helped to loosen the bonds holding the area together. The Provisionals, after some hesitation, realized that the flak aimed at the Officials was certain to damage them as well and asserted their own refusal to accept the church's dictate. Initially they had tried to use the reaction to the Best killing to divert support away from the Officials and towards themselves. But that was much too delicate a manoeuvre to come off and was quickly abandoned.

The Officials' leadership in Dublin called a ceasefire three weeks after the Best affair on 23 May. They insisted at the time that this had nothing to do with the 'peace women's' still buoyant campaign; few accepted this. What happened was that the elements in the Official leadership which had wanted, anyway, to call a ceasefire found the time ripe in the post-Best atmosphere. They had continued to insist that their organization was not engaged in any offensive, military operations – this despite the fact that since Bloody Sunday active service units had been doing little other than seeking out ways and means to shoot and blow up soldiers. This, insisted the leadership, was 'defence and retaliation', not to be confused with the offensive and sectarian behaviour of the Provisionals. The common people had continued to have great difficulty discerning the difference between the Officials defensively blowing up two soldiers in Brooke Park on 5 April and the Provisionals offensively shooting one a week later. The stated reason for the ceasefire was that military operations were aggravating the sectarian situation, forcing the Protestants into an even more intransigent position and leading on towards open civil war; the way forward was to concentrate on politics.

The Provisionals, meanwhile, were getting on with it. They had no hang-ups about Catholicism. 'All our volunteers go to mass on Sunday.' Nor did they espouse any un-Irish theories of revolutionary socialism. They had in their ranks most of the 'Old Republicans' whose presence helped confer on them a historical legitimacy denied the Officials. Theirs was a philosophy which presented the people of the area with no problems. One might disagree with it, and many did, but it was not in our tradition to disrespect it. 'Fitt and the rest are wasting their time,' said Martin McGuinness at a meeting in Brandywell. 'We are not stopping until we have a united Ireland.' That was clear enough. They recruited a few of the Official volunteers who had not agreed with the ceasefire.

They had become, by any standards, a brilliantly efficient

guerrilla army. Now that the Officials had 'given up' they claimed recognition as the sole inheritors of the Republican tradition, a status which, once assumed, cannot of its nature be subjected to democratic contestation. A resultant disregard for all proffered advice or criticism was sometimes upsetting, even to their own supporters. They were the front-line hooligans of 1969 in arms, young and urgent and now absolutely sure of themselves, with all the arrogance of their age and their race. They escalated the bombing campaign. Systematically, street by street, business house by business house, they continued to take the commercial area of the city to pieces. 'We are filling in the gaps,' they would say. They became very good at it. They were rarely caught. And, still, they did not injure civilians, nor did they blow themselves up, both of which things still seemed to happen with tragic regularity in Belfast. And still, commentators would denounce them as mindless thugs and eminent churchmen would damn them to hell. Politicians continued to urge the people to 'get rid of the terrorists' and experts on guerrilla warfare talked learnedly about 'a strategy to detach the gunmen from the civilian population'. It is not easy to envisage the strategy which would 'detach' the sons and husbands of the area from the 'civilian population' of it, a consideration which seemed never to strike experienced experts on the situation, such as Mr Whitelaw who continued to repeat the phrase as if repetition might magically endow it with meaning. (About a week after Ranger Best was shot I argued on a street corner with a lady who had been vigorously supporting the 'peace campaign', in the course of which I alleged against her that, 'I suppose if you knew who did it you would give the names to the police.' At this she stalked away saying that she had been trying to conduct a sensible discussion and if I was not going to take the matter seriously . . .)

One of the Provisionals' reasons for rejecting all entreaties to call a ceasefire was that they had not yet been recognized as a 'legitimate' political tendency. British ministers of both major parties had pledged repeatedly that they would not 'sit down with terrorists', 'shake the blood-stained hands of', 'have any discussion with the vile perpetrators of', and so on. The more unequivocal the pledges given the more clearly the Provos recalled Cyprus, Aden, Kenya and Ireland in the twenties. At the end of June Whitelaw agreed to talk terms with them and a truce was called. After nine days, on 9 July, it collapsed when Provisional leaders in Andersonstown in Belfast were unable to restrain Catholics' anger at what appeared as open army support for militant Protestants in a sectarian housing dispute. The war continued. The first bomb of the renewed campaign exploded in Derry within a few hours.

The disparate movement for peace and for Mr Whitelaw to be 'given a chance' persisted. The SDLP was its political expression. There was a degree of liaison between the two tendencies. The 'peace women' met Provisional chief Sean MacStiofain and Mr Hume was seen acting as chauffeur for the man sometimes described as the Provisionals' 'top Northern strategist'. During the truce Hume and the local Provisionals had jointly negotiated the dismantling of three barricades with one of Whitelaw's aides. This nervous alliance fell apart when the truce collapsed and the barricades went up again. A soldier was shot dead on 11 July. The Provos celebrated the twelfth with the biggest bomb offensive to date, detonating a total of five hundred pounds of explosives around Waterloo Place alone in the afternoon. As usual hundreds gathered to watch the bombs go off. Businessmen, as they watched their premises crumble, said that it was the last straw and berated army officers standing around – 'call yourselves security forces?' – and demanded to know 'why you don't go into the Creggan and shoot every one of the bastards'. Our teenagers cheered: 'Fucking right. We're never going to own it. We might as well destroy it.' But once again it was teenagers who were doing all the cheering. There was no one in the area willing to sell the Provos out. They were our people. But there were some – not peace women necessarily – who thought that for what we were going to get out of it it was maybe not worth going on.

Pressure from Unionist politicians, and more effectively from the UDA, who were setting up their own Protestant no-go areas in protest against the Catholic enclaves, mounted on Whitelaw to move in on Free Derry. The re-erection of the barricades dismantled during the truce was taken as proof that they could not be talked down, that Hume and the peace women could not deliver the area up. Whitelaw's office began signalling unmistakably that the army was going to move in. The Provos understood this more quickly than most. They understood that Whitelaw had agreed to the truce in order to talk the barricades down, and they had been willing to go along with this, bargaining, barricade by barricade, for political position. That was no longer on the agenda.

Had the army moved in before direct rule it is certain that thousands of people could have come out to face them, guns or no guns. Now, however, the detested Stormont was gone. The peace women had emerged, bringing the SDLP along in the slipstream of their petticoats, back towards the centre of the political stage. What the area lacked now, which it had had prior to direct rule, the Best killing and the Official ceasefire, was single-mindedness. Without that single-mindedness it was not possible for the Provos, or anyone else, to contemplate a protracted set-piece battle to repel a determined British advance. There was little discussion of the question in the area. Everyone knew it was just not on; that the army, after a year, was going to get in.

They came, naturally, in the morning (at 4 a.m. on 31 July), unceasing lines of them in convoy, Ferrets, Whippets and APCs, Land Rovers, Saladins and Centurions coming up Rossville Street past the High Flats and into Lecky Road, searchlights playing down from the city walls, bulldozers and earth movers beginning to grapple with the barricades, men shouting, machinery screaming, noise everywhere.

'Jesus Christ,' said Tommy McCourt, watching from West-land Street and getting his military parallels slightly crossed in his awe, 'it's like bloody Dunkirk.' All over the area volunteers were melting into the darkness and short back-and-sides. In McCafferty's in Beechwood Street Tommy, the American writer Jack McKinney and I made tea and dis-cussed the theoretical implications of the changed situation. 'Are you three going to sit there,' asked Mrs McCafferty, 'and let those tanks come right into our street?' Ten minutes later an unmolested Centurion rolled round the corner from Elmwood Road and roared up the hill towards the barricade at the top. 'Annie, Annie,' shouted Mrs McCafferty across the street to a neighbour, 'would you come out and see what they are doing? They're taking down our barricade.'

Before the day was out meetings had been held protest-ing about the army having killed two unarmed youths in Creggan, Seamus Bradley and Daniel Hegarty, who had appa-rently got in their way. The requisite instant broadsheet was on the streets:

Now, more than ever before, it is necessary that every hour of every day every British soldier is made to understand that in the eyes of the people of the area, he is a leper... Our area was an insult to Tories everywhere. Here we had a community which organized and ran itself without any 'help' from all those institutions which are supposed to be necessary, and we man-aged well enough ... The only thing we demand of them or want from them is that they get the hell out of our area and out of our lives so that we can build our own future in a free, socialist, Ireland.

We had it printed by the *Derry Journal* and distributed seven thousand copies of it around the area. It was very well received. But Free Derry was finished, for the time being anyway.

The local Provo leadership had retreated over the border and into itself. Mr Hume said that the people were 'resent-ful but resigned'. The Provos were not really resigned, of course. They were shortly to re-emerge with blithe disregard for the seemingly inevitable, the old cause still begetting the old indomitable persistency. The Officials faced the future wondering how one conducted 'the political struggle' now. Mr Hume knew how he wanted it conducted. Next Friday's *Journal* carried the front-page headline: 'Hume Calls for Continued Restraint'. 'Now there,' said McGurran, 'there's a turn-up for the books.'

Part 3

It is often said that Irish people pay too much attention to history. This is not true. Irish people pay very little attention to history.

Some Irish people do pay attention to a mixture of half-truths and folk mythology about the past. At meetings in Free Derry Republican speakers would quite unself-consciously reel off the names and speak with natural emotion of those who had gone before in the fight against oppression and of the fate which had befallen them. Each name triggered remembrance of that particular phase of the struggle and excited the tingling realization that what we were about was yet another episode – perhaps, hopefully, the last – in the long chronicle of our nation's distressed indomitability. 'If you really love me,' wrote Sean Heuston to his sister in 1916 just before the British shot him, 'teach the children the history of their own land and teach them the cause of Caitlin ni hUllachain never dies' (*Capuchin Annual*, 1966). Sean can rest content that we were well enough taught.

There is a large body of opinion in Catholic Ireland which holds that that is half the trouble: that since 1922 successive Southern Irish governments, aided by the media, have bombarded the people with propaganda about the evils done to Ireland and about the continuing evil of partition; that the Catholic schools, including those in the North, have pumped children full of history, and a history distorted so as to idealize the gun. Thus, the theory goes, young men in places like the Bogside turn easily to the waging of unnecessary war.

It is an easy point of view to argue. The traditional

Catholic view of Irish history does contain a great deal of myth which it is not difficult to debunk. A Catholic child in the Bogside, for example, would gather at an early age that Wolfe Tone, who led the United Irishmen's rising in 1798, was a Protestant who came over to our side. One would not gather that Tone, the 'Father of Irish Republicanism', took his inspiration from the French Revolution, was as bitterly opposed to the Catholic church as any Orangeman and, if he had had his way, would have sponged the church from the face of the Republic he hoped to build. One gathered too that in every subsequent generation the Irish people – or at least the majority, Catholic section of it – rose against the English oppressor, sometimes in arms, sometimes in constitutional movements, and that there were direct links between each stage of the struggle. This is not true either. The Irish people as a whole never rose. Whole peoples rarely do. And there was little organizational or political continuity between the movements which did arise. The Catholic emancipation movement which was led by Daniel O'Connell in the 1820s, for example, owed nothing to Tone's ideas. It was conservative, constitutional and anti-republican. The radical and thoroughly unconstitutional Fenian movement of the 1860s had nothing in common with O'Connell. And so on.

But underlying all the mythology there is a deep stratum of truth. The Irish people, particularly the Catholic Irish people, *were* exploited and oppressed for hundreds of years by Britain. The overwhelming majority of them were born in misery and reared in squalor. They lived from day to day, fighting to tear some dignity from life, most of them finally to die amid the ugliness in which they first saw the light of day. And knowing that one of the reasons for their condition was that the country was ruled by Britain.

If the movements they threw up lacked any continuity neat enough to please the detached historians' sense of order, they did not lack in the desperation of their adherents' search for a remedy. Irish history is hair-raising.

In that it is not dissimilar from the history of many other countries. History almost everywhere is terrible. The main reason why Republican rhetoric about the past continues to evoke a gut response from many people in Ireland is that most of it is true. That it is encrusted with myth alters nothing essential. Some people need myths, need them to glorify their history in order to push away the grim reality of the way they have to live now. If the traditional Republican account of Irish history has been most fervently believed in the Catholic ghettoes of the North, in the Bogside and Creggan, Ardoyne and Ballymurphy, it is because the people who live there, ground down by oppression and with no apparent possibility of escape, have needed an ennobled history, have needed to postulate a line of continuity between the glorious struggles of the past and a liberation yet to come. When a man lives in a world of bookies' slips, varnished counters and Guinness spits he will readily accept an account of the past which tends to invest his living with dignity. Observers such as C. Cruise O'Brien, such circumstances of life being beyond their range of experience, may find it difficult fully to understand this.

Protestants, too, have had a mythology, and it has supplied source material for an equally rich fund of educated sneers. It too is now being derided, by a growing section of 'enlightened' Protestant opinion. Protestants have believed that for almost four hundred years their community has been besieged by rapacious Catholic hordes intent on the destruction of the civil and religious liberty won by the Reformation, and that it was the Orange Order which provided the organizational framework for the successful prosecution of their struggle; that every movement against the link with Britain, or against Partition, has been motivated, however hiddenly, by a desire to extend the hegemony of Rome over them and that the retention of the link with Britain guaranteed against this. Rome Rule meant return to the dark ages, envelopment in black superstition, the loss of civil and religious liberty, the loss of the right of a sturdy people to think for itself won, at terrible cost, when the Reformation shattered medieval papal power. Some of this is true. Moreover, the organizations embodying the Orange mythology – the Orange Order and its associate institutions – offered the people of crumbling areas like the Shankill in Belfast and the Fountain in Derry a sense of vigour and a colourful life-style in sharp contrast to the workaday drudgery which was their normal lot.

The difference between the two traditions is most sharply evident in accounts of the founding of the Northern state. There is a Catholic folk-myth which holds that in the early part of this century the Protestants, blackmailed and befuddled by sectarian loyalist propaganda, chose, against their own interests as Irish people, to retain the link with Britain; that had it not been for the agitational activities of Carson and Craigavon, supported by the British Tories, the Protestant masses might well have seen that their real interests lay in joining with their fellow Irishmen in the South to create an independent republic. As against that, there is a Protestant legend telling that in order to prevent their economic ruin and their ideological domination by totalitarian Catholicism the Protestant people rose and, by setting up the Northern Irish state, won freedom for their community.

Before partition the Protestant myth was promoted by a powerful section of the British establishment. This did not happen because the British establishment believed it to be true or that endorsement of it would lead to equitable political arrangements in Ireland. They endorsed it because its practical implications met the requirements of the overall British interest in Ireland. When Randolph Churchill decided in 1886 to 'play the Orange card' he did so because his class, then in its imperial heyday, was best served by meeting the central Unionist demand – that Ireland remain within the Empire. When, in the changed circumstances of 1912–20, the Unionists gave up hope of holding all Ireland within British rule and campaigned instead for partition, they were, again, and for precisely the same reason, supported by the British Conservative Party and their cause was trumpeted by *The Times*.

The fact was, and is, that the Republican tradition, for all the distortions of history contained within it, stemmed from a genuine, if episodic, anti-imperialist struggle; the Orange tradition was, objectively, pro-imperialist.

After partition the two traditions provided the official ideologies of the new states. The North became a 'Protestant state for a Protestant people' and the Protestantism of the state was demonstrated by the destruction of local government democracy in areas where Catholic representatives were in power, the systematic exclusion of Catholics from the civil service and from sectors of private industry, and the use of state forces and of the law to discourage Catholics from attempting to change this situation. The ideology was most stridently expressed when sizeable sections of the Protestant people broke, or attempted to break, from the Unionist Party. When that happened the Unionists' unique political apparatus, the Orange machine, went into action, drowning dissident voices with bible-and-thunder rhetoric, herding the masses back into Orangeism and isolating those who refused to return. For a long time it was very successful. Although the Unionist Party and the system over which it presided was never able to supply the Protestant working class with the means for a decent life – despite discrimination – it managed on the whole to retain mass Protestant support.

One of the reasons why it was so successful was that in the South of Ireland the counter ideology was being promulgated with equal vigour. All the main parties in the South have until very recently described themselves as 'Republican' and insisted that the main purpose of their activity was to bring about a united Ireland. Much of the argument between them, particularly during election campaigns, has been about which of them was best equipped to do this.

What lent plausibility to Unionist propaganda were not

actual attempts by Southern governments to assimilate Northern Ireland but their ceaseless, strident declarations that Northern Ireland *ought* to be assimilated into the South. Which is a very different thing. This rhetoric was accompanied by the gradual institutionalization of Catholic teaching in Southern law so that the state into which Southern leaders said the North ought to be incorporated became, more and more clearly, a Catholic state. The more Catholic it became the more repulsive to the Northern Protestants did united-Ireland rhetoric sound.

Any ideology which is propounded or accepted by a large group of people is based on the economic interest of a class. Protestant Unionism was based on the interests of the owners of land and industry in the North of Ireland. Nationalism was based on the interests of the owners and potential owners of industry in the South.

The owners of land and industry in the North of Ireland needed, for commercial reasons, to retain the link with Britain. Potential capitalists in the South, if they were going to have an industrial infrastructure at all, needed protection from British competition. In 1922 the two classes agreed to part. By that time the essential characteristics of the movements they led and the ideologies of those movements had already been decided.

For almost four decades they went their separate ways. In the South, through successive changes of government and variations in economic strategy, the attempt to build up native Irish industry proceeded. It involved a short-lived 'economic war' with Britain, 'Buy Irish' campaigns, opposition to – and sometimes destruction of – foreign goods being offered for sale. The fierce anti-British, 'Ireland-for-the-Irish' propaganda which constituted the official ideology of the state was a reflection of all this. In ideological terms it expressed the economic needs of the establishment. It served too, to divert the attention of those elements – workers and small farmers – discontented with their lot under the new order, away from the rising Dublin bourgeoisie towards putative and more distant culprits. The Catholic church was used, and was more than willing to be used, to isolate and politically to destroy anyone who threatened seriously to disrupt the set-up.

In the North the constant reiteration that 'Ulster-is-Protestant-and-British' was, equally, an ideological refraction of the economic needs of property. Here, unlike the South, there was no need after partition to create anything new, rather a need to retain access to British markets and sources of raw material already enjoyed. The 'threat' from expansionist, Southern, Catholic Nationalism without which no speech from a Unionist leader was complete encouraged the preservation and intensification of a creed, as opposed to a class, consciousness; encouraged the Protestant community, all classes within it, to act and react as a whole, under the leadership of the established political bosses. That is, under the leadership of those making the speeches.

North and South, it was a neat arrangement. Each ideology fed on the other. But it could not last.

By the nineteen-fifties things had changed. In the South the industries created behind a protective tariff-wall had reached the limits of their growth. Further development could not be sustained by the small home market. The economy ground to a halt, almost went into reverse. It became necessary to discard economic isolationism and to seek reintegration into wider, commercial empires. That meant, in effect, reintegration into the British market.

Something similar happened in the North. The industries which had given the Northern economy its original dynamic – linen, shipbuilding, heavy engineering – were in decline in the years after the Second World War. The nature of the economy changed as the slack created by this decline was gradually taken up by new enterprise. The new enterprise was financed from outside, mainly from the British mainland.

By the end of the fifties the economic basis of partition

was being eroded. The interests of the dominant classes, North and South, converged. And, by the same token, the British interest in Ireland changed.

While British economic interests in Ireland were concentrated in the North, successive British governments, Liberal, Tory and Labour, were content to allow the Unionist Party to get on with the job of ruling in whatever way it saw fit and using whatever means it claimed were necessary. On occasion this meant allowing the armed supporters of the Unionist Party to massacre Catholics. But once the South tore down the tariff-walls and the barriers to outside investment crumbled, things changed. The British interest now lay, not in giving uncritical support to an Orange government in the North, but in balancing between the Orange and the Green, between North and South, between Protestant and Catholic capitalism in Ireland. That was to become very significant in August 1969.

At the beginning of the sixties it did not occur to the economic planners who were guiding Northern and Southern Ireland closer to one another, and guiding them, together, towards a closer economic relationship with Britain, that the gutters of Belfast and Derry might run red as a result. But the gutters in the Falls and the New Lodge Road, the Shankill, Ballymacarret and Bogside did, and the reason why they did was that ideologies and the political institutions which embody ideologies do not necessarily exist in a constant state of adaptation to the changing needs of the class in whose interest they were originally built. They can resist change. They can have a life of their own and in certain circumstances they fight for their life.

As the more far-seeing sections of the Belfast and Dublin establishments moved hesitantly towards one another they were, in effect, betraying the beliefs which, for decades, they had claimed to cherish and which they had *demanded* that their people, under pain of national apostasy, accept as eternal truths. The anti-British, united-Ireland propaganda which had blared forth from Dublin for decades had to be stilled. The anti-Catholic, pro-partition hysteria which had been the stock-in-trade of Belfast governments for just as long had now to be calmed. It was inevitable that there were those who would shout 'traitor'. In other circumstances that might not have mattered. In other circumstances it might have been possible to dismiss the objectors as 'backwoodsmen', gradually to isolate them and to move forward into a new era – rather as the British Conservative Party dealt with those who objected in principle to postwar welfare legislation.

That could not happen in Northern Ireland. The main political representatives of Northern capitalism, the Unionist Party, had not just proclaimed their ideology from election platforms – which is all their more fortunate Southern counterparts had ever found it necessary to do. The Northerners had had to put their ideology into practice. They had had to create a vast and intricate apparatus which, day in, day out, ensured that political decisions and public life in every part of the state conformed to a predetermined pattern. The apparatus was the Orange machine, as remarkable a piece of political equipment as has existed anywhere. It involved tens of thousands of people, each of whom had an interest in the machine retaining its central position in the power structure – indeed in its retaining its position *as* the power structure. And that interest did not forever coincide with the overall needs of the Northern Ireland economy. By the sixties it was in sharp conflict with it.

The Unionists had had to create such a machine. Discrimination was necessary in Northern Ireland. It was necessary in order politically to disarm the Catholics. It was necessary, too, if the Unionist Party was going to retain the vital allegiance of its 'own', the Protestant community. Because, contrary to the image of Northern Protestants commonly projected backwards into history, all classes within that community did not automatically act and react together. What emerges most starkly from a study of the Orange machine is not the ease with which it was able to contain the mass of Protestants, but the continual difficulty it experienced; not its efficiency but its fragility. There has not been a decade since the foundation of the Unionist Party in which it has not been challenged from within for the leadership of the Protestant community. Thus the machine needed constantly to be tended, needed to be fuelled and refuelled with the spoils of discrimination – jobs, houses and social prestige – which could be paid out to the faithful to endow them with a sense of privilege. The threat from without had constantly to be inflated and 'dealt with' in order to discourage and buy off the threat from within, if for no other reason.

The new economic pattern in Ireland in the sixties made the Orange machine redundant. Northern-Protestant and Southern-Catholic capitalism could not come together as economic common sense demanded while the main political expression of Northern Protestantism continued to brow-beat the Catholics within its territory.

Hence 'liberal-Unionism'. And thus the heightened expectation of Catholics that they were about to get their 'rights'. And, in reaction, the habituated response of the Orange machine. And thus 5 October and August 1969, the British army. The British army enmeshed in the machine, internment and Bloody Sunday. Direct rule: Northern Ireland up for grabs, chunks of political masonry falling from the monolith; the Provos blazing, going for bust, now at last to destroy it for ever. Furtive Protestant guerrillas in twos and threes with small-arms at night in the back streets of fringe areas of Belfast, waiting. British cabinet ministers wringing their hands in horror on the telly and talking on about 'gunmen'. 'The psychopaths have taken over,' chirruped Mr Roy Hattersley, former Secretary of State for the Army.

The psychopaths have not taken over. There is a war in Ireland because capitalism, to establish and preserve itself, created conditions which made war inevitable. Essentially, there is no other reason. There rarely is for war.

Part 4

I

The Orange apparatus was constructed in the second half of the nineteenth century by industrialists and landowners in north-eastern Ireland in order to capture and keep the loyalty of the Protestant masses. The all-class alliance contained within it was fraught with contradictions and consequently fragile. It has frequently threatened to disintegrate. The motivation of the Orange leaders was and is economic self-interest. At each point of crisis their primary consideration has been the 'necessity' not so much to repel Catholic encroachment as to prevent Protestant defection. Historically, Irish Protestant property owners' attachment to 'the link with Britain' has in no way been sentimental. This was clearly demonstrated by their reaction to the disestablishment of the Church of Ireland by the British Liberal government elected in 1868.

Disestablishment removed the formal legal basis of the Protestant ascendancy in Ireland. The instinctive reaction of a major section of the ascendancy was to withdraw its support for the union with Britain. 'It is hardly surprising', said the *Belfast Newsletter*, 'that with the pages of history open before them, with the mire of their ancient privileges scattered all around, Protestants should care little to maintain a union which for them appears henceforth to have little value' (16 May 1870). At the same time the two Dublin Protestant papers, the *Irish Times* and the *Evening Mail*, flirted with Home Rule. Issac Butt, leader of the Irish Parliamentary Party, noted that those attending the meeting in May 1870 which founded the Home Rule Association were 'principally Protestants and Conservatives ... all men of some mark and station'. The 61-man committee elected by the meeting contained 28 Conservatives, 10 Liberals, 17 Constitutional Nationalists and 6 Fenians, of whom 36 were Protestants and 25 Catholics. Protestant Conservative control of the HRA lasted only a few months, but the fact that they even attempted to take the leadership of the movement indicates that their primary concern was to pre-serve their own position in society, not the constitutional *status quo*. It was when Home Rule leadership eluded them that they turned to other things.

Within a few years the ascendancy was to be threatened by something much more formidable than a reforming Liberal government. In October 1879 the Irish National Land League was established under the effective leadership of the radical Michael Davitt. The League demanded a re-duction in rents, state aid for tenants to buy out the land they worked on and an end to evictions. The League's tac-tics included the 'boycott' of landowners and agents evict-ing or attempting to evict tenants. It arranged that all evictions were 'witnessed by gatherings of people'. The witnesses in the nature of things were wont to set about the evictors. The success of the League can be gleaned from the fact that in 1881 there were 4,439 'agrarian crimes' com-mitted in Ireland, an increase of 900 per cent over the 1877 figures (Special Commission, vol. iv, p. 515).

The Land League was based in the south and west of Ireland among Catholic peasants, but its economic de-mands were also clearly in the interests of the Protestant peasants in the north-east who, although they enjoyed security of tenure, were by no means comfortably off. They had, moreover, been hard hit by a slump in the prices of agricultural produce in the late 1870s, and by the fact that the 1879 harvest was the worst since the famine of 1845–7. To minimize the chances of the Land League's gathering Protestant peasant support, northern landowners reverted to a tactic which had worked in the past and which was to prove so reliable in the future. All talk of Home Rule forgotten, they strove to give their tenants to understand that the Land League was a militant Catholic movement intent on the destruction of Protestantism by taking Ireland out of the United Kingdom and creating Rome-rule throughout the land.

One prominent Orange leader appealed to all 'Protestants and Orangemen': 'Are the Protestants of the south and west to be shot down like rotten sheep?' (N.P. Palmer, *The Irish League Crisis*, p. 301). 'Shot down like rotten sheep' was putting it a bit high, but the speaker's basic point – that the Land League was attacking Protestants – had some substance.

Most of the Land League's targets in the south and west were Protestants. But it could not have been otherwise. There were very few Catholic landlords in any part of Ireland available for attack. Impatient of such hair-splitting the Orange Order established the 'Orange Emergency Committee' in April 1881 to oppose the League and to support its 'victims'. Its main activity was the organization of squads of blackleg harvesters to save the crops of boycotted landlords.

The landlords and the Orange leaders appealed to the communal solidarity of Northern tenant-farmers as Protestants, Davitt to their class interests as peasants. And Davitt was not wholly unsuccessful. By the autumn of 1880 branches of the Land League had been established in Armagh, Enniskillen and Belfast. In January 1881 Davitt addressed a meeting in Armagh chaired by the Grand Master of the local Orange lodge. Around the same time an observer recorded that after a Land League meeting in Lurgan 'Orangemen joined the league in vast numbers' (private letter in Belfast Public Records Office, D 1481). Somewhat euphorically Davitt claimed that 'had I had a few more months I would have brought the whole province into the League'.

The nervousness excited by Davitt's radicalism and by the 'excesses' which accompanied the 'witnessing' of evictions was not confined to the landlord class or the Protestant religion. Most of the Catholic clergy and almost all the Catholic bishops opposed the campaign. Charles Stuart Parnell, leader of the Irish Parliamentary Party, was titular leader of the Land League. He was a landowner by birth and a moderate man by resultant nature. His formal leadership of the Land League, however, led to his arrest and detention in Kilmainham prison in October 1881, following which there was much uproar in the Irish countryside. In January 1882 the Vatican intervened. Pope Leo XIII denounced the Land League in a letter to the Irish hierarchy and urged the people 'not to cast aside the obedience due to their lawful rulers'. The hierarchy endorsed the Pope's communication and issued a pastoral letter instructing Catholics 'not to resist the law' (quoted in *The Revolutionaries* by Sean Cronin, p. 131). As a result the land campaign weakened, as did Mr Parnell's resolve.

In the spring of 1882, in accordance with the terms of the 'Kilmainham Treaty', Parnell called off the land agitation in return for an Act which gave tenants limited rights in the land and reduced rents by twenty per cent. He was released from prison.

The ending of the land war ruptured the few tenuous links laid down by the Land League between the southern Catholic and the northern Protestant tenant farmers. The concessions gained by Parnell were more meaningful for the former. The Protestant tenants, after all, for the most part already enjoyed in practice the rights in the land conferred by the Act. The 'Kilmainham Treaty' thus reduced the differential between the Protestant and Catholic peasants while not significantly benefiting the former. Thereafter the movement which Parnell proceeded to build on the ruins of the League had no appeal at all for the Protestant masses.

In October 1882 Parnell formed the National League, in which, as the name implied, land reform took second place to the demand for Home Rule. In order to combat Davitt's ideas Parnell and his lieutenants actively sought to recruit the Catholic clergy. An average county convention called to select parliamentary candidates comprised 150 laymen and 50 priests (C. C. O'Brien, *Parnell and His Party*, p. 130). Davitt and some others bitterly but unsuccessfully opposed the granting of such decisive influence to the clergy, but they did not break formally with Parnell.

The effect of this development on the north was predictable. Protestant tenants had seen a movement which claimed to be fighting for their social and economic emancipation transformed into one which offered them nothing and which was steeped in Catholic clericalism. Those who had broken with their traditional leaders to support the Land League were betrayed. The warnings of those – their landlords, most vociferously – who had claimed all along that it was merely a devious anti-Protestant plot were validated. Not for the first time in Irish history and by no means for the last a 'moderate' leadership of a mass national movement had operated in conjunction with the Catholic clergy to defeat an emerging radicalism and thus to shatter any possibility of the movement's crossing the sectarian barrier in the north to make contact with the Protestant masses. The real beneficiaries were the northern landlords. The all-class Protestant alliance in the countryside was preserved, indeed strengthened.

The Parnellite movement, actively supported by the clergy, gathered strength. In 1885 it won 86 of the 103 parliamentary seats in Ireland and held the balance of power between the Tory and Liberal parties at Westminster. Gladstone bought their support with the promise of a Bill to give Ireland Home Rule. It was in the campaign in Ireland for and against the 1886 Home Rule Bill that the Orange-Unionist machine was built and the future pattern of Irish politics determined. The most passionate opponents of Home Rule were the businessmen and industrialists of the Belfast area. They joined the Orange Order, helped create the Unionist Party and for the first time began to assert themselves, as opposed to the rural squires, as the dominant class in northern Irish politics.

By 1886 the Belfast area was industrialized. This was not true of the rest of Ireland. Northern industry had developed on the basis of the land tenure system – the Ulster Custom – which gave tenant farmers security of tenure, thus encouraging improvement to holdings and modest capital accumulation. The industrial background of some of the Protestant settlers facilitated a turn towards small-scale part-time cotton and linen manufacture. For a time both trades prospered. Competition between individual operators and the development of associated technology led to the gradual elimination of small-holding spinners and weavers and the concentration of manufacture in factory units, mainly in the Lagan Valley. In the early nineteenth century the cotton industry was hit by a slump and cotton manufacturers switched to linen production. Belfast was by 1830 the centre of a prosperous expanding linen industry, and the sons and daughters of tenant farmers were swarming into the city to become wage-earners in the mills. It was on the basis of the profits generated by the linen industry that shipbuilding and engineering became established in the Belfast area. The first iron ship built in Ireland was made in Belfast in the 1840s. The first major shipbuilding company began production at Queen's Island in 1850. The population of the city increased from less than thirty thousand in 1813 to more than a hundred thousand in 1851. Coal for the industries came from the Scottish mines. British banks supplied credit. The Empire provided both raw materials and secure markets. In 1886 Belfast, for practical economic purposes, was part of industrial Britain.

The economic situation in the rest of Ireland was in stark contrast. The factors making for industrialization in the north – the land tenure system and the presence in large numbers of 'industrially-oriented' settlers – had not operated. Attempts in the early eighteenth century artificially to inject linen manufacture into the south had failed.

The Irish Parliamentary Party had no industrial base. What most of the Parnellites wanted was not dramatic change in the economic set-up but the opportunity, under a Dublin parliament, to have a say in the distribution of patronage. It was open to northern industrialists to negotiate – and there is no reason to suppose that it would have been difficult to negotiate – an arrangement which, within a Home Rule framework, would have guaranteed them continued free access to the British market. The Home Rule parliament envisaged in Gladstone's Bill would not, anyway, have had control of customs. There were other factors, however.

Other movements nearer home were causing anxiety in the northern business community. The decade before the introduction of the Home Rule Bill saw the development of effective trade unionism in Belfast. For the previous half-century the owners of industry had been fortunate indeed in this regard. Sectarianism had prevented effective working-class organization. Since the early years of the century Catholics, fleeing from starvation on the land, had poured into Belfast to compete with Protestants for jobs. Grimy ghettoes grew up side by side. By the 1850s sectarian riots were a regular feature of Belfast life. Owenism and Chartism passed Belfast by. In the 1870s, however, the relative industrial peace was disrupted as a labour movement struggled into existence. There were strikes against wage cuts involving both Catholic and Protestant workers in the linen and shipbuilding industries in 1874, 1881, 1883 and 1884. The Belfast Trades Council was formed in 1881. The workers of whom it had been said by Sir Robert Bateson in 1838 that 'no men had ever conducted themselves better in their very depressed conditions' (Green, *The Lagan Valley*) were now flexing their muscles and gingerly testing their strength. In 1885 the Belfast Trades Council nominated the first Irish 'Lib-Lab' candidate, Alexander Bowman, a Protestant, for North Belfast. The Home Rule issue was heaven-sent to industrialists wishing to discourage such class differentiation. They set about welding Protestants of all classes more firmly together. They were marvellously successful. The instrument for integration was the Orange Order.

Up to then the Order, although useful at times, had not received any sizeable support from the respectable classes. The official history of the Order records that it 'had been very much a labouring and poorer artisan class Protestant movement'. The respectable classes joined now, however, in great numbers and with great enthusiasm. 'The introduction of Gladstone's Home Rule Bill gave the Order a membership which was to transform it completely to make it a highly respectable and exceedingly powerful religious, political organization' (Rev. S. E. Long, *Orangeism*, 1967).

The political effect of this on the developing workers' movement was devastating.

The Orange Lodges provided the basis of an effective political machine while their tradition of fraternal equality between members tended to blur class distinctions and helped to reconcile the Protestant proletariat to the leadership of landlords and wealthy business men. (J. C. Beckett, *The Making of Modern Ireland*, 1966, p. 399)

Virulent anti-Catholicism had been the ideology of the Orange Order since its foundation as a Protestant peasants' defence organization in 1795. Hitherto the business classes had been above that sort of thing. Now, however, in one of the biggest mass conversions in Irish history since St Patrick baptized ten thousand clansmen into Christianity in one afternoon on Tara Hill, they rediscovered the Fundamental Truth of the Bible, discerned on the southern horizon the gathering hordes of the Scarlet Women from the banks of the Tiber, and urged the labouring masses to gird themselves for battle to defend their civil and religious liberty. In January 1886 the Irish Unionist Party was formed by a meeting at, suitably enough, the Carlton Club. It was opposed to Home Rule for any part of Ireland, and its leaders were quite explicit about their motives. One of the first establishment figures to join the Order, Colonel Saunderson, an ex-Liberal, had said that he did so because it was the only organization 'capable of dealing with the condition of anarchy and rebellion' (T. W. Moody and J. C. Beckett, *Ulster Since 1800*, 1, p. 91). Lords Londonderry and Hamilton favoured a Protestant alliance on the grounds that the Home Rule movement was 'menacing to the rights of property and so order' (quoted in Jeff Bell's *This We Will Maintain*). The Belfast Chamber of Commerce was against Home Rule because it believed that 'commercial prosperity' would thereby receive 'lasting injury' (pamphlet issued by Irish Loyal and Patriotic Union, 1886). The *Northern Whig* of 21 January 1886 said: 'Our Commercial and manufacturing classes are devoted to the Union because they know that Trade and Commerce would not flourish without the union.' More succinctly, a 'Belfast Merchant': 'The birth of a Dublin Parliament would be the death of credit' (Bell).

British commercial interests had a wider reason to oppose Home Rule: to grant it might set a dangerous headline for the inhabitants of other colonial countries. 'It [Home Rule] is a Right,' said Joseph Chamberlain, 'which must be considered in relation to the security and welfare of other countries in juxtaposition to which Ireland is placed and whose interests are indissolubly linked' (*Home Rule and the Irish*, p.34).

'If we can stir up the religious feeling', wrote the Rev. Henry Henderson, 'we have won.' They did win. Religious feeling was stirred up so effectively that sectarian war erupted in Belfast, leaving many dead, hundreds injured and many Catholic houses burned out. And what, most importantly, they won was not the guaranteed preservation of the union but the political allegiance of the Protestant masses. The Liberal Party in Ulster collapsed into the Unionist Alliance. The Conservative (and Unionist) Party which had hitherto had little formal existence outside the Belfast area spread into the countryside as the new respectable Orange Lodges created, or in some cases more or less became, branches of the party.

The northern industrialists' stated reason for mobilizing against Home Rule – that 'commercial prosperity' would thereby suffer 'lasting injury' – was not based on any fear that Parnell and what he represented threatened 'commercial prosperity'. Parnell did not. Nothing in the Home Rule Bill which he agreed with Gladstone would have interfered with the profitable conduct of business. Nothing in Parnell's political philosophy would have hampered the reconciliation of any section of the proletariat to the leadership of landlords and wealthy businessmen. His own attitude to class and to organizations tending to emphasize class distinctions was recorded by Davitt.

What is trade-unionism but the landlordism of labour? I would not tolerate, if I were at the head of a government, such bodies as trade unions. They are opposed to individual liberty and should be kept down, as Bismarck keeps them down in Germany ... (quoted in Andrew Boyd, *The Rise of the Irish Trade Unions*, p. 59)

Nothing there to cause the class-conscious nineteenth-century industrialist to lose sleep. A Dublin parliament, as envisaged in the Home Rule Bill and headed by Parnell, would clearly not have been the 'death of credit'.

But the Unionist fears were not entirely fanciful: because what they really feared was the propertyless masses behind Parnell. *Their* interests were certainly inimical to 'commercial prosperity', and there was no guarantee that Parnell could 'hold the line' against them. Indications were that he could not. The Act implemented with Parnell's support after the Kilmainham Treaty had not solved the land question. Eviction and resistance to eviction continued, although the statistics for 'agrarian crime' show a falling-off after the record year of 1882. Davitt himself was enormously popular at grass-roots level. In 1886 a 'Plan of Campaign' was launched by John Dillon and William O'Brien against Parnell's advice. Basically the 'Plan of Campaign' involved tenants of a particular estate uniting to prevent the eviction of any of their number whose offer of a 'fair rent' had been refused by the landlord. It lacked the scale and intensity of the 1880–2 land war, but it was enough to convince propertied observers that dangerous radical ideas were still contained within the Home Rule movement.

What the Unionist leaders feared was that within a Home Rule Ireland they, *despite Parnell*, would not for long be able to preserve their privileged position, the more especially since their 'own' masses were chafing at the bit. It was not the policies but the composition of the Home Rule movement which made them nervous.

It was precisely to combat such ideas that Parnell had recruited the Catholic clergy in 1882. In other words the tendency within the Home Rule movement which represented 'Rome-rule' was precisely that which did not threaten the interests of property. But the fact that it was the dominant tendency invested the slogan 'Home Rule is Rome-Rule' with plausibility. And the fact that the tendency opposed to Rome-rule, that which did threaten propertied interests, was not clearly differentiated from Parnellism in the public mind, and had no separate organizational expression, prevented it from rebutting convincingly Unionist allegations that it too, for all its radical phrase-mongering, was a part of the plot to subjugate the Protestants.

The Catholic ideology introduced into the Home Rule movement was of crucial assistance to the Unionist leaders as they strove to combat radical ideas simultaneously emerging from the Northern Protestant community. Ever since, the two ideologies most powerful in Irish politics, Protestant Unionism and conservative Catholic Nationalism, have been complementary, and have operated together to keep Ireland safe from 'anarchy and rebellion'.

The 1886 Bill was defeated, as was Gladstone's second Home Rule Bill in 1893. After that the immediate threat to Ulster Unionists receded. And as the threat receded the pressure for the maintenance of the Protestant alliance weakened; the alliance still had internal contradictions which sooner or later were bound to come to the surface.

The conditions of the working classes in north-eastern Ireland at the end of the nineteenth century and the beginning of the twentieth were such as to make inevitable some sort of rebellion against the political *status quo*. However, the conditions of sections of the Protestant working class relative to that of the Catholics placed difficulties in the way of fomenting rebellion among them.

Belfast was a very unhealthy city for workers to live in. Tuberculosis and bronchial diseases were almost epidemic. In 1897, 27,000 people were treated for typhus (Beckett and Glasscock, *Belfast*, p. 117). The 1901 census showed that there were 17,919 one-room tenement dwellings in Ulster in which 50,000 people lived. In 1906 the Commissioners for National Education in Ireland reported that schools in Belfast were 'the most backward in the British Isles'. Emigration from Ulster in this period was at 8 per cent per year, as high as that from any other part of Ireland (Thom's *Directory*, 1908). There were 90,000 'farms' with a rateable valuation of £10 or less, relatively the highest figure in Ireland with the exception of Connemara.

Agricultural labourers were atrociously paid. The highest rate paid in Ulster (that is, Co. Down, at 12s. 5d. per week) was lower than the lowest rate paid in England, Scotland or Wales (Orkney to Shetlands, 14s.) (J. W. Boyle, *The Rise of the Irish Labour Movement*, unpublished thesis, p.34). The situation of urban workers was slightly different. Wage-rates for shipbuilding and engineering workers (35–38s. per week; J.W. Boyle, p. 48) were in line with those for Britain and higher than those in Dublin. Moreover, Protestant workers were doing better than Catholics. In 1901 Catholics formed 24.3 per cent of the population of Belfast, yet held only 10.1 per cent of jobs in engineering, 15.5 per cent in carpentry, 11.6 per cent in plumbing and 6 per cent in shipyard work (1901 census).

The result was that while there was considerable discontent among the Protestant lower classes this discontent did not automatically link up with the grievances of the Catholic workers, who naturally wanted, among other things, 'fair' distribution of whatever jobs were going. Thus the radical challenge to Unionism which arose in the Protestant community in the early years of this century at first spoke not at all to Catholic interests. In 1902 an Independent pro-union candidate won a by-election against a Unionist for the rural East Down seat on a platform of compulsory land purchase. In the same year the Unionists lost South Belfast to Tom Sloan who stood as an Independent Unionist and campaigned for fair rents, higher pensions and trade-union rights.

After the election Sloan was suspended from the Orange Order and in June 1903 he helped form the Independent Orange Order. The first Grand Master of the IOO was Lindsay Crawford, a journalist. On 12 July 1904 the IOO demonstration was 2,000 strong. Its leaders were in no way 'soft' on the Home Rule question: they were, if anything, more fierce than the official Order in their denunciations of popery. But in the process of elaborating a political programme in opposition to that of the Unionist leadership gradually and inexorably they were driven to oppose Unionism as such. A speech by Crawford in December 1904 indicated that the IOO was developing a critique of unionism more radical and more broadly based than the platform on which Sloan had stood in 1902:

Not until the Irish Roman Catholic placed the reasonable claims of his country before the impossible demands of his Church, not until the Irish Protestant inscribed in indelible characters 'Not that I love the Empire less but that I love Ireland more' would there dawn on the dark horizon of Irish politics a single ray of hope for the cooperation and consolidation of all classes and creeds, for material progress and prosperity of this country … The woes of Ireland are mainly attributed to British misgovernment, to the fact that Ireland is governed not on national but on sectarian lines. (J. W. Boyle, 'The BPA and the IOO', *Irish Historical Studies*, XIII, p. 132)

By July 1905 the IOO had moved further. In the *Magheramore Manifesto* they remarked:

We consider it is high time that the Irish Protestants should consider their position as Irish citizens and their attitudes towards their Roman Catholic countrymen and that the latter should choose once and for all between nationality and sectarianism. In an Ireland in which Protestant and Catholic stand sullen and discontented it is not too much to hope that they will reconsider their position and in their common trials unite on a basis of nationality.

At this time there were seventy Independent Lodges in the North.

During the same period, and for the same reasons, the Labour movement began to reassert itself. In 1893 a branch of the Independent Labour Party was established in Belfast. In the 1897 municipal elections a reformed (household) franchise enabled six Labour candidates to win seats in Belfast Corporation. In 1905 William Walker, a pro-union Labour candidate, came within 500 votes of winning a by-election in North Belfast against the Unionist nominee.

The 1906 General Election presented the Ulster Unionist leadership with the most formidable electoral challenge it had yet faced. Walker lost again in North Belfast, but Sloan retained South Belfast and the Nationalist Joe Devlin won West Belfast. The IOO supported all three anti-Unionist candidates in the city. Two other candidates supported by the IOO won seats from Unionists in North Tyrone and North Antrim. In Ulster as a whole the Unionists won only 14 of the 33 seats. The Protestant Alliance within Unionism was fragmenting.

It was into this situation that the syndicalist labour organizer Jim Larkin arrived at the beginning of 1907, as Belfast organizer for the National Union of Dock Labourers. The political opposition to Unionism from the Catholics on the one hand and the Protestant masses on the other had been separate oppositions. Ulster Catholics, like Catholics in the rest of the country, voted solidly for the conservative Nationalist Party, Parnell's party, then led by John Redmond, and although the IOO had supported the Nationalist Devlin against a Unionist in West Belfast it had done so on the principle of the lesser of two evils, rather than in any confidence that Devlin stood for or would defend Protestant working-class interests. Between the politics of Devlin and Sloan there was scarcely any contact, much less common ground. Devlin was closely connected with the Ancient Order of Hibernians, the miserable Catholic mirror-image of the Orange Order. He was as solicitous for the interests of the church as any bishop, and as instinctively conservative as any ascendancy landowner. Neither Sloan nor Devlin, neither the IOO nor the Nationalist Party was offering to the Catholic and Protestant working class in Belfast a political philosophy or a programme of action which invited them to come together against a putative common enemy: although, clearly, the IOO was tending in that direction. Larkin, as a syndicalist, was short on political philosophies but long on programmes for action. What he was to do within a few months of his arrival was, by the application of trade-union tactics more militant than any which Belfast had experienced before, to challenge Protestant working-class radicals and their leaders to break from Unionism, and Catholic working-class conservatives and their leaders to break from Nationalism. The result was, if nothing else, interesting.

Larkin went quickly into action and won the majority of the dockers away from the moderate Carters Association. In June 1907 he led 500 dockers into strike for higher wages. When the employers resisted he introduced them to the sympathetic strike. At the beginning of July the carters struck. The coal merchants, whose supplies were thus frozen, locked out their employees. The next section of the Belfast proletariat to be infected by the militant virus was the police, whose members downed batons for higher pay and better conditions. The strike involved both Catholics and Protestants.

Larkin was a Catholic and was outspokenly opposed to the Union, and this was naturally used against him by employers appealing to Protestant workers for 'loyalty'. He offered to resign his leadership of the dispute to head off attacks from this direction, but his offer was refused by Protestant trade unionists whose spokesman Alexander Boyd was firm that 'men of all creeds are determined to stand together in fighting the common enemy'. The IOO backed the strike and Sloan and Crawford spoke at strike meetings, answering the employers' attacks on Larkin. Crawford wrote in the *Ulster Guardian*: 'The best reply to make to the opponents of Mr Larkin is to point to the fact that the employers have been compelled to raise wages and reduce hours all round since Mr Larkin organized the men' (Emmet Larkin, *James Larkin*, p. 28). After riots on the Falls Road, leaflets were distributed in both the Falls and the Shankill urging workers not to be 'misled by the employers' game of dividing Catholic and Protestant'. Grand Masters of seven Loyal Orange Lodges resigned to join Larkin. On 12 August he led a non-denominational parade through the city – in memory of both the besieged and the besiegers of Derry (Lysaght, *The Making of Northern Ireland*, p. 21).

The strike ended messily. The London leadership of the National Union of Dock Labourers, alarmed by reports of what their revolutionary representative in Belfast was up to, denounced Larkin. At the beginning of August troops moved in and the leaders of the police mutiny were arrested. The carters settled for a wage rise in mid-August. The dockers were finally broken in September.

In terms of the development of Northern Irish politics the most significant aspect of the summer's events was the antics (it is the correct word) of Joe Devlin and the Nationalist Party. Many of the strikers and the families of the strikers were from Mr Devlin's 'natural' constituency – the working-class Catholics of the Falls Road. At the outset he could not afford to be seen to be opposing the strike. He made no comment until 11 August, when he attended a strike meeting addressed by both Larkin and Crawford and explained, plausibly enough, that he had been silent until then lest his intervention give the Unionist Party an opportunity to represent the strike as Nationalist-inspired. Mr Devlin's party, however, controlled and funded as it was by the Catholic business community and led at local level by the clergy, had as little use as Unionist industrialists for 'Larkinism' and soon made it clear that this was the wrong tune to play. Within a few weeks, as the strike collapsed, Mr Devlin insisted, with as much protestation as a Fianna Fail Prime Minister sixty-six years later explaining that he had never met a Provisional IRA man in his life: 'Let me say I knew nothing about the strike in its progress, and I do not think I even know at the present moment what the absolute results of the strike were ... I have never spoken to Mr Larkin in my life but once ... I have never received a communication from Mr Larkin or anyone connected with the strike during its progress, before it commenced or after it ended' (Emmet Larkin, *James Larkin*, p. 34). Mr Devlin made it clear that henceforth class antagonisms would not disrupt his struggle for Home Rule.

The effect of Devlin's desertion on Protestant working-class politics was in line with the effect on the Protestant peasantry of Parnell's suspension of the Land War. The burgeoning discontent of the Protestant masses having led a section to break from the official Orange machine and to begin to break from Unionism itself to rally to a radical standard – despite the fact that the standard had been raised by a Catholic and a believer in Home Rule – Catholic conservatism in politics operated to repel them and to direct them back into the certainties of the Orange Order from which they had emerged. In his capacity as a trade-union organizer Larkin could win the loyalty of Protestant workers despite the fact that he was a Home Ruler. But he could not break down the Protestant workers' opposition to Home Rule as such unless he detached, or at least was seen to be striving to detach, the Catholic workers – who were already Home Rulers to a man – from the clerical conservatism represented by Joe Devlin. Once the radical content of 'Home Rule' was smothered, the only distinguishing feature remaining was its conservative Catholic Nationalism, a feature which tended not only to be repugnant to Protestants anyway, but, as an added bonus for the Unionist bosses, to validate all prior warnings about the treacherous intent of the Catholics who had been presuming to preach to Protestants. Larkin's weakness was that as a syndicalist he did not 'believe in' politics. Thus he was not involved in any attempt politically to argue against, much less defeat, Devlin in Belfast, and had not consciously set out to build a 'movement' at all, except in the vague sense of ultimately capturing power through militant trade unionism. For all that it was a political defeat which Larkin suffered with the collapse of the strike movement. In Belfast 'Home Rule' still meant Devlinism, and as long as that situation obtained every day was a field-day for Orange platform orators intent on reminding Protestant workers that to break the link with Britain meant, inevitably, to be put in thrall to Rome. As Devlin resumed his role as unchallenged master of Falls Road politics the sectarian straitjackets were once again wrapped around the ghettoes of the city.

The exit from the Orange machine which the IOO had taken had led them straight up Joe Devlin's garden path. Those who had supported the IOO began to draw back into the fold. Membership declined sharply. In 1908 it formally condemned Home Rule and expelled Crawford, but it was too late and this did little to revive its fortunes.

The results of the General Election of January 1910 showed how devastating to the fortunes of Labour and Independent Unionism events since 1906 had been. The Ulster Unionist Council directed its main attack not at Nationalists such as Devlin in West Belfast but at the non-Unionist supporters of the link with Britain, such as Sloan in South and Robert Gageby who was representing Labour in North Belfast. The line of attack came over loud and clear in the editorials of the *Belfast Newsletter* during the campaign:

It is a fight for the maintenance of the union in the South and North divisions as in the West. (3 January 1910)

Of William McClaw, Independent Unionist candidate for South Antrim:

He must be a Home Ruler, no matter what he says or thinks. (6 January 1910)

Orangemen must vote for every supporter of the Government, for it is only by doing so that they can prevent the Nationalists and priests from becoming masters of this country ... The Sloanites are prepared to betray their fellow Protestants. (6 January 1910)

Beware of the danger to the cause of the Union that lies in the candidates of Mr Sloan and Mr Gageby. (20 January 1910)

Gageby was beaten in North Belfast. Sloan lost his seat in the South. Two other Independent Unionists lost seats to the official party in the countryside. In all, the official Unionists won 18 of the 33 Ulster seats. The Unionists had been able to present the election as a choice between Catholic Nationalism and Protestant Unionism in which it was necessary for voters decisively to opt for one or the other. They had been able to do this because Larkin had failed to build out of his trade-union activities any movement which could have connected with the consciousness of the Protestant workers who had supported his strikes. Devlin's victory over Larkin – for that is essentially what happened in 1907 – handed the Protestant masses back to the Unionist Party.

The Unionist Party sorely needed the Protestant masses during the next few years. In April 1912, the Liberal Prime Minister Asquith, dependent for his majority on eighty-two Irish Nationalist votes, introduced the third Home Rule Bill at Westminster. The House of Lords used their power to postpone its application for two years. It seemed therefore that Home Rule would be a reality by 1914. The Unionist leaders mobilized to stop it. The 'Ulster Covenant', a pledge to resist the Bill, was signed, allegedly by half a million people, in September 1912 and mass anti-Home Rule rallies were held throughout Ulster. The Ulster Volunteer Force was formed as the armed wing of the Orange Order and began drilling and training. Sir George Reilly Richardson, hero of the Boxer affair in China and of similar engagements against the native in Afghanistan, Waziri, Tiri, the Zhod Valley and other points east, was imported with due ceremony to take command of the force. Orange justices of the peace rubber-stamped UVF applications for arms licences. Sir Edward Carson – appointed Unionist leader in 1910 – and his lieutenants promised, with the support of the leaders of the British Conservative Party, to go to war to stop Home Rule and, if they failed to stop it, to set up an Ulster parliament of their own. The outbreak of the First World War interrupted developments. Home Rule was, by common consent, postponed for the duration. By 1918 the overall situation had been altered dramatically. Events following the Easter Rising in Dublin in 1916 had virtually destroyed the Irish Nationalist Party. Leadership of the movement against the Union had passed into other hands. One thing, however, had not changed – the determination of the Unionist Party to have no part of an independent Ireland.

3

In the second decade of this century, the economic profile of Catholic Ireland was significantly different from that existing in the 1880s. The series of Land Acts, culminating in Wyndhams Law in 1903, created a vast new class of peasant proprietors. (In the six years after the 1903 Act, 270,000 tenants bought out their holdings; Lysaght, *The Republic of Ireland*, p. 31.) This accelerated the growth of the Catholic middle class. In 1905 this class formed a political party, Sinn Fein, which accurately articulated its interests.

It is in the nature of small property-owners to want to become big property-owners. Sinn Fein's economic policy was designed to create the conditions whereby an independent Irish manufacturing class could come into existence. The keystone of the policy was protection against foreign competition. The official document, 'Sinn Fein Policy', put it clearly: 'Protection means rendering the native manufacturer equal to meeting foreign competition. If a manufacturer cannot produce as cheaply as an English or other foreigner only because his foreign competitor has better resources at his disposal, then it is the first duty of the Irish Nation to afford protection for that manufacturer.' As a slightly theatrical expression of its seriousness, Sinn Fein tried to set up its own bank and to print its own stamps. The founder of the Party, Arthur Griffith, was no insularist and by no means unambitious for his class. Noting that the English, the French, the Germans and others were plundering Africa, Asia and Latin America for colonial booty, and refusing as a patriot to believe that Irishmen were inherently incapable of playing a full part in this process, he looked beyond immediate horizons to envisage in the fullness of time an Irish 'commercial empire' taking advantage of the links forged with Africa and Latin America by Irish Catholic missionaries. Griffith was opposed to trade unionism and was later to join with the Catholic church and the employers in denouncing it during a 1913 lock-out in Dublin. He summed up his nationalism as follows:

> The right of the Irish to political independence never was, is not, and never can be dependent on the admission of equal right in all other peoples. It is based on no theory of, and dependable in no wise for its existence or justification on the 'Rights of Man', it is independent of theories of government and doctrines of philanthropy and Universalism. He who holds Ireland a nation and all means lawful to restore her the full and free exercise of national liberties thereby no more commits himself to the theory that black equals white, that kingship is immoral, or that society has a duty to reform its enemies, than he commits himself to the belief that sunshine is extractable from cucumbers. (Introduction to Mitchel's *Jail Journal*, quoted in Liam de Paor's *Divided Ulster*, pp. 94–5)

Sinn Fein, inspired by the tactics of the Hungarian Nationalists against the Austro-Hungarian Empire, advocated abstention from Westminster and the establishment of an Irish parliament to challenge the authority of the British government. Its initial impact was negligible. However, the uprush of emotion after the execution of the leaders of the 1916 Rising carried it to the forefront of the movement for independence. In the 1918 General Election it won 75 of the 103 parliamentary seats, and in January 1919 constituted the First Dail (Parliament). Only in the North where the Catholics' embattlement made them cling more closely to traditional leaders and values was Sinn Fein unable once and for all to break the grip of the Nationalist Party.

From the point of view of the Unionist Party, Sinn Fein's 'Home Rule' was crucially different from Home Rule as envisaged by Parnell or John Redmond. Griffith's economic policies, unlike theirs, did pose a direct threat to Northern industry. Had the linen, shipbuilding, and engineering industries been cut off from British markets and sources of raw materials by 'protective' tariffs they would have gone to the wall. More threatening still, Sinn Fein had within it and around it advocates of wide-ranging social revolution, who were as much interested in the overthrow of economic structures as they were in a Dublin parliament, who saw the latter, indeed, as a step towards the former.

Once again it was the composition of the movement against the link with Britain much more than the stated policies of its leadership, and the fear that the masses might burst through the limits set by the leadership, which most unnerved Northern businessmen and their British allies. In 1907 the Irish Unionist Alliance defined the situation thus:

In Ireland the classes that are inevitably against Home Rule... include the following: the capitalists, the manufacturers, the merchants, the professional men, and indeed all who have anything to lose. (*The Case against Home Rule*, p. 33)

In 1912 the Marquis of Londonderry bluntly summarized the contrasting class interests involved:

The opposition to Home Rule is the revolt of a business and industrial community against the domination of men who have no aptitude for either. The United Irish League is remarkably lacking in the support of businessmen, merchants, manufacturers, leaders of industry, bankers and men who compose a successful and prosperous community. (*Against Home Rule*, p. 165)

In 1913 *The Times* editorialized:

By disciplining the Ulster democracy and by leading it to look up to them as its natural leaders the clergy and the gentry are providing against the spread of revolutionary doctrine and free thought. (9 May 1913)

The Times need not have worried. The revolutionary doctrine and the free thought referred to got short shrift, not from the clergy and the gentry of the North, but from the clergy and the leaders of the movement for Home Rule in the south. Advocacy of wide-ranging social revolution was not to be included in the ideological baggage of the movement for Irish freedom.

One of the leaders of the 1916 Rising, James Connolly, was a Marxist, as much opposed to native as to foreign capitalism. In 1913 he had been an organizer for the Irish Transport and General Workers' Union and during the lock-out which convulsed the city for months he and Larkin had armed the picket lines and created the Irish Citizen Army, 'the first Red Army in Europe'. It was partly due to Connolly's and the Citizen Army's impatience for action in Ireland while Britain was distracted in Europe that the Easter Rising had been launched. Yet Connolly's ideas left little imprint on the movement which arose in the wake of the rising.

Connolly shared Larkin's central weakness. He did not understand that revolutionary theory, like revolutionary action, is impotent unless expressed through and guided by a revolutionary party. He did not build such a party. Thus, after his death, there was no organization which was clearly seen as the repository of his thought and it was possible for 'labour leaders' of various opinions and dubious intent to present themselves as his heirs. Before the 1918 General Election one of the Sinn Fein leaders, Eamon de Valera, declared that 'Labour must wait' in the interests of 'national unity', and Connolly's epigones agreed. As a result the fight for the hearts and minds of Catholic Ireland in 1918 was between constitutional nationalism and aggressive middle-class republicanism. The workers' role was to vote. All the time the new class of Catholic aspirant-capitalists was increasing in numbers and power. Catholics ran small leather, textile, paper-and-printing, milling and glass industries and two banks, the National and the Hibernian. Between 1910 and 1920 Irish joint stock bank deposits increased from £62½ million to £200 million (Lysaght, *The Republic of Ireland*, p. 64).

The failure of the Labour movement to play any active independent political role in the years after 1916 was a disaster. It need not have happened. Working-class militancy was increasing. In September 1918 Dublin papers were comparing the labour situation with that of 1913. At the beginning of 1919 industrial struggles were more noticeable in Southern Ireland than the guerrilla campaign getting underway in the countryside in the south-west. Between 1916 and 1920 membership of the Irish Transport and General Workers' Union went up from 5,000 to 100,000. Despite this, Labour's only distinctive contribution to the struggle for independence was a series of one-day strikes for short-term objectives, for example an anti-conscription strike in April 1918.

The immediate result of this was that middle-class nationalism was unchallenged as it established itself as the dominant ideology of the new struggle against Britain.

Connolly's ideas on education, for example his demand for popular control of schools and an end to clerical domination – an issue which loomed large in the Protestant mind – were quite forgotten. Moreover Sinn Fein began to attract many who had recently condemned it. The more far-sighted supporters of the Nationalist Party realized that a bandwagon was rolling, and as moderate Irish Catholic politicians were ever wont to do – and still are – on such occasions they leapt aboard and, having leapt, contrived to look as if they had been there for years. One of the founders of Sinn Fein was later to write bitterly :

We did not realize it at the time but what had happened was not that Sinn Fein had captured Ireland, but that the politicians in Ireland and those who make them, all the elements which sniffed at Sinn Fein and libelled it, which had upheld corruption and jobbery, had realized that Sinn Fein was going to win, and had come over to it en masse. They gave their votes and their support to a programme, every item of which was anathema to them, but in their hearts they remained corrupt, still just politicians. (P. S. O'Hegarty, *The Victory of Sinn Fein*, 1924, p. 29)

The bishops, too, with scant regard for episcopal dignity, scrambled hurriedly aboard. They had denounced the 1916 Rising. But by the election of December 1918 they were neutral between Sinn Fein and the Nationalist Party. In the North, Bishop MacCrory personally parcelled out candidacies between the two parties, lest a split Catholic vote hand winnable seats to the Unionists. As Labour dutifully waited, Sinn Fein drifted to the right. The clear lines of Griffiths original prospectus for the Irish middle class became blurred and hazy. As the guerrilla war in the countryside developed and increased in savagery through 1919 and 1920 it was clear that Sinn Fein wanted independence. It was now far from clear what it wanted independence for. It is not to be wondered at that to the Protestants in the North Sinn Fein looked like the Nationalist Party with a gun, the more so since in the North there was no contest between the parties.

This was a great pity, because in the years after the First World War the Unionist leaders were again having trouble with 'their' working class. There had been a strike of Belfast shipyard workers in December 1917, which the British government, anxious that the war effort should not be disrupted, settled quickly by encouraging management to concede the claim. There were more protracted strikes by druggists and municipal workers in Belfast and Portadown at the beginning of 1918. And as the war came to a close the issue of the forty-four-hour week began to dominate labour relations both in Britain and in the north of Ireland. In the December 1918 General Election the Labour Representation Committee put up four candidates in Belfast (Belfast had nine seats at the time), all of whom were equivocal on Home Rule and tried to confine the campaign to economic issues. The LRC candidate in Shankill declared that 'there is always a war going on, a war between rich and poor, between capitalist and worker'. They demanded a forty-four-hour week, statutory minimum pay and equal pay for women. This was the first election in which women (over thirty) were able to vote and the first under full manhood suffrage. All four LRC candidates came second in their constituencies, taking perhaps a quarter of

the Protestant vote despite passionate appeals from Ca...
and others for a closing of the Protestant ranks.

In January 1919, the Belfast District Committee of the
Federation of Engineering and Ship-building Trades balloted
for a strike for a forty-four-hour week. The result was
20,225 to 558 for strike action. The Belfast Committee was
denounced by the FEST leadership in London but supported
by shipbuilders in the Clyde, Humberside and Tyneside.
(Blithely ahead of their time workers on the River Forth
were meanwhile demanding a thirty-hour week.) At 4 p.m.
on Saturday 25 January the power-stations workers signalled the beginning of the strike. The trams stopped and the
street lights did not come on. On Monday the factories and
the shipyards were silent. The Orange Order condemned the
strike. The Unionist-controlled corporation called on the
British government to send in the army. Joe Devlin suggested 'impartial arbitration'. It snowed heavily on Tuesday,
which improved the chaos.

The workers involved were overwhelmingly Protestant,
but the chairman of the strike committee, Charles McKay,
was a Catholic. Another member of the committee was later
to become a cabinet minister in a Unionist government. The
committee was 'non-political'. It did not, even by implica-
tion, see the strike as a direct challenge to the political
authority of the Unionist Party – or the political influence
of the Nationalist Party, which still held sway in the
Catholic ghettoes.

After a fortnight the Clydeside strike leaders were arrested. A week later troops moved in to reopen public services
in Belfast. On the recommendation of the strike committee
the workers accepted a forty-seven-hour week as a compromise, and the 'Belfast General Strike' was over.

The strike was only partly successful but it did demonstrate that the Protestant workers were by no means
imprisoned within the Orange machine, that, on the trade-
union level at least, they were as ready as workers in any
other part of the British Isles to take on the Establishment

and to ignore the advice of the 'traditional' leaders of their community. Nor was there any truce after the Belfast strike ended.

There were major strikes throughout the province during the rest of 1919. Even farm labourers struck in Co. Donegal and Co. Down, and despite the strike leaders' insistence that there was nothing political in what they were doing, political conclusions were inevitably drawn.

On 20 February, as the Belfast strike petered out, the Unionist MP for East Antrim resigned. In the subsequent by-election G. B. Hanna, an Orangeman, went forward as an Independent Unionist. His politics were those of Tom Sloan, highly diluted. At campaign meetings, he attacked the official candidate for the party's failure to support the strike. He was elected by a majority of more than a thousand in a constituency containing the loyalist strongholds of Larne and Carrickfergus. He was no radical, and after a few months at Westminster he accepted the Unionist whip. At the time, however, his election – and the manner of it – were indicative of the tensions within the Protestant community. Despite the fact that the official candidate was supported by the Unionist press and formally endorsed by Carson, Protestant crowds broke up his meetings, smashed his car and on one occasion pelted his wife with eggs.

In January 1920, the Belfast Labour Party, which had been formed from the trade-union-based Labour Representation Committee, put up twenty candidates in the municipal election. Thirteen were elected. A Labour candidate, Sam Kyle, topped the poll in Shankill and shocked the Unionist psyche. James Baird, one of the local leaders of the Boilermakers' Union, outraged Unionist burghers by turning up at council meetings in overalls. At the first meeting of the council after the election Labour further infuriated the Unionists by nominating their own candidate for mayor, which showed that not only were they disrespectful enough to get elected; now they were presumptuous with it.

In March 1920, shipyard engineers gained a wage rise

which took their earnings to a minimum of 83s. 6d. – sustantially higher than those on Clydeside. This plunged one of the yards, Workman, Clarke and Co., into financial crisis. At the end of April, Northern building workers won the forty-four-hour week. On 28 June the shipyard workers demanded a £5 minimum wage.

When, in February 1920, Lloyd George's government published the 'Better Government of Ireland Bill', offering Home Rule to a partitioned Ireland, the Northern Protestant community was not at all united. It was beginning to tear itself apart along the lines of class cleavage. The significance of the 'Holy War' which erupted in Belfast in July 1920 was that it welded the classes within the Protestant community together again.

On 7 July Carson discovered a 'Bolshevik-Sinn Fein Alliance' (an alliance which, is still regularly being discovered in such places as the front page of the *News of the World*). At the demonstration of 12 July he declared: 'What I say is this, the men who came forward posing as friends of Labour care no more about Labour than does the man in the moon. Their real object, and the real insidious object of their propaganda, is that they may mislead and bring about disunity among our own people, and in the end, before we know where we are, we may find ourselves in the same bondage and slavery as in the rest of Ireland in the south and west.' In other words, Labour, by tending to fragment the all-class Protestant alliance, was helping to sell the Protestants into a Rome-ruled republic. The argument had an attractive simplicity, and nothing in the content of the developing independence struggle in the South seemed to refute it. Had there been in the south and west, and within the Catholic community in the north, a political tendency believing in national independence but opposed to – and opposing – the degree of 'bondage and slavery' which existed, this would have been a much more difficult point for Carson to make. But there was not.

Nine days after Carson's speech Protestant engineers at

Workman, Clarke and Co. met on the company premises and decided to expel all 'Sinn Feiners' (i.e. Catholics). As the Catholics were leaving, one defiant spirit shouted 'Up the Rebels'. That was enough. There was a hail of rivets from the Protestants, and for the next two years Protestant and Catholic workers in the North cut each other to pieces, the Catholics, being in a minority and in an economically inferior position, coming off much the worse. Working-class solidarity shrivelled in the heat of sectarian passion.

A pattern was established. In Belfast and in other towns, once a factory was cleared of 'disloyal elements' the Union Jack was raised over it as a sign of victory. At one such flag-raising ceremony, held in company time at the valve and brass-finishing department of Harland and Wolff's shipyard on 14 October, the future prime minister, Sir James Craig, set the official seal of Orange approval on these activities:

Before he sat down he would like to ask three questions and if they answered as he expected he would take back those answers to Sir Edward Carson when he returned to London (cheers). Would they hang on for ever to the old Union Jack, the emblem of their loyalty to King and Empire? ('Yes' and Cheers). Did they still refuse to go under a Sinn Fein parliament in Dublin? ('Yes' and Cheers.) Well, as they had answered those questions it was only fair that he should answer one that had not been put to him. 'Do I approve of the action you boys have taken in the past?' He said yes. (Cheers.) (*Northern Whig*, 15 October 1920)

In all, 10,000 workers were driven from their jobs. They were not all Catholics. Protestant radicals were, logically enough, included. Among those victimized were Charles McKay, James Baird and J. A. Hanna, one of the prominent Orangemen who had supported Larkin in 1907.

The effect on trade-union activity was immediate. On 18 October, four days after Craig's triumph at Harland and Wolff's, the workers there agreed, in the interests of 'good order', to waive the claim for a forty-four-hour week. One imagines that the management considered the wages paid for the afternoon of the meeting was money well spent. In December 1920 engineering wages were actually cut without any opposition from workers who, less than two years previously, had been in the vanguard of the struggle for more pay and fewer hours. The building workers were forced to abandon their own forty-four-hour week. When the Carpenters' Union launched a national strike throughout Britain against wage-cuts the Protestant joiners in the shipyards (there were no Catholics left), to a man, scabbed.

On the political level the effect of the sectarian war was equally disastrous for the Labour movement. At the election for the first Northern Ireland Parliament held under proportional representation on 24 May 1921, none of the four Independent Labour candidates in Belfast was elected. (The Labour Party did not officially fight the election.) James Baird received 875 first preference votes. His three colleagues mustered a thousand between them.

At no time between 1918 and 1921 did the labour agitation in the North link up with the contemporary struggle for independence. There was no basis on which it could have done so. In the first place, the trade-union leadership in Belfast was insistently 'non-political'. More important, the tendencies competing for dominance within Sinn Fein were united in one matter – that the class was irrelevant to their struggle, that labour must wait. The struggle for independence had nothing to do with the struggles of Belfast workers. There was no organization meaningfully active in Irish politics in the period after the First World War which offered the Protestant masses a united Ireland, in which they would get a better deal than was likely in a disunited one, no anti-Unionist organization which in the public mind had clearly differentiated itself from the conservative Catholic nationalism which infused the Sinn Fein movement. In that circumstance appeals to the Northern Protestants to join with their Catholic compatriots 'as Irishmen' in the fight for independence from Britain were, in the literal sense of the word, impertinent.

Larkin, who had been jailed in the United States while on a lecture tour, issued a call from his cell in Sing-Sing for a 'war for the workers' republic', but one needs soldiers to wage war and there was no socialist army left in Ireland.

Given the strength of the Orange Order and Orange ideology in the Northern Protestant community at the time, the sectarian propaganda of Carson and his colleagues would, anyway, have had an effect. But it would not have been as effective as it was had not the Sinn Fein movement resembled in many respects the ogre described. It was, as Carson said, a Catholic movement, in that it did not object at all to Catholic control of large areas of public life in Ireland. Its protectionist economic policies, had they been applied to all Ireland, would, as Carson said, have precipitated disaster in the North. The loyalist posters which festooned Belfast in 1921 depicting Royal Avenue and the shipyard choked with weeds and inscribed 'Belfast under Home Rule' may have been caricatures. But they contained an element of truth as important to the Protestant working class as to the leaders of the Unionist Party. The workers in the Belfast shipyard and in the engineering factories had nothing to gain and their jobs, possibly, to lose in the United Ireland which was on offer. Within an Orange Northern Ireland state they were able to retain a privileged position vis-à-vis Catholic workers, and through their involvement in the Orange Order able to feel that they played a real role in the affairs of the state. Republicanism, steeped in Catholicism, had nothing to offer. The main reason why Protestant workers were easy meat for Orange demagogues was that the Republican movement was not based on the working class.

The absence of a vigorous labour organization within the Republican movement and the resultant success of the Unionist leaders in containing the Protestant masses within Orangeism meant that in 1920–22 when the future shape of Ireland was being negotiated the only Irish interests being *considered* were those of Northern capitalism and Southern potential-capitalism. These interests, with the ready agreement of Britain, partitioned the country between them.

Partition was readily accepted by the Unionist Party, and the Northern Parliament opened in June 1921. It was not accepted by any major group in the South until January 1922. Thus Northern Protestants usually date the division of the country from 1921, Northern Catholics from 1922.

4

Partition left the Catholics in the North isolated, confused and afraid of the future. In Derry there were a number of local, complicating factors.

The 1916 Rising had made little impact on Derry Catholics. The *Journal* said that: 'It is agreeable to be able to state that despite the many exciting rumours and alarmist reports which have been floating about ... the conduct of all classes of the citizens, and of the north-west generally, has been admirably cool and sensible' (28 April 1916). In an editorial the attitude of the hierarchy and of the Nationalist Party leadership was faithfully reproduced:

(An) official message says that after the building had been shelled troops 'occupied Liberty Hall, the headquarters of the Sinn Fein force'. These phrases tend to show that the originators of the insurgent outbreak were not really the Sinn Feiners as a compact force in themselves, but rather the very considerable body of men who frequented Liberty Hall and who are known in Dublin as the Citizens Army. These are followers of the notorious Syndicalist Larkin. It is to be feared that many of these men have not had sufficient education to gauge correctly the dire consequences that must ensue from a mad-headed endeavour to carry into effect the principles underlying the teachings of Larkin and desperate characters of that type. From the publications which they have issued and the speeches these 'leaders' have made it seems evident that they are disciples of

159

men like Proudhon and Bakunine (*sic*) . . . The urging of people like the Dublin dockers with little political sagacity and less discriminative capacity to senseless and positively suicidal action is deplorable beyond power of expression.

Three days after the rising was crushed the *Journal* headlined the 'Irish people's disapproval of the wild deeds in Dublin' (1 May). Two days later it referred to Easter Week as the 'Red Week' and informed the populace:

The latest news from Dublin and the few other localities in the country where lawless outbreaks have recently occurred is to the effect that the authorities have succeeded in suppressing disturbance and restoring order. This is highly satisfactory. (3 May)

And two days after that, proof positive of a highly satisfactory outcome:

Valuable machinery nearly all intact. (5 May)

By the end of 1918 Northern Catholic bishops and businessmen, like their Southern counterparts, had shifted towards the Sinn Fein position, which, now that the views of the notorious syndicalists had been put aside, seemed much more reasonable anyway. In the December 1918 General Election Bishop MacCrory allocated the candidacy in the Derry seat to the Sinn Fein nominee, John MacNeill. The Nationalist hopeful, Major William Davey, obediently stood down. However, in Derry itself the Nationalist Party was much stronger than Sinn Fein, and the election campaign was, in effect, a Nationalist Party campaign for a Sinn Fein nominee. It opened with a parade through the Bogside led by the Hibernian band and speeches from the Rev. J. O'Doherty and the Rev. J. McGlinchey. The *Journal* weighed in with banner headlines urging the electors to 'Vote early, for MacNeill, for Derry and for Ireland' (13 December 1918). MacNeill was duly elected and in January 1919 took his seat in the Dail, but it was the Nationalist Party which still held sway in Catholic Derry.

Derry remained peaceful throughout 1919 while the guerrilla war spread like bushfire in the South. Trouble came the following year. One of the reasons for it was that in January 1920 Alderman H. C. O'Doherty became Mayor of the City. The *Journal* described this as 'An Historic Victory', which it was. Alderman O'Doherty was the first Catholic to become First Citizen since Colonel Cormac O'Neill was Chief Magistrate of Derry in 1688.

For a number of years the Unionist Party had been finding it more and more difficult to keep control of Derry Corporation. For one thing, the Catholic majority in the city kept increasing. For another, the municipal franchise had progressively been extended during the second half of the nineteenth century (the Municipal Corporations Act, 1840, the Towns Improvement Act, 1854, the Local Government Act, 1898). In 1896 a Londonderry Improvement Bill, redrawing the ward boundaries in the city, had been rushed through Westminster to prevent a threatened Catholic takeover. (The Londonderry Improvement Bill as originally submitted by Derry Unionists provided for city limits enclosing an area as big as that of contemporary Berlin. This section was amended at Westminster.)

By 1919 the Catholic majority in the city had grown to more than 5,000 and the boundaries were changed again. In that year the Local Government (Ireland) Act was passed instituting proportional representation at municipal elections and requiring ward boundaries to be drawn so as to give 'equal representation on the basis of population'. The new ward boundaries in Derry did not do that. However, the proportional representation system can flummox even the most experienced electoral fixers, and in the event the Nationalists in January 1920 won seats which had not been intended for them and found themselves with 21 members on the 40-man corporation. 'HISTORIC TRIUMPH IN DERRY,' exulted the *Journal*. 'NATIONALISTS WIN CORPORATION. "NO SURRENDER" CITADEL CONQUERED

AFTER CENTURIES OF OPPRESSION. OVERTHROW OF ASCENDANCY: CELEBRATION OF POPULAR VICTORY' (21 January 1920). In the Bogside bands paraded late into the night, crowds sang in the streets and bonfires blazed everywhere. There was 'a wild demonstration of enthusiasm' (*Journal*, 21 January 1920) at a victory meeting in St Columb's Hall in Orchard Street. The first meeting of the new Corporation was held in the Guildhall on 30 January.

When Councillor Logue declared that Alderman Hugh C. O' Doherty had been elected Mayor for the ensuing year there was a scene of wild enthusiasm among the crowd which thronged the Chamber. Cheering continued for a couple of minutes, and broke into a lusty rendering of 'God Save Ireland' and 'The Soldier's Song' ... (*Journal*, 30 January 1920)

In the late forties and in the fifties when I was running around the Bogside old people would sometimes say to one another when the talk turned to politics: 'Do you remember the time we won the Corporation?' And of course they did. After all, we never won it again – not until 1973, when everything was changed anyway.

In the spring of 1920 Derry was still relatively peaceful, although reports from the rest of the country conveyed something of the deepening chaos attending the War of Independence. A single page of an April edition of the *Journal* contained the following headlines:

Appalling Arklow Affair, Troops run amok, Civilian shot dead, Soldier killed in Limerick, Kerry policeman wounded, More hunger-strikers released unconditionally, Three mighty forces favour Irish freedom, Barracks besieged, Desperate Wexford encounter, Mysterious Cork arrests, Riots in Limerick, Soldiers and civilians in conflict, Belfast joins hunger strike, Derrymen released, Liveliness in Leitrim, Series of outrages, Wholesale slaughter the British method, Tyrone barracks blown up, Police-sergeant disarmed, Secession of Ireland; British Ambassador's statement.

Such reports generated nervous excitement. The Catholics saw the capture of the Corporation in the context of this wider struggle, as a preliminary to the capture of the whole country. The Protestants made a similar estimation of its significance, but saw it in a different light. The Catholics, locally, were now in control. That made the possibility of the greater outrage, Home Rule, more real, perhaps, to Protestants in Derry than in any other part of the North. Alderman O'Doherty had told them in his inaugural address:

Rest assured mighty changes are coming in Ireland. Do you Protestants wish to play a part in them? The Unionist position is no longer tenable; your leaders are abandoning it ... Do you not see that Englishmen are prepared to sacrifice you if they can only secure the goodwill of the rest of Ireland? Is it not time that you reconsidered your position? ... Ireland's right to determine her own destiny will come about whether the Protestants of Ulster like it or not. (*Journal*, 30 January)

It was hardly reassuring.

The riots began on 18 April. Shots were fired from the city walls into the Bogside. Police bayonet-charged a Catholic crowd in Ferryquay Street in the city centre. Soldiers of the Dorsetshire Regiment fired into an isolated Catholic street, Bridge Street. The Lecky Road police station in the Bogside was besieged by a large crowd. On 1 May shots were fired from the Fountain at Catholic houses in Bishop Street, at the edge of the Bogside. On 15 May fighting – 'the fiercest that has ever been experienced in the history of the city' (*Journal*, 17 May 1920) – broke out in Bridge Street. As police bayonet-charged, one of their number was shot dead. A four-hour gun battle between soldiers and a local IRA unit ensued. On 18 May the UVF emerged in strength and took over Carlisle Road near the city centre. Neither the police nor the army interfered. Twenty-one-year-old Bernard Doherty from Ann Street in the Bogside was shot dead. On 18 June Catholic houses in the isolated Prehen area were attacked. Notices were displayed locally warning that 'Any Sinn Feiner found at Prehen or Prehen Wood will be shot at sight'. On 19 June the UVF took over the Diamond and Guildhall Square and launched an attack on the

Long Tower area of the Bogside. Five Catholics were shot dead. On 23 June the *Journal* reported: 'Two more Catholic citizens murdered ... From the city walls bullets were rained on a portion of the Bogside.' On 25 June the UVF entered the grounds of St Columb's College and were dislodged by the IRA. Catholics were driven out of houses in Carlisle Road, Abercorn Road and Harding Street and fled into the Bogside. Rioting and shooting continued and attitudes hardened on all sides. 'To become hewers of wood and drawers of water for Sir Edward Carson,' said the Catholic bishop, Dr McHugh, 'Catholic Ulster will never submit' (*Journal*, 17 November 1920).

Trouble flickered on in 1921. In the May election – the first Northern Ireland general election – the alliance in the North between Sinn Fein and the Nationalists held. Twelve Home Rulers were elected to Stormont, as were forty Unionists. As far as the Unionists were concerned, that was that. Northern Ireland was established. Catholics did not agree, especially in places like Derry. As far as they were concerned nothing had finally been settled. The war in the South was continuing. Sectarian fighting in Belfast continued unabated (15 killed and 68 wounded on 10 July alone). Matters were still being contested.

Even when the terms of the Treaty recognizing Partition were announced in December 1921 and accepted by a majority in the Dail in January 1922 it did not occur to many Catholics in the North that that was an end to argument. They seized on the provision for a Boundary Commission to determine the line of the border, reasoning that some at least of Northern Ireland's territory – Derry, for example, with 23,000 Catholics as against 18,000 Protestants – would have to be ceded to the South. The Treaty, taken as a whole, was regarded not as a blue-print for the Ireland of the future, but as further clear evidence of inexorable and accelerating progress towards full independence. Said the *Journal*: 'We see the sinister power of a central citadel of the Unionist ascendancy brought down to the dust' (9 December 1921). At the beginning of 1922 most Northern Catholics, fearful of what the future might bring if they were left to the mercy of an Orange administration, looked to the South with nervous confidence for salvation. They had reason to believe that this was not a forlorn hope. Even those who had signed the Treaty had done so, they said, because they believed it to be a 'stepping-stone to freedom'. No one in the Sinn Fein leadership was going to tolerate partition for long.

5

This is one of the best-loved Irish modern myths – that the Sinn Fein leaders agreed to partition only with the utmost reluctance and that the Civil War in the South which followed the signing of the Anglo-Irish Treaty was fought between those who reluctantly accepted and those who rejected partition. In fact partition was scarcely mentioned in the Dail debates on the articles of the treaty in December 1921 and January 1922. When Mr de Valera, the leader of the anti-treaty faction, did mention it it was to liken the South's claim to the North to Britain's lately relinquished claim to the whole of Ireland. The argument between Treatyites and anti-Treatyites was about the precise nature of the future relationship between the 26-County State and Great Britain. It is true that there was a widespread feeling among IRA volunteers in the countryside that the exclusion of the Six Counties was a sell-out, and that this reflected the conservative attitudes of the Treatyites on a wide range of social issues; and this feeling was used by Mr de Valera to give impetus to his anti-Treaty campaign. However, the initial split in the Sinn Fein leadership was not about the border. When the County Councils of Tyrone and Fermanagh declared their allegiance to Dail Eireann and were as a result dissolved by the Unionists, no one, either pro- or anti-Treaty, is on record as suggesting that something might be done about it. When Mr de Valera's irregular anti-Treaty forces went into action in the Civil War it was never seriously suggested that they direct their military attentions to the North.

The Cumann na nGael Party – the pro-Treaty faction of Sinn Fein which formed the first Independent 26-County government – represented large farmers and commercial businessmen who wished, as far as it was possible, to minimize economic friction with Britain and to obtain for themselves as comfortable a position as they could within a colonial situation. Many, like Kevin O'Higgins, were fearful of the effect of high tariffs on existing Anglo-Irish trade. Mr de Valera's minority faction (representing small manufacturing capitalists) held to the original Sinn Fein policy of protectionism and represented those who wanted to wage an economic war against British domination and thereby quickly to build their own Irish industrial structure. Being, thus, necessarily more anti-British than the Treatyites, they were able to represent themselves as the heirs of 'true Republicanism', and were consequently more popular among Catholics in the North.

Their Republicanism was expressed in their opposition to the office of the Governor-General and to the Oath of Allegiance to the British Crown which, under the Treaty terms, members of the Dail were required to take. Mr de Valera stumped the country promising to 'wade knee-deep through Irish blood' before he would accept 'this heinous document'. Which thing he then proceeded to do. He waded knee-deep through Irish blood and then he accepted the Treaty. Those of the IRA who still had stomach for a fight rallied to him. They believed, and were encouraged by Mr de Valera to believe, that they were fighting against the border, against the Governor-General and the Oath. (Most of them were also against the 'law and order' which the new government was imposing on the countryside. Peasants in some areas, assuming that since the revolution had happened they might properly make some revolutionary changes in their own lives, had taken over large estates. Mr Cosgrave explained to them that this was a misinterpretation of the situation and sent the army to clear them off the land. Workers who took over creameries and created 'soviets' were similarly disillusioned. Mr de Valera tended to be reticent on this aspect of the Cumann na nGael sellout.)

It was a very bloody war. Anti-Treaty prisoners, untried, were shot by their former comrades-in-arms. More Irishmen (approximately 650) died than had been killed in the war against the British. It can still excite fierce passions. A verse of the song 'Take it down from the Mast' tells of four of Mr de Valera's followers who were shot without trial by the Treatyites in 1922:

> They have murdered our young Liam and Rory,
> They have butchered young Risteard and Joe,
> Their hands with their blood are still gory,
> Fulfilling the work of the foe.

'Joe' was Joe McKelvey from Belfast. In August 1969 on the gable wall at the corner of Cyprus Street in the Lower Falls area someone wrote in foot-high letters 'Remember Joe McKelvey'. In Letterkenny in 1970 I heard Mr Neal Blaney rouse an election crowd to fever-pitch with the cry: 'Remember Drumbo.' (The Treatyites had shot two anti-Treaty volunteers there.) 'REMEMBER DRUMBO' they roared back, clenched fists raised in the air, believing now with the same honest passion which had excited the two martyrs that it had been another noble sacrifice for the Republican ideal. Which in a sense it was. It all depends on what one means by 'Republican'. Because really, objectively, in terms of the politics of the leaders of the two sides, the Irish Civil War was a faction fight between gombeen-men and tiny capitalists trying to grow up, between those who wanted to retain a role as middle-men for British business in Ireland and those who wanted to lay their own hands on the profits accruing to British business, between the grubbers and the grabbers.

The pro-Treaty forces won the Civil War. They were supported by the majority of the people not so much because there was widespread enthusiasm for the Treaty but because the people were weary of war and the Treatyites offered them peace. Cumann na nGael held office until 1932. Under it, land consolidation continued and most industries were not protected.

The Cosgrave government had, by any standards, a fairly difficult task. With the loss of the North through partition it was deprived of 29 per cent of the population and 40 per cent of Ireland's taxable capacity. Belfast alone had handled a third of Irish trade. Still, within the limit of its own ambitions it was not without achievement. Roads and railways were rebuilt. Fisheries were improved and an afforestation programme begun. A sugar-beet factory was set up in Carlow, the Barrow was drained, and a hydro-electric plant was built on the Shannon, all by direct state enterprise. In 1927, an Electricity Supply Board was set up to distribute the power produced by the Shannon scheme. The number of jobs in industry began to increase, but slowly, from 103,600 in 1926 to 111,000 in 1931 (J. Bowyer Bell, *IRA: The Secret Army*, p. 119). Working-class organizations were, however, thoroughly demoralized. The failure of Independence to effect any dramatic economic change in their conditions and the failure of the Labour Party and of 'left-Republicans' within Mr de Valera's party to suggest what concretely should be done about it weakened the impulse to maintain organization. Between 1923 and 1929 trade-union membership declined from 130,000 to 85,000 (Lysaght, *The Republic of Ireland*, p. 89). The lack of any clear perspective was reflected in the fissiparous nature of the Parliamentary Labour Party. Of 17 Labour TDs elected in 1922, three were Independents by August 1923. Of 14 elected then, one was an Independent by June 1927. Of 13 elected in June 1927, four were Independents by 1932.

Agricultural labourers were badly off. By the early thirties wages had fallen to 21 shillings per week. When unemployed, which was often, they were eligible for no state benefits. By 1932 unemployment had reached 130,000. The economy was totally dependent on Britain, which took 92 per cent of exports. A quarter of a million people emigrated in the first decade of independence.

Until 1927, Mr de Valera's followers refused to take their seats in the Dail – which they regarded as a 'puppet-parliament' – and the Taoiseach William Cosgrave and his government, facing only the small, permanently disintegrating idea-impoverished Labour Party, had a comparatively easy ride considering the economic mess over which they presided.

Mr de Valera, 'excruciatingly articulate and precisely vague' (Bowyer Bell, p. 69), made as much as he could of the abounding discontent. He gave the populace to understand that in some inexplicable or at least unexplained way their economic problems resulted in great measure from the government's insufficiently anti-British attitudes. There was truth in this, but, as was to be shown, it was a tiny truth. His most important achievement during the years of Cumann na nGael government was to keep the Republican anti-Treaty coalition together.

By the late twenties the fragments of Radicalism, scattered during the 1916–22 débâcle, were beginning to coalesce. The 1929 slump encouraged a more radical analysis of the Irish malaise than that offered by de Valera. The IRA sprouted a rich crop of radical fronts (Saor Eire, Friends of Soviet Russia, Irish Labour Defence League, Workers' Revolutionary Party, Irish Working Farmers' Committee, Women Prisoners' Defence League, etc.). By September 1931 the Minister of Justice was voicing fears that 'a Republic of Soviet nature' would be imposed on the country (*Irish Independent*, September 1931). Mr de Valera had, of course, no intention of imposing a Republic of Soviet nature on anyone. But his rhetoric was occasionally radical enough to encourage those who were that way inclined to regard him as a lesser evil than Cosgrave, and he went into the 1932 election with the fairly enthusiastic support of the Republican left. By then one section of the population at least had had their minds wonderfully clarified about the nature of the 'Free State'.

The establishment of the new state enabled Protestants in the North to discover whether, in action, Home Rule was Rome-rule. They discovered that it was. The power of the Church was consolidated. It was, of course, already great, and even under the British the influence of the hierarchy and of the priests had often been decisive in forming public opinion. It was only with the establishment of an independent government, however, that it became possible actually to write Catholic teaching into the Statute Book.

By the end of the Civil War the hierarchy was thoroughly disturbed by the 'low level of degeneracy' (Bishop Hoare of Ardagh, *Irish Catholic Directory*, 3 August 1924, p. 589, quoted in J. H. Whyte, *Church and State in Modern Ireland*, p. 24). Traditional *mores* had apparently come to be observed with something less than proper piety during the upheavals of recent years. Now, given its head, the church set about putting all that to rights. The clergy spread out across the countryside, like beaters at a pheasant-shoot, flushing out sin. Sex took a terrible hammering. Pastoral letters foamed over with warnings against mixed dancing and similar occasions of sin. The Archbishop of Tuam observed with alarm that 'company-keeping under the stars at night has succeeded in too many places to the good old Irish custom of visiting, chatting and story-telling from one house to another, with the Rosary to bring all home in good time' (*Irish Catholic Directory*, 1928, p. 557). The Archbishop also noted that 'bad books, papers and pictures were finding their way into remote country places' (ibid.). The Bishop of Galway said in a sermon: 'It had been suggested that the present-day attraction for dancing was physical exercise. He did not believe it. If physical exercise were needed why did not the devotees of dancing go out and skip with a rope?' (*Irish Independent*, 9 April 1924). Nor did the clergy confine itself to exhortation. Many a courting couple was rooted out of a comfortable Irish hedgerow by a curate with a blackthorn-stick. (It is important to understand that none of this was regarded as being in any way eccentric.)

Such things were reported in the press and noted in the North, but much more crucial to the development of Northern Protestant attitudes to the South was the reaction of the Dublin government to the hierarchic aspiration for these attitudes to be incorporated in the law. The first example of Holy Writ being substituted for secular law was the Censorship of Films Act in 1923, which empowered a censor to ban films or passages of films deemed 'subversive of public morality'. The Intoxicating Liquor Act, 1924, reinforced by a further Act in 1927, reduced the opening hours and the number of pubs in the land, to the general approbation of the church. In 1925, the government moved to prevent the presentation of private divorce Bills to the Dail – the only way, under a system inherited from pre-Treaty days, that people in Ireland could obtain a divorce. Urging support for the measure, Mr Cosgrave made it clear that as far as the government was concerned the Catholic moral code had the effective status of enacted law: 'I have no doubt but that I am right in saying that the majority of people of this country regard the bond of marriage as a sacramental bond which is incapable of being dissolved ... Anything that tends to weaken the binding efficacy of that bond to that extent strikes at the root of our social life' (Dail debates, 11 February 1925). Four years later Mr Cosgrave's government removed two other daggers aimed at 'the root of our social life'. The Censorship of Publications Act provided for the banning of any book which 'in its general tendency' was considered 'indecent or obscene' or any newspaper or magazine which had 'usually or frequently been indecent or obscene'. The first censorship board consisted of one Protestant and four Catholics. One of the Catholics, a priest, was chairman. The act also made illegal advocacy of birth control.

By so institutionalizing Catholic teaching Mr Cosgrave hoped to establish Cumann na nGael not just as the party of Law and Order, but as the party of God's Law and Order. If he could do that he would be in a very strong electoral position. The church had branches in every constituency. Announcing the banning of a number of the IRA's radical outcrops in 1931, Mr Cosgrave explained that: 'Drastic laws are made only for the evil-doer, and there need be no fear of punishment in the minds of those misguided young men and women if they seize this opportunity to recognize that the observance of the laws of God and of the State is the only sure means of achieving the ultimate happiness and prosperity of the people. The authority of the State comes from God, and every organization that seeks to destroy the State is subversive of morality and religion.'

However, Mr de Valera had no intention of allowing Mr Cosgrave sole title to the franchise for pushing God's line in Irish politics. By 1929 he had led the majority of anti-Treatyites out of Sinn Fein and the IRA and into the new Fianna Fail Party. Dropping the abstention policy, they took their seats in the Dail. Many of Mr de Valera's followers had been excommunicated from the church during the Civil War, but once they entered Parliament it became clear that they did not hold this against the hierarchy. They facilitated the passage of the Censorship Act. One of the Fianna Fail leaders, the future President Sean T. O'Kelly, scotched any suggestion that Fianna Fail was less sound than Cumann na nGael on questions of faith and morals: 'We of the Fianna Fail party believe that we speak for the big body of Catholic opinion. I think I could say, without qualification of any kind, that we represent the big element of Catholicism.'

Indeed Mr de Valera's party began to 'play the Catholic card' with considerable adroitness, attacking Cumann na

Gael for neglecting to consult with the bishops when arranging an exchange of diplomatic representatives with the Holy See, and vigorously defending Mayo County Council's refusal to sanction the appointment of a Protestant librarian. Around the same time Mr de Valera went on record as being against Protestant doctors being allowed to cure sick Catholics (Dail Debates, 17 June 1931). Through all this Fianna Fail retained the effective support of the fringe 'Red' republicans.

6

Fianna Fail came to power in 1932, capitalizing on widespread disillusion with the economic effects of the 'Revolution', and except for two short periods of coalition government it stayed in office until February 1973. One of the first acts of the new 1932 government was to stop the payment of land annuities, monies due, under provisions of the Treaty, from Irish farmers in payment for land granted under the pre-Treaty Land Acts. (Mr de Valera, be it noted, did not stop completely the collection of the annuities. He merely halved them and stopped paying the collected half over to Britain.) Britain retaliated by imposing special tariffs on Irish imports, calculated so as to make good the loss to the British Treasury. Thus commenced the 'economic war' with Britain.

The one consistent policy motivating Mr de Valera throughout his political life was that Irishmen ought not to be exploited by foreigners while there were Irish exploiters available for the task. Thus the basis of Fianna Fail economic policy was protection and import substitution – in its broad outlines the 1905 Sinn Fein policy. The government consulted the import lists to discover which of the goods being imported could be manufactured at home. Tanning, boots and shoes, wholesale clothing, woollen and non-woollen textiles were the five categories first selected. It was estimated that the home market for these would provide 45,000 jobs. Production licences were issued to applicant manufacturers. A law was passed requiring that 51 per cent of the capital of new industries be in Irish hands.

In this hot-house atmosphere Irish capital tried to claw its way to self-sufficiency. Between 1932 and 1936 there was a 30 per cent increase in manufacturing output and a 40 per cent increase in industrial employment. An index of the increased governmental activity was that in 1935 alone the number of statutory rules and orders issued exceeded the total for 1922–32 (Lysaght, *The Republic of Ireland*, p. 132). However, the limits of this growth, based as it was on a relatively tiny home market, were soon reached. The economic war was launched on the slogan 'Burn everything British but their coal'. Coal, however, was a resource lacking in the 26 Counties, and by 1935 Fianna Fail had signed an agreement to import no coal but British, in return for increased cattle exports to her neighbour. A more extensive trade agreement in 1938, permitting the import of iron, steel, metal goods, machinery and chemicals, signalled the effective end of economic hostilities, the end of the only period in Irish history when national capital tried to assert real independence.

It had not, in truth, been a very determined effort. British capital in Ireland itself had remained untouched, not least because to take it over might have suggested to malcontented elements that Irish capital, too, might usefully be expropriated. Nor was there any ban on profits 'earned' in the 26 Counties being invested abroad. The proportion of the Irish national product invested abroad and the per-capita income from that investment is and has been one of the highest in the world. To facilitate this, Fianna Fail did not disrupt the link between Irish currency and sterling. Irish interest rates are still coordinated with British bank rate no matter what the state of the domestic Irish economy.

The attempted drive against British economic domination and towards self-sufficiency encouraged an 'anti-imperialist' stance abroad, and necessitated internal repression and reaction. Irish capital, fighting for its existence, could not permit militant opposition. Sinn Fein and the IRA – that is, those who refused to follow Fianna Fail into the Dail in 1927 – were first given fairly free rein to smash the crypto-fascist 'Blue Shirt' movement. That done, Mr de Valera turned on them.

He found it the more easy to do so since the radicalization which had bubbled up in the ranks of the IRA in the late twenties and early thirties had found no clear organizational expression. IRA leaders had continued to regard Fianna Fail as much less evil than Cumann na nGael. 'Many retained close personal relations with the Fianna Fail hierarchy. Peadar O'Donnell, one of the IRA's most incisive and Marxist-inclined thinkers who, in 1931, had been urging 'workers and working farmers to seize control of production, distribution and credit' (*An Phoblacht*, 28 February 1931), was, in 1932, urging the same people to 'give Fianna Fail a chance' (*An Phoblacht*, 2 April 1932). When Mr de Valera called a General Election early in 1933 to consolidate his position, an IRA manifesto demanded 'the scrapping of the Treaty, the abolition of partition and complete severance from the British Empire ... public ownership of the means of production, distribution and exchange ... We ask the people of the 26 Counties to return the Fianna Fail government on these terms' (*An Phoblacht*, 14 January 1933). What exactly was meant by voting for Mr de Valera 'on these terms' was not explained.

The IRA's problem was that it had never emerged from the misty nationalism which had shrouded the movement since its inception. That is, it had never really detached itself from the politics of national capitalism, just as Davitt had never really detached himself from Parnellism. As it urged revolutionary socialist change it was simultaneously in the vanguard of an ultra-chauvinist campaign against the importation of foreign, and especially British, items of all descriptions: 'If Irish cannot be bought, then let American, French or German, or any other product *except British* be bought ... Why should [British firms] be allowed to foist their chocolates on Irish people? Why should Bass, made from British barley, be distributed here? Have we not Irish sweets and Irish ales?' (*An Phoblacht*, 29 October 1932). We had, indeed; they were being churned out in great quantities by Irish capitalist enterprise.

Cinemas where newsreels containing items about the British royal family were on show were attacked, as was 'the wave of jazz which is sweeping the country' (*An Phoblacht*, 7 January 1934). The reason why the banks ought to be nationalized was not, or at least not primarily, that they were capitalist institutions, but that 'the power of the banks will, in all probability, be exercised in England's interest' (*An Phoblacht*, 23 July 1932).

As Mr de Valera in office began actually to develop national capitalism and as this began to involve the smashing of strikes and the holding-down of wages, the contradiction within the IRA between its nationalism and its socialism became acute. The most prominent left-wingers – O'Donnell, George Gilmore, Mick Price – were forced out. They formed the 'Republican Congress', but it too advocated support for Fianna Fail in certain circumstances, hoping to win over the Fianna Fail rank-and-file. However, there was little it could win them to, since Gilmore and others were arguing that 'the congress is not a party but a coordinating centre for anti-imperialist activities by people who may or may not be members of various parties and organizations'.

In the end de Valera broke definitively with the IRA and its offshoots on a straightforward class issue. Dublin transport workers struck in March 1935 for the restoration of wage-cuts and against the arbitrary dismissal of a bus driver. The strike lasted eleven weeks. The government sent in army lorries to ferry people to work. The IRA then called for a general strike, arguing that the strike had now gone beyond the bounds of a normal trade dispute and that the government was clearly not neutral.

The IRA's offer of help to the strikers created something akin to hysteria in the ranks of the state and church establishment. There was already much nervousness abroad. Unemployment was rising towards 130,000, despite the new industries. In January there had been street-fighting in Dublin in the course of a struggle for union recognition by shop workers. Now, with the city paralysed, the awful possibility loomed of the IRA, with the methods and the weapons appropriate to its tradition, being grafted on to an aggressive mass movement of workers. On 28 March all copies of *An Phoblacht* were seized, not for the first or the last time. De Valera entered the lists, drumming up anti-IRA feeling: 'Those who remember the old IRA know that it always regarded itself as the army of the nation, pledged to defend the rights and liberties of the whole people. It stood for the maintenance of order. No one could conceive it as an instigator of sectional strife or as lending itself out as if it were some racketeering organization.' In pastoral letters the bishops denounced the strike and 'the specious arguments of the unCatholic people' (Archbishop Byrne). Forty-three members of the IRA and of the Republican Congress were arrested.

Despite this the strikers soldiered on until late May, when they won substantial wage increases. But the inability of the IRA to capitalize on the situation was evident within a few weeks, when, at the annual Bodenstown demonstration, Sean McBride – the present-day international, all-purpose Liberal – detailed IRA units to tear down Congress banners on the grounds that they were offensively left-wing. Meanwhile the Congress itself was beginning to fall apart in a welter of argument and recrimination about the precise organizational form it should adopt. De Valera weathered the storm.

Surveying the débâcle and searching around for an explanation, with ninety-six of its militants in Irish gaols, its newspaper being seized by the man it had hoisted into office, and its best thinkers peeling off to search in a left-wing wilderness for a new way forward, the IRA finally came up with: 'FIANNA FAIL ELECTED IN ERROR' (*An Phoblacht*, 27 April 1935).

In repressing disruptive communistic elements Fianna Fail had a powerful ally in the church. In fact relations between church and state were never better. On taking office Mr de Valera dispatched a note to the Pope expressing the government's 'respectful homage' and its intention to 'maintain with the Holy See that intimate and cordial relationship which has become the tradition of the Irish people'. (By 'the Irish people' Mr de Valera clearly meant 'the Catholics of Ireland', relationships between the Northern Protestants and the Holy See being neither intimate nor cordial.) In 1933 a tax was placed on imported newspapers, which helped to stem the tide of alien porn, please the bishops and, as a quite useful bonus, raise revenue. In 1935 in an effort to rid the country once and for all of family-planners Mr de Valera took time off from suppressing the IRA and breaking strikes to ban the import and sale of contraceptives. In the same year the problem of mixed dancing was faced up to, with the Public Dance Halls Act, which required persons intending to organize dancing activity to apply for a licence to the district court. But it is on none of these acts that Mr de Valera's and the Fianna Fail Party's reputation as the most willing hierarchic stooges in recent Irish history will rest. It is the 1937 Constitution which will ensure that that verdict is passed upon them.

The 1937 Constitution is crucial to any understanding of the political attitudes of both Catholics and Protestants in Northern Ireland: because, unlike the 1922 Constitution operated by Cumman na Gael, the 1937 document claims to be the Constitution of all Ireland, containing a blunt assertion of the Dublin government's right to legislate for the whole national territory. It provided for the abolition of the office of Governor-General and the election of a President of all Ireland. The 1937 Constitution also spelled out for Northern Protestants the social content of the united Ireland which was being wished upon them.

The *Irish Catholic* described the constitution as 'a noble document in harmony with Papal Teaching', and went on: 'There is substantial evidence of a sincere desire on the part of the drafter to be guided by the principles laid down in such encyclicals as "Immortale Dei" and "Rerum Novarum" of Leo XIII, and "Quadragesimo Anno" of the present pontiff. No sincere Catholic can fail to be impressed' (quoted in 'Article 44', pamphlet of the BICO, November 1972, p. 5). (The *Irish Catholic* did not speculate about what sincere Protestants might have thought.) The *Derry Journal* described it as a 'magnificent confession of Faith ... an inspiring enthronement of our tradition in the Faith ...' (ibid., p. 4). The Archbishop of Tuam praised the Constitution as 'founded on the rock of Christian and Catholic principle', and ingeniously, as a tourist attraction:

Ireland was always an interesting country to visit, but when it is realized that our new Constitution will put it before the world with its own distinctive characteristics, outsiders will be more interested then, and eager to see on what lines we develop ... they will come to see for themselves what kind of people we are ... (ibid., p. 4).

Indeed. With a characteristic mixture of historical inaccuracy and supernatural fantasy, Mr de Valera expressed the thinking behind the Constitution in a radio broadcast to America.

The historical phenomenon which turned Europe into Christendom, and barbarism into civilization, the historical phenomenon which made Christendom the leader of the world and centre of the world order, was the recognition by that continent of the simple but fundamental fact that man is created for a supernatural end. Our people are a conservative people. For fifteen

179

hundred years they have preserved the tradition and practised the Rule of Christian life. We stand in the world for the public worship of God in the way in which He has shown to be His will. (ibid., p. 5)

And 'the way in which He has shown to be His will' was, as the detailed provisions of the Constitution made clear, the Catholic way.

Article 41 begins with a brief statement of Catholic teaching on the family:

The state recognizes the Family as the natural primary and fundamental unit of Society, as a moral institution possessing ... rights antecedent and superior to all positive law.

Therefore:

No law shall be enacted providing for the grant of a dissolution of marriage.

Articles on Education (42) and Private Property (43) paraphrased the relevant encyclicals. Article 44 recognized the 'special position of the Holy Catholic Apostolic and Roman Church as the guardian of the faith professed by the great majority of the citizens', although, in truth, the special position of the Catholic Church was already clear from the previous articles.

It has been argued since, especially in November 1972 when a Referendum on the section giving a 'special position' to the Catholic Church was being held, that the 1937 Constitution merely reflected the statistical fact that within the 26-Counties area the great majority of people were Catholics, that it was never intended that such a Constitution could or should apply to the whole of Ireland. This is not so. At the time Mr de Valera was quite explicit that this was the Constitution under which Northern Protestants would be expected to live in the event of a united Ireland:

There are 75 per cent of the people of Ireland as a whole who belong to the Catholic Church, who believe in its teachings, and whose whole philosophy of life is the philosophy that comes from its teachings ... If we are going to have a democratic state, if we are going to be ruled by the representatives of the people, it is clear their whole philosophy of life is going to affect that, and that has to be borne in mind and the recognition of it is important. (Dail Debates, 4 June 1937)

Both Cumann na nGael (now after some changes renamed Fine Gael) and the Labour Party supported the Constitution.

The Fianna Fail regime was, as Dr Whyte put it, 'from the hierarchy's point of view in many ways a model administration' (op. cit., p. 88); and from the same point of view, Labour and Fine Gael formed a model opposition.

The years 1923–37 reveal, so far as religious values are concerned, a remarkable consensus in Irish society. There was overwhelming agreement that traditional Catholic values should be maintained, if necessary by legislation ... The two major parties, bitterly though they differed on constitutional and economic issues, were at one in this. Mr Cosgrave refused to legalize divorce; Mr de Valera made it unconstitutional. Mr Cosgrave's government regulated films and books; Mr de Valera's regulated dance-halls. Mr Cosgrave's government forbade propaganda for the use of contraceptives; Mr de Valera's banned their sale or import. In all this they had the support of the third party in Irish politics, the Labour Party. The Catholic populace gave no hint at protest. The Protestant minority acquiesced. (Whyte, op. cit., p. 60)

By the end of the 1930s it was difficult to see what there was or could be in common between the Northern Protestants and the Southern state – except that both were in the business of hammering the IRA.

7

Once the Northern state was established the Unionists set about organizing affairs in such a way as to guarantee, they hoped, that their power could not be broken. They did this by disenfranchising Catholics as far as was possible and by taking measures to deny political expression to any discontent coming from the Protestant lower classes; by building the Orange machine into the structure of the state.

Orange power was already a reality in many parts of Northern Ireland. Through the Unionist Party the Order controlled local government authorities in Protestant areas and was in a position to dispense patronage to its supporters in those districts. The Order, as we have seen, was also influential in many sectors of industry. In October 1920 the Order's armed wing, the Ulster Volunteer Force, was constituted by Westminster as a Special Constabulary. Thus, when the Government of Ireland Act was passed, setting up the Six Counties state, the immediate concern of the Orange leaders was not to create an administrative apparatus but, thus freed from direct and occasionally inhibiting Westminster control, to tighten the grip they had already taken on the existing apparatus. They showed fair determination. They were supported by the majority of the British Conservative Party.

The UVF, now the Specials, and other supporters of the Order went into action during the election campaign leading to the first Northern Ireland Parliament. Sinn Fein, Nationalist and other anti-Unionist candidates were arrested, gaoled, beaten up or otherwise intimidated. The *Manchester Guardian* commented: 'No sooner had it been discovered that a man was Sinn Fein election agent for a district than he has disappeared' (21 May 1921). A projected Labour rally in the Ulster Hall on 17 May was broken up by Specials, who thereupon cabled Sir James Craig: '... have captured Ulster Hall from the Bolsheviks' (F. Gallagher, *The*

Indivisible Island, p. 258). Observing the election campaign, one British journalist wrote:

The Unionists have one important ally – they have a coercive police force of their own ... Some of them [the Specials], the A class, become Regular RIC; the rest, the B and C classes, parade their districts at night with arms, harassing, threatening, beating and occasionally killing their Catholic neighbours and burning their homes. ('Special Correspondent', *Manchester Guardian*, 19 May 1921)

Almost the first legislative activity of the new Parliament was the drafting and passage of the Civil Authority (Special Powers) Act, introduced in April 1922 to give unusual powers to the government and the police force (which, when they were mobilized, included the Specials). Its second major Act was the Local Government (Northern Ireland) Bill, passed in October 1922. It abolished proportional representation for local government elections and gave the Minister of Home Affairs power to alter electoral boundaries. The purpose of the two Acts was to make Northern Ireland safe for the economic ascendancy.

In the first few years of its existence the most immediate threat to Northern Ireland and the source of greatest hope to the Catholics within it was the possibility that the Boundary Commission might cede some of its territory to the South. Under the terms of the Anglo-Irish Treaty the Boundary Commission was charged with determining 'in accordance with the wishes of the inhabitants, so far as may be compatible with economics and geographic conditions, the boundaries between Northern Ireland and the rest of Ireland'. The areas where Catholics were in a majority and where anti-Unionists held local government power lay precisely along the border. Tyrone had 79,000 Catholics to 63,000 Protestants, Fermanagh 35,000 Catholics to 27,000 Protestants. The biggest border towns, Derry, Armagh, Newry, were in Catholic hands. Had the Boundary Commission taken as its criterion the wishes of the inhabitants area by area as expressed in local government elections – and that, on the face of it, would have been the logical way to proceed – Northern Ireland would have lost almost all the border areas, practically half its territory. One of the few things about which all parties in Ireland were agreed was that if that happened the remaining Unionist-controlled territory would not have found it easy to maintain itself as a viable entity.

For three years the Unionists refused to appoint a representative to the Boundary Commission, thus preventing it from starting work. What they did appoint was a Commissioner with the power of judge to visit various areas and to recommend changes in local government electoral boundaries. The Commissioner, Mr John Leech K.C., was a characteristically clear-minded Unionist functionary. With regard to Strabane Rural Council, for example, he accepted without amendment a scheme submitted by Mr William T. Millar. Mr Millar was the local Unionist MP and stalwart of the local Orange Lodge. In Clogher boundaries drawn up by the Unionist MP for the area, William Coote, were similarly accepted. The Unionist Party in Cookstown had its suggestion duly rubber-stamped. And so on. The effect of the boundary changes, coupled with the abolition of proportional representation, was dramatic. In Co. Tyrone, for example, *every* rural council hitherto controlled by Catholics became Unionist. The councils of Castlederg, Clogher, Cookstown, Dungannon, Omagh and Strabane (rural) – in the areas of each of which Catholics predominated – were Unionist by 1924. Fermanagh county council passed into Unionist hands, as did the Enniskillen, Lisnaskea and Irvinestown Rural Councils, despite a Catholic majority in each. The figures for Omagh Rural Council illustrate the process. The electorate broke down: 61·5 per cent Catholic, 39·5 per cent Protestant. Before the changes the Council comprised 26 Nationalists and 13 Unionists. After Mr Leech had finished his task this changed to 18 Nationalists and 21 Unionists. William Millar summed it up well: 'The chance that we had been waiting for for so long arrived. We took advantage. We divided the country in the way we thought best' (12 July 1923). Only those areas with such a massive Catholic majority as to make effective gerrymandering impossible – for example Newry, Keady and Strabane Urban District – were left in Nationalist hands.

Derry City was, of course, the area which the Unionists were most anxious to deal with. Not only was it the second largest city in the Six Counties, it was a sort of Orangeman's Mecca. Catholic control of its corporation was intolerable. Sure enough, the boundaries were redrawn – for the second time in three years – and this time, the abolition of proportional representation making the necessary calculations much simpler, there was no mistake made. The Catholics' brief moment of municipal power was over.

Their reaction was understandable. They refused to contest elections, opted out of public life and banked on the Boundary Commission to see that fair play would be done. A meeting in St Columb's Hall in November 1922 resolved not to contest a forthcoming election on the grounds that

In Derry City alone, where Catholics are an overwhelming majority of the population, they are, owing to the system of gerrymandering and other mean devices, being disenfranchised, permanently excluded in future from all share in the management of the city and placed at the mercy of a privileged, intolerant minority ... We rely on the provision of the Anglo-Irish Treaty to save us from an intolerable bondage and religious, political and economic servitude which would be unbearable, and we hereby resolve to press our claims before the Boundary Commission to be set up under the Treaty. (*Derry Journal*, 3 November 1922)

It was to be August 1924, when the British government acted over the head of Stormont, appointed a representative to the Commission and set it in motion, before anyone was able to press a claim. But that time the 'wishes of the inhabitants' of the border areas, as expressed in local government elections, were as much in line with Unionist thinking as it was possible for electoral ingenuity to make them. Still the Catholics did not bring themselves to believe that the Commission could possibly confirm the existing frontier. 'The wishes of the inhabitants', the Treaty had said. Surely there could be no argument about that, in places like Derry. 'They cannot deny that almost half the area of the Six Counties is held within the North by force,' said the *Journal* (26 August 1925) as the release of the Commission's report became imminent. In the Bogside optimism abounded as it was reported that, 'while the political barometer rises to the point of optimism in Dublin, the spirit of Belfast becomes correspondingly depressed' (*Journal*, 28 August). Ernest Blythe, a minister in the Cosgrave administration, 'had no doubt that the result would be satisfactory to the Free State' (*Irish Independent*, 28 August 1925). *The Sunday Pictorial* reported : 'It is understood that, though the Boundary Commission has not yet completed its report, the British Government is already in touch with the Free State on the matter. It is even stated that the Free State is preparing to take over certain of the disputed territories' (30 August 1925). *Journal* editorials became positively lyrical – 'The Boundary Commission is about to give an early and inevitable decision ... It is not the Shamrock but the Orange Lily which is withering on Irish soil today' – and reported that customs officials in Co. Donegal had made arrangements to move over the border into Derry to man the new frontier at two hours' notice (2 September 1925).

It was not to be. Catholic political leaders had reacted to the activation of the Boundary Commission by presenting detailed statistics about the religious make-up and voting patterns of various areas. But it was brute force, not statistics, which was to decide the matter. The Unionist Party greeted the arrival of the Commission by mobilizing the Specials. There were 35,000 Specials at the time. In villages and towns along the border at weekends the Specials would parade in arms to be reviewed by cabinet ministers down from Belfast for the purpose. On 2 September 1924, for example, 1,000 Specials paraded in East Fermanagh (*Irish Times*, 3 September 1924). Two days later another 1,000-strong parade was reviewed by the Parliamentary Secretary to the Minister of Home Affairs in the adjoining and equally disputed area of South Tyrone (*Belfast News-letter*, 5 September 1924). In Derry there were numerous parades and open-air 'training sessions'. The intention was to impress on the Commission and on the British government that all hell would break loose if the border were tampered with and on local Catholics that it would be they who would experience this hell. In the Catholic village of Garrison in Fermanagh Sir James Craig assured an audience of 'Protestants and Loyalists' that 'they had their platoons and their system of defence and he could assure them that if necessary they would have twelve platoons of Specials' (quoted in F. Gallagher, *The Indivisible Island*, p. 188). That the mobilization of the Specials was designed specifically to ensure the unwilling inclusion of Catholic areas within Northern Ireland was made clear later by Winston Churchill: 'While the Boundary question was in suspense Sir James Craig and his Government felt it necessary to maintain between 30,000 and 40,000 armed special constables in various degrees of mobilization ... but so soon as this settlement was reached Sir James Craig informed me that he would be able to proceed immediately with the winding up of the Special Constabulary ...' (*Hansard*, 8 December 1925).

The British government had no intention of taking on the Unionists for the sake of democracy or to fulfil the provisions of a Treaty. The Unionist Party was the most direct representative of the British establishment in Ireland.

At the beginning of October 1925 Irish papers reported 'an astonishing rumour' (*Journal*, 2 October 1925). The rumour was to the effect that, far from there being a recommendation for the secession of Northern areas to the South, some Southern territory was to be handed over to the North. Nationalist Party representatives hurried to Dub-

lin to confer with the government as the press reported:
'Alarm in Donegal' (*Journal*, 20 November 1925). The
Journal's shamrock withered quickly enough as Derry
Catholics, bemused by the sudden blight that had afflicted
their hopes, joined now in demanding: 'HANDS OFF
DONEGAL. NOT A SOD: NOT A SLATE' (*Journal*, 30
November 1925). The Dublin government was not going to
go to war about the North either. To pre-empt any loss of
its territory it pushed through a measure confirming the
existing boundary. In the Bogside there was bitterness, bewilderment and apprehension, and a mind-numbing understanding of its own impotence. 'Gerrymandered, gagged
and throttled, the harassed Catholics of the Six Counties are
left in bondage.'

Preserving the original boundaries of the state was vital
for the Unionists. It was just as vital that they keep the
Protestant bloc intact. And in order to do *that* the Unionist
Party had to be in a position to deliver some sense of
privilege to the Protestant masses. After the seizure of the
local government machinery there was no real problem.
Jobs and and houses are what working-class people need
more than anything else, and local authorities have jobs
and houses to distribute. The success of the Unionist Party
over a period of time in staffing key local governmental
positions with their own supporters was shown by a 1957
study of County Council administrative officers:

Tyrone (55·3% Catholic) had 60 Protestant and 6 Catholic
officers.
Antrim (22% Catholic) had 93 Protestant and 4 Catholic
officers.
Armagh (46·5% Catholic) had 47 Protestant and 3 Catholic
officers.
Derry (43·1% Catholic) had 48 Protestant and 4 Catholic
officers.
Down (30·1% Catholic) had 71 Protestant and 7 Catholic
officers.

Fermanagh (54.3% Catholic) had 60 Protestant and 6 Catholic officers.
(Figures from Gallagher, op. cit., p. 210.)

Thus the Unionist majorities elected to Councils on the basis of the 1922 Act, by appointing safe men to key positions, ensured that there would be little high-minded reluctance to operate their policies. Local government jobs and publicly-financed houses were allocated not according to need but according to the politics/religion of applicants. It is unnecessary to give figures. No one now denies this. Private enterprise played its part too, which was but natural, the owners of local industry being almost to a man prominent Unionists.

Other state institutions were drawn into the mesh. One third of the membership of the RUC was recruited directly from the Specials, who in turn were recruited exclusively from the Protestant community and almost exclusively from the ranks of the Orange Order. The Specials' chain of command linked directly into that of the RUC. Appointments to the Bench and to the magistracy were decided on a sectarian-political basis. The magistrate who sentenced Bernadette Devlin for her part in the events of August 1969 in Bogside was a former Unionist candidate for the constituency of which she was a sitting member. Of the three judges who heard and refused her appeal, two were members of the Orange Order and one a former Unionist cabinet minister.

There is a theory, currently fashionable in 'liberal' circles in Ireland, that gerrymandering, discrimination, and so on were unfortunate but natural reflections of the sectarianism of both communities in Northern Ireland, that, given the Protestants' understandable fears of Home Rule, it was simply inevitable that such things would happen, and that no one essentially was to blame for it. A pity, but it was the way things had to be. (For a more long-winded exposition of this point see Garret Fitzgerald, *Towards a*

New Ireland.) This was not the way things had to be. It was the way things had to be if the Northern state was to continue to exist and that, *pace* Dr Fitzgerald, is a very different thing. The classic statement of the Orange position was made by Sir Basil Brooke (later Lord Brookeborough) on the Twelfth in 1933 in words which thousands of Catholic schoolchildren in Northern Ireland know by heart:

There were a great number of Protestants and Orangemen who employed Roman Catholics. He felt he could speak freely on this subject as he had not a Roman Catholic about his own place. He appreciated the great difficulty experienced by some of them in procuring suitable Protestant labour, but he would point out that Roman Catholics were endeavouring to get in everywhere. He would appeal to Loyalists, therefore, wherever possible to employ good Protestant lads and lassies. (*Fermanagh Times*, 13 July 1933)

A few months later Sir Basil was equally explicit about the reasons why Catholics should not be allowed to work:

You people who are employers have the ball at your feet. If you don't act properly now, before we know where we are we shall find ourselves in the minority instead of the majority. (*Londonderry Sentinel*, 20 March 1934)

In other words: the Catholics will outbreed us unless we force them to emigrate. Catholics by that time had already got the point. They were not wanted.

Discrimination was, for obvious reasons, most acutely felt in the western border areas where Catholics were in a majority – in Tyrone, Fermanagh and around Derry City. These were, by neat coincidence, the areas which were, anyway, most vulnerable to economic trends. The staple industries – linen, shipbuilding, and engineering – were largely concentrated in the Lagan Valley around Belfast and, as capital attracted capital, the economic disparity between the eastern and western parts of Northern Ireland increased, a natural tendency which the Unionists were not at pains to reverse. The situation round Derry went from bad in 1920 to worse. The border cut off part of the natural hinterland. The city was never more isolated. In 1920 the Strabane Canal Company had closed. In 1921 a large distillery in William Street went out of business. In 1922 a tailoring industry collapsed. In April 1923 a 'Derry Employment Committee' suggested that the local unemployed might be 'placed in colonies'. In 1924 the Derry shipyard, which had employed 2,000 men during the war, went out of business. In 1925, a flag, bunting and lingerie factory closed, as did a hosiery factory. The shirt industry marked time. In 1926, the male unemployment figure for the city was 28 per cent. Given widespread discrimination, it can safely be assumed that almost all of these were Catholic men and that the figure for male unemployment in the Bogside was nearer 40 per cent. Parts of the Bogside were still unsewered. The population density of the district was 106.2 per acre. In the next ten years three thousand men emigrated. Lord Brookeborough, no doubt, was relieved that whatever virility was left in them would not be exercised in Protestant Ulster.

The Unionist leaders as pragmatic men were not against Catholics because of Catholic dogma, the Virgin Mary or the transubstantiation of bread and wine. They encouraged anti-Catholicism because they wanted to stay in power and thereby to preserve the economic position of their class. The Catholics had to be browbeaten into submission in order that the state could exist. The Protestant lower orders had to be bought off by the marginal privileges accruing from Catholic second-class citizenship.

Many Protestant workers, however, remained stubbornly unbought, which was not really surprising. Northern Ireland came into existence with an overall unemployment rate of 22.9 per cent and by no means all the jobless were Catholics. Sir James Craig's seven-man government included one industrialist, one titled landowner, one prosperous solicitor and three past presidents of the Belfast Chamber of Commerce. It was to be expected that Protestant working-class opposition to such a regime would reassert itself once the jingo-religious hysteria which accompanied the foundation of the state diminished. It reasserted itself fairly quickly. In a Stormont by-election in May 1923 an Independent Unionist in the tradition of Sloan defeated the County Grand Master of the Belfast Orange Lodge for the Protestant seat of West Belfast. In the next two years passions continued to cool, and many of the workers expelled from their jobs in 1920–2 began to drift back to work. The Labour Party was reorganized in Belfast.

The second Northern Ireland General Election was held in 1925, while the Boundary Commission was deliberating and the Specials were showing the Catholics the flag. The Unionist Party, as always, tried to fight on the sole issue of 'The Constitution'. But the results showed that the trick was not working nearly as well as it had done in the rather special conditions of 1921. In Belfast there were four four-member constituencies. Eight candidates appealed for a Protestant anti-Unionist vote. Only one failed to get elected. There were three Labour and four Independent Unionist MPs in the new Parliament. Unionist representation went down from 40 to 32.

Sir James Craig and his cabinet colleagues were not prepared to stand idly by while a trend such as that gathered momentum. Within two years they had determined to alter the rules of the game. Proportional representation was abolished. Explaining why this was necessary, Craig told a Twelfth Rally in 1927: 'Mr Devlin and his party are the natural opposition. Why then should any loyalist constituency add strength to it and weaken the influence of my colleagues and myself?' (*Belfast Newsletter*, 13 July 1927). Introducing the bill to abolish proportional representation early in 1929 he went on: 'What I have been afraid of under the proportional representation system was that certain members might be returned to the house who in a crisis on the one point of vital importance to the Ulster people might not stand on whichever side it was intended they should stand when they were elected to this house. Therefore, I personally will welcome this opportunity to get down to simple issues instead of the complicated ones that are inevitably brought before us under the old plan' (*Hansard* (N.I.), Vol. 10, 28.29). The 'simple issues' were the border, whether Catholics should be allowed to sweep the floor in the City Hall, and so on. The 'complicated ones' were unemployment, houses, rents, wages and such things, irritatingly being 'brought before us under the old plan'.

The first election under the new system was held on 21 May 1929. Craig's party faced ten Independent Unionists, eight Labour candidates, and six Liberals as well as tenants', unemployed and ratepayers' nominees. There were also twelve representatives of the natural opposition. The abolition of multi-member constituencies enabled the Unionists to pose their simple issue in starkly simple terms: for or against the maintenance of the state and no messing about the condition of the working classes. On polling day the *Belfast Newsletter* carried the final Unionist message in banner headlines: 'BEWARE OF INDEPENDENTS: UP ULSTER: SCATTER YOUR ENEMIES: HONOUR YOUR FRIENDS'. The Unionists increased their representation to 37. The Independent Unionists lost one and the Labour Party two seats. The sole Liberal MP was also defeated. It was a highly successful exercise from the Unionist point of view. For the moment they had checked the disintegration of the Protestant alliance. The abolition of proportional representation, Nationalist mythology notwithstanding, was not aimed against the Catholic population. It was designed to destroy Protestant working-class political organizations and it almost did.

However, the continuing fragility of the Protestant alliance was to be demonstrated dramatically three years later, when Protestants and Catholics in Belfast joined together to fight the police. The issues were unemployment and the pay for outdoor relief workers.

Northern Ireland, a depressed area at the best, so to speak, of times, was hard hit by the economic collapse at the beginning of the thirties. In 1932 a third of the total workforce was unemployed. There were 45,000 out of work in Belfast alone, including thousands of Protestant shipbuilders and engineers. Relief rates were farcical. A man and his wife received 8s. per week. This was increased to 12s. for couples with one or two children and to a maximum of 16s. for larger families. Most single men and women got nothing. Some unemployed were given outdoor relief work – digging roads and drains – for which labour they received their payments in cash. The idle unemployed were paid in kind. In these circumstances it was difficult for many Protestants to feel as privileged as Craig assured them they were.

On 30 September 1932 an Independent Unionist at Stormont demanded an immediate debate on the unemployment situation. The Speaker refused, and a Labour member threw the mace at him. On Monday 3 October the outdoor relief workers struck. Fifteen thousand marched to a mass rally and endorsed a demand for a minimum of 18s. 3d. a week for a single person, 23s. 3d. for a married couple, and 2s. extra for each child. On Tuesday men lay on the tramlines and halted the traffic. On Wednesday they hijacked the trams. Three hundred men demanded entrance to the Poor House as paupers. The next morning they asked for eggs for breakfast and were thrown out. At the week-end food was collected and food parcels given out to the most needy cases. There was rioting in Sandy Row (Protestant) and in Divis Street (Catholic). The unemployed appealed for a general strike and were ignored by the local trades councils. They called a rent strike and a school strike to begin on Monday 10 October and for a mass rally on the eleventh.

The strikers were to march to the rally from five points in the city in both Catholic and Protestant areas. The government used the Special Powers Act to ban the marches.

The Falls Road contingent tried to defy the ban and were attacked by the RUC. What happened in the Shankill as a result was described by a journalist on the spot:

On the Shankill Road crowds of growling men lounged about waiting ... Suddenly a big red-faced woman with a black shawl thrown over her shoulders, wisps of hair hanging over her eyes, appeared almost from nowhere. Wild-eyed and panting from exertion she ran to the crowds of men and in quick tense language told them that the unemployed and the police were in conflict in the Falls Road – one man was killed and others were wounded – and the fighting was still going on.

'Are you going to let them down?' she shrieked ... A cheer went up.

'No, by heavens, we are not,' they roared back and in a twinkling a veritable orgy of destruction had begun. (J. J. Kelly, *A Journalist's Diary*, Capuchin Annual, 1944)

This lady was obviously a mischief-maker of the type referred to in a *Belfast Telegraph* report:

There was an exchange of mischief-makers all over the city so as to confuse the police force. (Quoted in *An Phoblacht*, 22 October 1932)

A few days later the government and the Poor Law Guardians announced increases in relief payments – 20s. for a man and wife plus 4s. for each two children up to a maximum of 32s. a week. At a mass meeting on Saturday, the strikers accepted the terms. The chairman of the strike committee, Tommy Geehan, said:

What we have achieved is in direct contradiction to the statements of those who said that the workers could not unite and could not fight and the past fortnight will be recorded as a glorious two weeks in the history of the working-class struggle. We saw Roman Catholic and Protestant workers marching together and on Tuesday last we saw them fighting together. (Quoted in *Workers' Fight*, No. 19, p. 8)

The 1932 riots were described in the Unionist press as 'the worst rioting the city had experienced in fifty years' (quoted in Jeff Bell's *This We Will Maintain*, p. 7). They were not the biggest riots or the most destructive (only two dead). What the Unionists may have meant was that these were a more pernicious class of riot than the city was used to. Certainly the Unionist leaders were shaken if not by the extent of Protestant defection then certainly by the intensity with which it was expressed. The digging of trenches on the Shankill Road to draw police off from the Falls did not fit into the expected pattern of Northern politics. Sir James Craig was quickly on the job, warning 'the mischief-makers' that 'if they have any designs by the trouble they have created in our city . . . that this is one step towards securing a Republic for all Ireland, then I say they are doomed to bitter disappointment' (*Belfast Newsletter*, 13 October 1932). For the next few months the local press was filled with dire warnings from government spokesmen to Protestants that persistence in such foolish agitations might well lead to the annexation of Northern Ireland by the Vatican, Dublin, Moscow or all three. It was on the next 12 July that Sir Basil Brooke publicly congratulated himself on not having a Catholic around the house and urged others to seek the same purity. And significantly, the main Resolution on that Twelfth dealt with the newly apprehended danger of communism : 'We desire to impress upon all the loyal subjects of the King the vital necessity of standing on guard against communism, whose aim and object is to overthrow authority, the will of the people and everything we hold sacred in our domestic and public lives' (*Belfast Newsletter*, 13 July 1933). The Unionist Party held its vote in the 1933 General Election.

As had happened in 1907 and in 1919, there had been no effort by anyone involved to give political direction to the 1932 strike. The Labour Party had equivocated, the natural opposition was silent and the Republican movement was politically confused and more concerned with 'giving Fianna Fail a chance' in the South. Against all the odds a few Protestant workers did draw political conclusions and turned up with socialist banners at the 1934 Republican march to Bodenstown to commemorate the death of Wolfe Tone. But the IRA was in the process of expelling its left wing and the Northern contingent, like the Congress group, was beaten up by Mr MacBride's 'pure Republicans', who objected to their disruptive left-wing slogans. They went back to Belfast and there is no record of their ever appearing again at Bodenstown.

In 1932 the unemployment situation in Derry had been, as always, much worse than that in Belfast. But the trouble did not spread. In the summer of that year there were happier things on the Bogside's mind. There was a carnival atmosphere about. Brightly painted, intricately constructed arches spanned the narrow streets and flags and bunting fluttered. A 'Eucharistic Congress' was to be held in Dublin. Every school and parish was organizing a contingent to attend, to hear the masses, join in the prayers and listen to Count John MacCormack singing 'Panis Angelicus', the highlight. The streets were decorated so that those who stayed at home could make a 'spiritual pilgrimage'. 'The Holy Father loves Ireland,' alleged the *Journal* (22 June 1932).

On 10 October there was a march of unemployed to the Guildhall, but no violence attended. A deputation was received by the Corporation and demanded an end to the means test, and submitted fourteen suggested schemes for relief work. The Corporation was non-committal. The *Journal* was pleased by the dignified bearing of the Derry destitute and, correcting any impression that it was only the Unionist Party which disapproved of the unruliness in Belfast, declared that: 'Every right-minded person, and especially every friend of the unemployed and sympathizer with the plight of the vast army of hungry men and women, will deplore the happenings in Belfast yesterday' (12 October 1932). The *Journal* was then owned by Mr J. J. McCarroll, the Nationalist MP for the Foyle constituency.

One of the reasons for the lesser reaction to unemployment in Derry was that Derrymen were used to it. It was natural. Moreover the unemployed in Derry were almost all Catholic and tended as a body to look, not for changes within Northern Ireland, but for an end to Northern Ireland, as a solution. They had turned their backs on Belfast and looked to Dublin, although by this time it was beginning to dawn on some that perhaps Dublin was not terribly interested. 'It seems that we get nothing more from Southern parties,' said local Republican Neil Gillespie uneasily, 'than a pious wish that at some time or other Ireland will be united' (*An Phoblacht*, 15 January 1933).

In the 1933 Stormont General Election Mr McCarroll was opposed by a Sinn Fein candidate, Sean McCool, from Ballybofey, Co. Donegal. It was typical of the times that the election campaigns had very little to do with Derry. There was little mention of an unemployment problem, much less recent agitation on that score. Mr McCarroll advocated support for Fianna Fail as the best way of ensuring that at some time or other the country would be united. The IRA had not yet got rid of its most left-wing members, a fact to which Mr McCarroll was not slow to draw attention. Leaflets, printed by the Derry Journal Ltd, were distributed under such headlines as; 'The truth at last!', 'Communists backing McCool' and 'The Communists want McCool to win; do you?'

McCool's organization countered with declarations of traditional republican defiance which, if they lacked solid content, were frequently splendid in their expression:

> Give the answer from the North,
> O'er the border send it forth,
> Let them shout for all their worth,
> 'Keep to law and order.'
> Craig and Devlin save your face,
> Now, McCarroll, leave your place,
> Here's a man that's no disgrace,
> McCool is on the border.

But it was a defiance increasingly overlaid with romance, as Northern Republicans, trapped in the Six Counties and lacking any adequate analysis of why that situation seemed yearly to be solidifying, warded off despair with nostalgia and sentimentalized their hopelessness.

And here were the young boys and girls of Derry hurling revolution at the very gates of Empire. *Och, a Dhia!* What a long hunger has been on them all these days. (*An Phoblacht*, 2 December 1933).

Mr McCarroll, with the solid support of the clergy, had a comfortable victory.

In the North the rest of the thirties followed now-established patterns. The July Twelfth demonstration in Belfast in 1935 sparked off sectarian fighting. Nine people were killed and hundreds of Catholic families burned out. The city coroner commented: 'The poor people who commit these riots are easily led and influenced almost entirely by the public speeches of men in high and responsible positions. There would be less bigotry if there were less public speech-making of a kind by the so-called leaders of public opinion' (*Irish News*, 21 July 1935). Things were back to normal.

Derry remained fairly peaceful in 1935. In the Bogside people read of what was happening and raged about the terrible wrong of it, but there was nothing anybody could do.

15 July : Five dead and seventy-three wounded in Belfast.
Catholic districts again invaded.
Police use machine-guns.
Dastardly shooting of Catholic girl.

17 July : Brutal treatment of Catholics.
New areas attacked by mobs.
Catholic houses marked with crosses.

19 July : Heart-rending scenes.
Hundreds of Catholic refugees.
Catholics ordered to clear out.
Twenty-four hours to leave or homes wrecked.

22 July : New phase of Belfast pogrom.
Catholic girl workers attacked.
Two more deaths in Belfast.

24 July : Belfast Orange mobs active.

(*Journal*)

At least there were some things worse than being a Cath-, olic in Derry : being a Catholic in Belfast for one.

1936 saw a further turn of the screw in Derry, but the reaction was resignation rather than revolt. The problem was that despite emigration the Catholic population kept increasing. In one of the wards carved out in 1922, the North Ward, the Protestant majority had steadily decreased, from 618 in 1922 to 406 in 1928 and, in a by-election in May 1936, to 352. It was time for another change in the boundaries. Local Unionists drew up a scheme reducing the number of wards from five to three and the number of corporators from forty to twenty. At a public inquiry Mr A. Halliday, a prominent local Unionist, explained : 'There is a fear that the Unionist majority in the North Ward will in the course of a year or two be wiped out.'

Counsel for the Nationalist Party : 'And this is the purpose of the scheme?'

Mr Halliday : 'Oh yes.' (Quoted in F. Curran, *Ireland's Fascist City*, p. 23.)

Conveying the decision of the inquiry to the Corporation the Ministry of Home Affairs wrote :

Very considerable opposition was offered to the scheme at the Inquiry, while the evidence put forward in support of it was of a most unsatisfactory character. The new line proposed as a boundary ... followed in some places a course very difficult to define and no evidence was given in justification of the complication. (Quoted in *Ireland's Fascist City*, p. 24)

The letter went on to say that despite these reservations the plan was acceptable. In the municipal election of 1938 (the Nationalist Party having by now dropped the abstention policy) the scheme proved its worth. Two Protestant wards returned twelve Unionist corporators. The Catholic South Ward returned eight Nationalists. In all there, were 7,444 Protestant and 9,691 Catholic electors.

However, not all the news was depressing. The *Journal* reported that events in Spain were more encouraging: 'Bilbao's fall: Joybells greet Nationalist triumph. Franco pushing on to Santander.'

In 1938, Craig called a General Election, saying: 'We are asking for the return of the Government on the paramount issue of partition. I would appeal with all the earnestness at my command for a closing of ranks against the common enemy' (*Belfast Newsletter*, 21 January 1938). The Unionist Party won 39 seats, its best performance since 1921. The unemployment rate for the province as a whole was 28 per cent.

On the eve of the Second World War the rulers of Ireland, North and South, had reason to be pleased with their performances to date. The industrialists and landowners who ran the Unionist Party had successfully corralled the Catholics outside the political process and the Protestant masses inside their own party. The small-time capitalists of Fianna Fail had, by a short, sharp burst of protectionism, managed to build some sort of industrial structure while isolating the Republicans and making peace with the Catholic church. Both governments were firmly in control of their respective territories.

They had reached these positions by moving steadily apart. In the South industry had been developed by the application of economic policies which would have been catastrophic for the North, while year by year Catholic doctrine had been allowed to seep into the criminal code until the statute book was sodden with it. In the North Protestant power was steadily strengthened. Northern and Southern capitalism had needed to develop separately. Each had to hand an ideology which simultaneously mystified its 'own' community and repelled the other. Those who refused to be mystified were brutalized.

It can seriously be doubted whether the Northern state could have survived the first two decades of its existence had not the 'Free State' become increasingly repellent to Protestants. The Unionist Party had to fight unceasingly and at times desperately to hold the support of the majority of Protestants. That it succeeded was mainly due to the fact that the only alternative to the Union with Britain appeared to be sectarian Catholic Rule from Dublin.

No one consistently canvassed a third alternative. No one was with equal vigour fighting sectarianism North and South, no one was actively supporting and attempting to politicize the economic militancy of Protestant trade unionists and, at the same time, seeking to destroy clerical conservatism in the South. There was no anti-partitionist organization which the Protestant rioters of 1932, for example, could have turned to, because there was no anti-partitionist organization which had put up even a token fight against the lengthening list of objectively anti-Protestant laws in the South, none which had clearly detached itself from bourgeois-Nationalist politics.

The 1929 Northern Ireland General Election coincided with Mr Cosgrave's Censorship of Publications Act in the South. The 1932 unemployment riots took place eight months after Mr de Valera's election and his tendering of 'respectful homage' to the papacy. The 1938 election came in the wake of Fianna Fail's theocratic constitution. And all the time Cumann na nGael and Fianna Fail sprouted anti-partitionism, unceasingly declared their firm intention some day to take the North. Neither party in power made a single move to do any such thing. Once again the tendencies within Catholic Irish politics which were most sectarian and therefore more repellent to Protestants, and which yielded to no one in their verbal anti-Unionism, were precisely those which had no intention of, and no interest in, subverting the North. Their Catholicism and their anti-partitionism were the twin components of an ideology designed not to oust the Unionists but to mystify the Southern Catholic masses. The only effect on the Unionist Party was repeatedly to strengthen it.

W. T. Cosgrave and Eamon de Valera were the crutches on which the Unionist Party staggered through the twenties and thirties. The people who really lost out in all this were the Northern Catholics. Condemned to second-class citizenship within the Northern state, they were encouraged, during election campaigns, at commemorative functions for dead heroes and by the regular speeches of Dublin politicians, to believe that if they held fast a little longer succour would come. The actions of Southern governments simultaneously ensured that nothing actually would or could be done. So in places like the Bogside, enclaves of muffled unrest, people suffered on, and waited.

8

The Second World War interrupted developments. Both North and South did fairly well out of the war. In the South, which was neutral, the value of bank deposits more than doubled during the hostilities (Lysaght, p. 169). In the North, war production and an influx of allied troops generated a minor boom. After the war the weakness of both economies was exposed.

In 1947 Southern Ireland had a trade deficit of £91,823,000 (Lysaght, p. 170), four times the largest pre-war deficit. Employment in agriculture continued to decline, while stagnant industry provided no alternative jobs. To develop further, Irish industry needed access to international markets. But the very conditions of its initial formation and growth made this impossible. Protection had had the disastrous side effect of cosseting inefficiency and technological backwardness. (At the levels of productivity obtaining in the thirties the goods in the five categories first selected for protection and produced in Ireland by 45,000 workers could have been produced in Britain by 27,000 workers.) By the 1950s the number of industrial workers was falling. Between 1951 and 1961 the total employment in the South decreased from 1,217,000 to 1,053,000. The number of industrial workers fell from 664,000 to 637,000 (Garret Fitzgerald, *Towards a New Ireland*, p. 69).

There was an actual drop in output in 1957. In the first half of the fifties an average of 39,353 people were emigrating per year. In the second half the figure rose to 42,400. Successive post-war governments – two periods of inter-party government, from 1948 to 1951 and 1954 to 1957, interrupted Fianna Fail rule – reacted with a series of half-hearted development acts. In 1949 an Industrial Development Authority was set up. In 1952 grants were offered to investors in depressed areas. In 1966 industrial grants were extended to all areas. To little avail. The real problem was that industries built on the relatively tiny home market could not take off from the base constructed in the thirties. Access to international markets was a necessity; access to the Free State for international capital a necessity if that was to be achieved. Economic isolationism was redundant. With the cheerful pragmatism characteristic of the party Fianna Fail promptly abandoned the Sinn Fein economics on which it had first come to power. The Protection of Manufacturers Act was repealed in 1958 and, within a decade, the industrial infrastructure of the South was radically changed. Far from discouraging foreign investment Fianna Fail now went in search of it. Investment came in, attracted by tax concessions, low wages and unrestricted freedom to take profits out of the country. By March 1965, 234 new foreign projects had commenced operation in the state. Almost half of them were British. Between 1960 and 1966 profits increased by 54 per cent. Between 1961 and 1966 agricultural employment declined by 45,000, while employment in manufacturing industries other than textiles, clothing and footwear went up from 143,000 to 163,000. The new projects stimulated a boom in the construction and service industries. In the same period employment in the former increased by 14,000, in the latter by 22,000. The percentage of the population living on the land decreased steadily from 46 per cent in 1946 to 38 per cent in 1956 to 34 per cent in 1966 (Lysaght, p. 201). At the time it was all known as 'the Lemass miracle', being named after the new Taoiseach Sean Lemass, who symbolically had replaced Eamon de Valera as Fianna Fail leader in June 1969. (The Lemass miracle resembled most other Irish miracles in one crucial respect – that is, it never really happened. What had happened was that Fianna Fail offered foreign investors the chance to make a quick buck. The fact that there were those ready to accept the invitation cannot properly be regarded as miraculous.) The trend was formalized in 1965 when Lemass travelled to London to sign the Anglo-Irish Free Trade Agreement with Harold Wilson – one of the few recorded cases in history of one bankrupt managing to pawn his assets to another. The Free Trade Agreement provided for the dismantling of all economic barriers between the two countries over a period of ten years. It thus increased the dependence of the Southern economy on British capital. Not that that upset the nouveaux semi-riches who, barnacle-like, were beginning to encrust Irish parliamentary politics. As output continued to grow the whoops of delight in select lounge bars around St Stephen's Green in Dublin would have given the uninformed passer-by to understand that the Free State middle class had at last shrugged off its sexual inhibitions. But no. It was just that the talk had changed from horses to economics, from cross-doubles and Prendergast's chances at Ascot to unit costs, cash-flow and growth potential. Happy is the Tory with investment coming in and underpaid workers to boot.

While increased investment seemed to begin to solve the problems of the economy it would be a fundamental mis-understanding of economics to conclude that the economic problems of the people were thereby solved. For example: in 1965 there were an estimated 3,000 girls between 14 and 18 years old working full-time on the land. They worked an average 41 hours a week and earned £4 2s. 6d. Their male contemporaries were slightly better off, receiving £4 9s. 3d. for 41.9 hours. 24 per cent of men and 93 per cent of women workers were taking home less than £10 per week. In 1967, when Southern Irish manufacturing wages were the lowest in Europe, the state achieved the possibly unique distinction of simultaneously reaching the bottom of the European housing league. Comparative figures were: Austria 7, Denmark 9, Finland 7.9, France 8.5, Britain 7.6, Sweden 12.7, Norway 8.1, Holland 10.2, West Germany 10.0 houses built per thousand citizens. The Republic of Ireland: 4.2; and this despite one of the highest densities of persons per room (.9) and easily the lowest population increase. The seriousness with which the government of the day took the situation was indicated by the percentage of the Gross National Product spent on housing – 4.1, the third lowest in the Continent. In 1966 the number of houses built went down. In 1969, there were 20,000 people on the housing list in Dublin alone, even though it was far from easy to get on to it: one had to establish five years' residence in the city and have two or three children. There were a thousand vagrants sleeping rough in Dublin, and more than a thousand Dublin vagrants sleeping rough in London. Itinerant children died of exposure in rag tents in winter along the roadside. This is the decade on which Southern Irish politicians look back nostalgically, through the smoke and sulphur of the more recent troubles, as a period of peaceful progress, the full flowering of the Lemass miracle. Some miracle.

The extent of foreign economic control of Southern Ireland is indicated by the fact that of more than five hundred industrial projects started since the change in Fianna Fail's economic strategy fewer than one hundred and fifty were Irish-controlled. Of the rest, almost half were British. Government propaganda in such organs as the *Financial Times* continued to assure foreign capitalists that Ireland was a nation 'wedded to the free enterprise system. Taxation, legislation and social climate are all so shaped as to offer the private entrepreneur unimpeded scope for development ... Companies in Ireland may be wholly owned by non-nationals ... There is a degree of freedom from Government interference that is not matched in most other Western democracies' (quoted in the *Sunday Independent*, 11 March 1973). It can be doubted whether the 'degree of freedom from Government interference' is matched anywhere. Foreign companies have complete freedom to take profits out of the country. There is no check on how much profit they make and repatriate since they are not required to publish accounts – *any* accounts. However the US Department of Commerce estimates that in 1969 American companies in Ireland 'earned more than the total net profits of the biggest fifty Irish companies'. And the American stake was little more than half the British (*Sunday Independent*, 11 March 1973). Overall, foreign enterprise in Southern Ireland had been highly profitable. Estimates of profit-rate on foreign capital in 1970 are around 20 per cent. (See J. Palmer, 'The Gombeen Republic' in *International Socialism*, 51). The average profit-rate in Britain in 1970 was 13.4 per cent.

Meanwhile trade with Britain prospered as the Wilson-Lemass agreement of 1965 was implemented. More than half of all 26-Counties imports came from Britain. More than two thirds of exports went to Britain. In 1970 Southern Ireland became Britain's third biggest trading partner.

Economically, Southern Ireland by the end of the 1960s was a province of the United Kingdom with significant investment from other metropolitan countries. It had no independent existence.

Meanwhile in the North things were changing in a not dissimilar way. In the immediate post-war period agriculture, textiles and heavy industry including shipbuilding remained the staple industries. There had been little diversification. In 1951, 40 per cent of Northern employment was in such declining sectors. They continued to decline, and, as had happened in the South, there was a net drop in total employment within the state during the fifties, from 546,000 to 539,000. The Belfast like the Dublin government went in search of new industry. Potential investors were offered much the same inducements – capital grants, tax concessions, a large pool of unemployed and low wage structure. 'Advance factories' were built by the government in anticipation of overseas firms taking up tenancies. By 1966 217 new industries had been established, 117 of these in advance factories. By 1961, the proportion of people employed in the declining sectors of the economy had fallen to 30 per cent. It continued to fall, reaching 18 per cent in 1971. The most dramatic example of the changing shape of Northern economy during the sixties was the textile trade. Linen and cotton on which Northern industry was historically based declined rapidly (65,000 workers in 1951, 42,000 in 1961, 23,000 in 1971; Fitzgerald, p. 69). Simultaneously, the introduction of new synthetic textile plants helped to take up the slack. Between 1961 and 1967 the proportion of Northern Irish textile output represented by synthetics increased from 14 to 47 per cent and increased in value sevenfold. Between 1951 and 1971 the numbers employed in shipbuilding decreased from 23,000 to around 10,000, a loss of jobs offset exactly by the expansion of employment in construction from 40,000 to 53,000. Agricultural employment dropped from 98,000 to about 43,000 while the workforce in the service industries went up from 214,000 to 280,000 (Fitzgerald, p. 69). Over three quarters of the outside capital involved was British. 80 per cent of the new production was for the British market. Locally owned distributors and retailers were hit by the operations of British Home Stores (from 1965), Boots (from 1966), Marks and Spencer (from 1967), and the expanded activities of the Mace and Spar chains (since 1968).

By the middle of the 1960s the expanding sections of Northern industry were no longer in the hands of local businessmen. The tough-minded, self-made Northern Protestant businessman who had been 'the backbone of Ulster' and who controlled the Unionist Party and the Orange Order no longer wielded decisive economic influence. Both Northern and Southern native capitalism, which had developed in different periods and under very different conditions, were together drawn inexorably into the mesh of a changing British industrial complex. The contradictions between them which had underlain partition were fading away. The interests of each now lay in closer integration with Britain, as Britain herself moved into the EEC. In January 1965 Sean Lemass travelled to Belfast and took tea with the new Unionist leader, Terence O'Neill, an event which was interpreted by all but cynics as resulting from sudden, simultaneous upsurges of Christian charity in both their hearts. 'Economics and reason will end the border,' boomed the *Irish Press* (4 March 1968). And indeed, if economics and reason had been the sole political determinants the border would have begun to fade away. The real reason for its existence was disappearing. There were bourgeois visionaries – some such exist – in the early sixties who dreamed of the Six and the 26 Counties peacefully coming together, eventually to form some sort of Federal Ireland, under the benign gaze, not to mention the economic stranglehold, of Great Britain. It was not to work out like that. There is more to Irish politics than economics and reason.

9

The Unionist Party had retained the support of the majority of Protestants by constantly drawing attention to the alleged threat posed by the Rome-ruled Republic to the South. As has been shown, the social forces in the South responsible for the degree of Rome-rule which there was were precisely those which had least intention of subverting Ulster. There was nothing subversive about them.

No matter: the propaganda worked. The ideology was

transmitted to the masses via the remarkable political machine which the Unionist leaders had built, which carried the message and put it into effect in almost every town and townland in the state and which reached into the cabinet room to influence the selection of prime ministers as easily as it reached into the offices of an obscure rural district council in Fermanagh or Tyrone to influence allocation of houses. It was a machine which had been running fairly smoothly for more than half a century, grinding and crushing all opposition, siphoning into itself the spoils of the discrimination and automatically disgorging them to those who had to be bought. It was to prove damnably difficult to modernize it.

The changed pattern of British investment in Ireland and the changed relationship between the North and the South demanded reforms in Northern Ireland. If, as economics demanded, there was to be a *rapprochement* between Protestant business in the North and Catholic business in the South something would have to be done about the way Northern Catholics were being treated by their Protestant rulers.

Very little of note had happened in the Northern Catholic community in the decade after the Second World War. One year followed another and differed little from it. In Derry the male unemployment rate hovered around twenty per cent. Over a fifth of the population of the South Ward lived in houses where there were two or more persons per room (1951 census). The Nationalist Party maintained its grip, while the Republican movement began to wither away. Some may have taken vicarious pleasure from the *Journal*'s eager recording of further British reverses in international affairs ('British bluff called on Argentine meat' – 27 April 1951) or raged against the successful (allegedly British) plot to stop the Catholic General Douglas MacArthur dropping atom bombs on the Chinese Communists ('MacArthur takes hero's leave of Japan. Emperor Hirohito's precedent-breaking gesture' — 16 April 1951). There were minor riots after Nationalist parades in 1951 and 1952, but the local event which raised the Bogside's spirits highest was, necessarily, symbolic. Late on Easter Saturday, 24 April 1951, a local Republican, Manus Canning, climbed to the top of Walker's Pillar, which was set on the city walls and towers over the Bogside, and fixed an Irish Tricolour to the flagpost. The *Journal* report conveys the effect perfectly:

NATIONAL FLAG FLIES FROM WALKER'S PILLAR

... Small groups of people assembled in adjacent streets approaching midnight and stared in amazement at the unique spectacle ... Our reporter says that by the time the sky had cleared and in the light of the full moon the Tricolour could be quite clearly seen. It had been perfectly raised to the top of the tall vertical flag-pole and fanned by a slight breeze from the south-west it floated fully spread out and presented an impressive sight. It was right over the head of the Orangemen's hero, Rev. George Walker.

(In August 1973 the Provisional I R A blew the pillar up.)

Within a few years the external factors compelling a change in official attitudes North and South were operating to encourage Catholics in Derry and elsewhere to seek cause for more immediate and substantial satisfaction.

The industries which came in to replace declining, locally owned firms presented a new attitude. They had no intimate ties with any section of the local community. They were not dependent on the goodwill of Orangeism. The owners of Dupont (UK) for example, unlike the owners of many an old-established linen mill, had little interest in what religion, if any, a worker professed, as long as he laboured efficiently to create surplus value. Although unemployment remained high and Catholics continued to suffer disproportionately from it, within the new industries a section of the Catholic working class had access to skilled jobs and even lower managerial positions hitherto denied them, which tended to emphasize continued discrimination in the public sector. Equally important was the effect of the Butler Education Act and the Welfare State.

The Butler Act, passed in Britain in 1944, came into effect in Northern Ireland in 1947. It gave Catholic working-class children access to grammar-school and university education and thus, for some of those who wished it, access to the middle class. As the effect of the Act began to work its way through the age groups, the number of pupils at Catholic grammar schools and of Catholics at Queen's University, Belfast, steadily increased. St Columb's in Derry had 725 students on the roll in 1959, 1,125 by 1967. For them the contrast between aspiration and local reality was stark. In the early sixties a person like myself could easily get a place at university but would have been ineligible for a job as a lavatory-cleaner at Derry Guildhall, and that rankled.

The development of the Welfare State under the British Labour government in the immediate post-war period reinforced the effect. Compulsory national insurance, increased family allowances and the Health Service all helped to shield Catholics from the worst effects of unemployment and poverty. Pressure to emigrate was reduced. It was economically possible to stay at home and strive for better things. Census figures showed that the Catholic population had risen by 0·9 per cent between 1926 and 1951, but by 0·5 per cent between 1951 and 1961, a 66 per cent increase in the rate of growth. And since such benefits were not available south of the border the tendency to regard the achievement of a united Ireland as the only possible way to make things better began to weaken.

The overall effect on the Northern Catholics of post-war change was a lessening urgency about the border coupled with growing impatience about discrimination. At the end of 1956 the IRA launched a guerrilla campaign against the border. With the nonchalant disregard for reality which was, by now, typical of the movement, they proclaimed:

NEW DAY DAWNING
 Spearheaded by Ireland's freedom-
fighters our people in the six
counties have carried the fight
to the enemy.
(*United Irishman*, January 1957)

'Our people' were doing no such thing. The campaign evoked no deep response. It petered out by 1962, 'They mean well,' it was said in the Bogside, 'but aren't they living in the past?'

In 1963 the leaders of the Orange Order and of the Ancient Order of Hibernians held a widely-publicized series of secret talks about 'community relations'. The *Journal*'s editorial attitude to Unionist institutions softened : 'Nationalists readily recognize the extreme efficiency of the RUC in carrying out the normal duties of a police-force.' The Nationalist Senator Patrick O'Hare described the RUC as 'a fine body of men who are doing a good job' (*Journal*, 18 January 1963).

Shortly after the Lemass–O'Neill meeting in 1965 the Nationalist Parliamentary Party at Stormont agreed to accept the role of Official Opposition. Our Derry MP, Eddie McAteer, became Leader of the Opposition. They even appointed a Shadow Cabinet. (There were only eight government ministries, but nine Nationalist MPs. The matter was resolved by the expedient of appointing Eddie Richardson, a former athlete from South Armagh, Shadow Minister of Sport, even though there was no real Minister of Sport to be shadowed.)

Dogmatic economic rationalists might have issued very cheerful prognoses. Many people did. Every Belfast and Dublin newspaper welcomed the new spirit in Northern politics. From Westminster Mr Harold Wilson tossed in a congratulatory bouquet. No one in the parliaments in Belfast, Dublin and London is on record as believing that anything but good could come from the warm relationship

213

now being established between the warring tribes; or, to be more accurate, between the leaders of the warring tribes. Only on the far, Paisleyite right and the far Trotskyist left did there emerge shrill voices insisting that it couldn't and wouldn't work.

On the face of it there were grounds for optimism. In demanding an end to discrimination the Catholic leaders were not asking for anything which the more far-sighted section of the Unionist leadership was not willing to concede. The problem was: how to go about making the concessions without destroying the political machine which had served them so well.

From 1943 to 1963 the leader of the Unionist Party was Lord Brookeborough, formerly Sir Basil Brooke, a political antique. He had been the youngest member of the cabinet, a mere 59, when he became prime minister and was the type of man – not at all uncommon in Irish politics – who, if anyone had called him progressive, would have issued a writ for libel. He wasn't a very active prime minister because he judged that he did not have to be. O'Neill records that he would often spend no more than an hour a week dealing with affairs of state, and that for longish periods he would not emerge at all from the fastness of Fermanagh where he and his son John managed a large estate and rode to hounds at the weekends. (He was a sprightly man in some respects.) It is really a misnomer to talk of Unionist 'leadership' in the forties and fifties. There was no need for leadership because there was no debate about where the party should go. For almost two decades the machine was on automatic pilot. There were a few bumps on the road, but nothing serious. Most of the Independent Unionists had been absorbed into the party. Tommy Henderson, the maverick populist who ran, rather than represented, the Shankill was the only substantial figure to stay outside the machine and he was not opposed by the official Unionists after Brookeborough took over as leader.

Brookeborough did not do very well in the first post-war

Stormont election. In 1945 the determination of British workers not to return to pre-war conditions – which carried the Attlee government into power in a British election – was reflected in Northern Ireland and particularly in industrial Belfast. Labour took Dock and Oldpark from the Unionists. Brookeborough could muster only 33 seats, the lowest total since 1929. Despite that, conditions were generally much more stable than they had been in the twenties and thirties. There was little of the passion and almost none of the physical violence which had accompanied, or followed, earlier threats to the party's hegemony, not least because Unionist Party managers, after more than two decades of practice, were immeasurably more confident of their organization's ability to reimpose itself in the Protestant community almost at will. That their confidence was not misplaced was demonstrated in 1949, when Unionist candidates succeeded in every constituency in which they challenged Labour or Independent Unionist opponents. They were helped, again, by the events in the South. The coalition government elected there in 1948 finally took the 26 Counties out of the British Commonwealth and, following a Fianna Fail initiative, set up an all-party committee to disseminate anti-Unionist propaganda throughout the world. The world had its own problems and paid very little attention. Neither of the moves posed any threat to Northern Ireland, but the fact that they had been made at all was grist to the Unionist propaganda mill and sufficient to rekindle the Protestants' sense of embattlement.

It was not until 1958 that Unionist complacency was really shaken. The continuing high unemployment (between 1946 and 1959 male unemployment averaged 8·5 per cent) and the decline, now clearly apparent, of the staple industries generated unease and fear for the future not only among workers but also in business circles. This was reflected in the loss of four Unionist seats in Belfast to the Northern Ireland Labour Party. The soul-searching which followed concerned not only the loss of the seats (the Party still held thirty-seven) but the increasingly urgent need for a reappraisal of the Party's whole outlook – on industry, on community relations, on relations with the South – in the light of the vaguely apprehended and ongoing alterations in the overall situation. There was another election in 1962. The IRA campaign had just been defeated, and it was difficult for Lord Brookeborough and his colleagues to find a plausible threat to the state with which to beat the faithful into line. The NILP held its four seats in Belfast and the Unionists lost another three to an assortment of challengers. The next year Brookeborough was ditched and Terence O'Neill took over.

O'Neill wanted to lead the Unionist Party in a new direction. However, if he was going to lead it anywhere he had to remain leader. And if he was going to do that he had to show respect for the old symbols and the old traditions. He had to march on the Twelfth and, indeed, as an ex-Guards Officer he was able to strut, besashed, with the best of them. Apart from his visits to convents and Catholic schools he would hint occasionally that discrimination might be a bad thing and that gerrymandering might not be democratic. But he never actually did anything about them. If he had tried, the machine would either have turned on him and destroyed him or it would have fallen apart. Either eventuality would have meant the end of O'Neill. The machine existed to discriminate and arrange gerrymanders. It had been created in order to guarantee the continued ascendancy of Protestant business and landed interests, and that was the only way in which the guarantee could have been delivered. If it could not deliver minor privilege to the Protestant masses it could not deliver the Protestant masses on polling day. The Orange machine, in a real sense, was Northern Ireland. To attack it or to attempt to take away its power was to weaken the state itself. The very boundaries of the state had, after all, been determined by calculating what area the machine could effectively control. If the machine had not been clamped on to Catholic areas the state might never have existed. When in 1964 Paisley began to say loudly and Unionist back-benchers to mutter that O'Neill was 'betraying Ulster' they were right. He was betraying what the overwhelming majority of Protestants had been led to understand by 'Ulster'.

Moreover, the machine itself, over the years, had developed interests of its own. It had been created to serve a single class, but the people who operated it at local level had a vested interest in it for its own sake. They derived social prestige, local power and, in many cases, a degree of economic prosperity from being involved with it. They were not ready to give that up for vague reasons to do with trade figures.

In the sixties the Unionist Party found it difficult to adapt itself to a new situation because the institutions which it had created in different circumstances had developed an autonomy and set of interests of their own and did not automatically, or necessarily at all, adapt to the challenging overall needs of the business community.

10

The establishment in the South was better placed. There was no equivalent of the Orange Order, resistant to change and controlling central and local governmental apparatus. There was an official ideology, of course, Catholic Nationalism, which, like the Orange ideology, had become entrenched in a different period and which was now losing its relevance. But the Catholic Church was not in any practical way involved in day-to-day politics to the extent that the Order was. Its power was based on control of education – not on direct involvement in detailed decision-making. It was not connected to any one political party, there being no need. All major parties paid it homage. The Nationalist component of the official ideology had long been a matter

217

of platform rhetoric rather than practical politics. All parties were against partition and for a United Ireland. Passionately. But there was not – and still has not been – any government in the South of Ireland which has reacted to *actual* attacks on Northern Ireland other than by harassing, imprisoning and hanging those responsible.

The difference between the anti-Catholicism inherent in the official ideology of the North and the anti-partitionism inherent in the official ideology of the South was that, in the North, when a Unionist politician said on a platform that Catholic influence in a particular area would have to be ended, it was confidently expected that arrangements would speedily be made for this to be done; in the South, on the other hand, when a representative of any of the major parties said on a platform that partition would have to be ended, it was generally understood that anyone attempting to make arrangements to achieve this would be locked up. For that reason the renunciation of ideology was easier in the South. Which is not to say that there was danger of anyone being hurt in the rush to renounce. Far from it, as the Minister of Health in the 1948–51 coalition government was to discover.

In 1951 the Mother and Child Bill was introduced in Dail Eireann by Dr Noel Browne. The controversy surrounding it has since been dismissed as unimportant by the new mythologists of Irish history. But it was, and remains, very important indeed. The direct interventions of the Catholic hierarchy into Southern Irish politics in the twenties and thirties were almost invariably on matters of 'faith and morals'. That the hierarchy could have its attitudes on faith and morals framed as statutes was offensive to Protestants – and to others besides. But now it went one further. Dr Browne's Bill provided that 'each Health Authority shall make arrangements for the safeguarding of the health of women in respect of motherhood and for their education in that respect' and should give 'attendance to the health of children up to sixteen years'. On 4 April 1951 the Irish hierarchy met and concluded that the idea that the state should look after its children was 'opposed to Catholic social teaching' (letter from Archbishop McQuaid to Taoiseach John Costello, dated 5 April 1951). At the entry of the hierarchy into the debate the right hands of the leaders of all the coalition parties twitched instinctively towards their forelocks. The leader of Dr Browne's party, Sean McBride (the hero of Bodenstown, '34), wrote to him instructing him to resign from the government. Dr Browne resigned from both the government and the Party. The Bill fell.

In the subsequent Dail debate government ministers took turns to express their willingness to do what they were told. Mr Costello, the Taoiseach (Fine Gael): 'I, as a Catholic, obey my church authorities and will continue to do so' (Dail Debates, CXV, 784). The Minister for Social Welfare, Mr Norton (Labour): 'There will be no flouting of the authority of the Bishops in the matter of Catholic social or Catholic moral teaching' (ibid., 951-2). The Minister for External Affairs, Mr McBride (Clann na Poblachta): 'Those of us in this house who are Catholics, all of us in the government who are Catholics, are, as such of course, bound to give obedience to the rulings of our church and of our hierarchy' (ibid., 789). The Minister for Finance, Mr McGilligan (Fine Gael), told a party meeting that he personally was not the type of man to break the moral law and went on to make the interesting point that one had, on occasion, to rely on the hierarchy to interpret the moral law since one could not always be absolutely sure what the moral law was (Irish Times, 1 May 1951). Archbishop McQuaid wrote to the Taoiseach conveying the bishops' 'deep appreciation of the generous loyalty shown by you and your colleagues'.

The Unionist view, understandably, was different. The Ulster Unionist Council in a pamphlet, 'Southern Ireland – Church or State', commented that 'in any matter where the Roman Catholic Church decides to intervene the Eire Government must accept the Church's policy and decision irrespective of all other consideration' (quoted in Whyte, p. 232).

The coalition government fell (as a result of a dispute over milk prices) a few weeks after Dr Browne's resignation, and a General Election brought Mr de Valera and Fianna Fail back to power. Fianna Fail once again showed that it was no less punctilious in its observance of hierarchic diktat than was its predecessor.

In 1952 a Bill to legalize adoption was passed. To ensure that nothing in the Bill was contrary to Catholic teaching the archbishop of Dublin was allowed to go over every clause while it was being drafted (Whyte, p. 276). In July 1952 a White Paper on Health was issued, foreshadowing legislation which was to include some, by no means all, the provisions of Dr Browne's 1951 Bill. Still the hierarchy was not satisfied. A three-bishop committee was set up to deal with the matter. In late 1952 government ministers, including Mr de Valera and his Minister of Health, Dr Ryan, appeared before this committee on a number of occasions to discuss what changes the bishops thought necessary. The Bill, published in February 1953, contained one significant alteration from that outlined in the White Paper – the introduction of a means test. The bishops met on 13 April and decided that even this was not enough. On 17 April they sent a letter to all the national papers except the *Irish Times* (the *Irish Times* is owned by Protestants) setting out their objections. Before the letter appeared in the press Mr de Valera and Dr Ryan rushed to Drogheda in Co. Louth, where Cardinal D'Alton was presiding over a confirmation ceremony, and asked him to delay publication pending further consultation. On 21 April, at the residence of the President in Phoenix Park, Dublin, Mr de Valera and Dr Ryan met the hierarchy's health committee. As a result of the meeting seven amendments were made to the Bill, which finally became law in October 53.

In its final form the Bill was an eviscerated version of Dr Browne's proposals, attending to the health of children up to the age of, not 16 years, but 6 weeks. The importance of the issue, however, especially from the point of view of Protestant attitudes to the South, lies not in the extent of the changes made but in the manner of their being made. A minister had had to resign from a government because he refused to accept completely the bishops' instructions as to what type of law should be enacted. The drafting procedure of the next government – the only alternative government available – involved, apparently, appearances by government ministers before episcopal committees and comic-opera dashes to confirmation ceremonies. It was, if not 'Rome-rule' in the literal sense of the phrase, then rule by courtesy of and within the limits set by the representatives of Rome. And there was almost no one, seemingly, in Southern politics who thought there was anything wrong with this state of affairs. The episode was, and is, constantly referred to on Unionist platforms.

During the fifties, through another change of government (a further coalition held office from 1954 to 1957) and as the economic situation went from bad to disastrous, there was little or no direct challenge to the social power of the church. In 1955 the Bishop of Cork, Dr Lucey, said bluntly that the bishops were 'the final arbiters of right and wrong even in political matters' (*Irish Times*, 13 April 1955). There was only one (anonymous) objection from an Irish politician in the form of a letter to the press (Whyte, p. 313).

Then there was the case of the communist footballers. In 1955 the Southern Irish football team had arranged a match against their Yugoslav counterparts to be played at Daly-mount Park, Dublin, on Wednesday 19 October. On the fourteenth a representative of the Archbishop of Dublin phoned the Football Association, complained that the arch-bishop had not been consulted about the fixture, and asked whether it could not be cancelled, the objection being that the Yugoslav players were communists. The match went ahead and the Yugoslavs were welcomed by a front-bench member of Fianna Fail who happened to be President of the Football Association at that time. 21,000 people attended the game, their enjoyment marred only by the fact that the visitors won 4–1. It has been argued by Dr Whyte and others that the fact that a politician welcomed the Yugoslav team and that the public did not boycott the match indicates that even in 1955 attitudes were changing.

But much more significant was the reaction of the government and of state institutions to the archbishop's intervention. Radio Eireann decided not to broadcast a commentary on the game. The army band, which had been scheduled to entertain the spectators at half-time, was withdrawn by the Ministry of Defence. The President, who had accepted an invitation to attend the game, changed his mind. In other words one phone call from the archbishop's palace was sufficient to stop the state broadcasting service, the army and the elected President of the land from going to a football match. (The refusal of the Football Association of Ireland to cancel the game at the eleventh hour may well have resulted, not from a willingness to flout the archbishop's authority, but from genuine bewilderment at his request. Quite possibly it had not, until then, occurred to them that the arrangement of their fixture lists was a matter of faith and morals.)

In 1956 the hierarchy made it a mortal sin for Catholic youth to 'frequent' the traditionally Protestant university, Trinity College, a decree which pedants could and did interpret as threatening Dublin errand boys with eternal perdition.

It was not until Sean Lemass took over from Mr de Valera as Taoiseach and instituted the new economic policy that the Irish Parliament passed a law against the express wishes of the Catholic church authorities. This was the Intoxicating Liquor Bill, which legalized Sunday opening of pubs in rural areas. (They were already legally open in urban areas.) The Bill was not important in itself but, in Dr Whyte's words, 'in the history of Church-State relations it marks a significant landmark. For it provides the only example so far recorded of a recommendation from the hierarchy being simply rejected by an Irish Government.'

As the policy of economic nationalism was abandoned, the ideological superstructure associated with it began slowly to be adjusted. The next decade was to see more and more open demands for liberalization of the laws on censorship, contraception, divorce, and so on. At the same time, in coordination with the change in the attitude of the Nationalist Party in the North, the Republican rhetoric of the major Southern parties became much more muted. Many an ancient hatchet was buried beneath the flow of British investment.

Speaking for the Ancient Order of Hibernians on St Patrick's Day 1963, Mr P. S. Donegan, TD, said: 'The Stormont Government could be assured of the full cooperation of all true Hibernians towards the aim of peaceful co-existence' (Derry Journal, 2 March 1963).

There were many harbingers of change. Dr Garret Fitzgerald mused in a Jesuit magazine that 'One cannot resist the conclusion that in the 1930s and '40s the Irish Church took a wrong turning . . .' (Studies, winter 1964, p. 345). Declan Costello, son of the leader of the coalition which had ditched Dr Browne and his Bill and now Attorney-General in the new coalition, told a meeting in Dublin that: 'In the name of Catholic social principles movements towards social reform had been criticized and whilst condemning the reformer the conditions which he sought to reform are condoned' (quoted in Whyte, p. 34). In 1964 the Minister for Justice, Brian Lenihan, appointed a number of liberals (liberal by Southern Irish standards, that is) to the Appeals Board dealing with censorship of films. The following year 37 appeals were wholly or partly successful. (The 1964 figure was 6.) In 1966 a Bill was passed allowing the ban on outlawed books to lapse after twelve years unless specifically renewed. The banning rate – 600 books a year in the fifties – began to fall. The prohibition of contraceptives remained, but it became possible for newspapers to carry articles on family planning, even articles advocating it, without fear of legal reprisal. A plan outlined by the Ministry of Education in April 1967 to amalgamate Trinity College with the Catholic University College Dublin did not call forth denunciatory statements from the bishops.

Not all Bishops approved of such changes and there were frequent fundamentalist outbursts, notably from Dr Lucey of Cork and Dr Browne of Galway. (Dr Browne's place in a footnote in history is ensured by his delightful remark during the Second Vatican Council debate on freedom of conscience that there is a great difference between freedom for a conscience which is right and freedom for a conscience which is wrong.) But the majority of the hierarchy adapted themselves to the changed situation, the more easily because the basis of their real power was in no way being undermined. Catholic power in Southern Ireland derives from the church's iron grip on education. The expansion of manufacturing industry necessitated changes in the educational set-up. The technologists, managers and economists now needed could not be produced by a system which was designed to turn out a small number of civil servants and priests at the top of the scale, and boat loads of emigrants at the bottom. The state had to intervene with a series of measures to group tiny rural schools into larger units, expand and reform the curricula of post-primary schools and rationalize higher education (the proposed Trinity-UCD merger being one example). The fierce jealousy with which the church has traditionally defended its sole right to control education made it inevitable that at some points there would be conflict between it and the state, and indeed, there were a number of skirmishes between the church and the Department of Education. But at no time was there a set-piece political battle.

The majority of the hierarchy came quickly to understand that it was possible for the system to absorb the required reforms while they retained control, that the changes were necessary and that to oppose them blindly woud inevitably result in a confrontation which they might not win. Cardinal Conway, whose sensitive political talents have recently been accorded wide recognition, said of educational reform in 1966: 'The national aim of providing the best possible post-primary education is not merely welcome, but has the enthusiastic support of the church' (*Irish Times*, 27 January 1966).

Thus, with much talk of a 'new spirit' being abroad in the land, Fianna Fail and the church moved together serenely towards the seventies, with only occasional jockeying for position between them. They were never really challenged. The differences in economic strategy which had divided Fine Gael from Fianna Fail in past decades no longer existed. There was general agreement between them about what ought to be done, and the civil war was now dismissed as a 'purgative of blood' (*Irish Press*, 23 June 1968).

The church retained an important political role in the sixties which was not drastically different from that which it played in the thirties. Relatively rapid economic change coupled with widespread continued impoverishment gave rise to a potentially disturbed political situation characterized by a rapid increase in strike action and the first stirrings of mass radicalization. In such circumstances the establishment has need of a powerful institution disseminating propaganda hostile to class differentiation. It needed bishops to tell the faithful that 'no matter what type of society you have there will always be an upper class' (Bishop of Achony, *Irish Times*, 1 September 1970). It needed professors of ethics at Maynooth College to explain that 'strikes are a breakdown of humanity, a kind of disintegration, a descent into the sub-human' (Professor Father O'Donnell, 'Christus Rex', December 1967). It needed pastoral letters plugging peace on the factory floor. Ideally the more enlightened members of the Southern establishment in the sixties – for example Garret Fitzgerald, Declan Costello, Donagh O'Malley – would have preferred more quickly to discard antiquated aspects of Catholic social philosophy. But in the situation which obtained that would have added to the dangers already apparent. They still needed the church. It is probably for that reason, rather than intellectual inertia, that ideological change, while proceeding, lagged well behind economic innovation.

In the North the Unionists moved with more trepidation. But in one respect at least the establishment in each part of the country was singularly, and similarly, blessed – neither found any determined challengers from the left. Indeed the most remarkable thing about Irish politics in the sixties is not that at the end of the decade the existing structures began visibly to weaken, but that they had such a relatively trouble-free passage until then. By now the Republicans were, by general consent, irrelevant. It was from the labour movement that any challenge to the twin establishments would have to come.

In the North, the Northern Ireland Labour Party, having retained in 1962 the four seats won in the 1958 General Election from the Unionists, devoted itself to what its leaders used to call 'consolidating our position'. Basically, this meant advancing cautiously, taking due care not to alienate any pockets of potential support. Fairly exhaustive research reveals no single occasion when the Party mounted a concerted attack on the Unionists. The Party frequently congratulated itself on the fact that 'the abilities of our four MPs as parliamentary strategists are known' (Erskine Holmes in *Impact*, March 1965, p. 32). In 1963 the Party almost tore itself apart over the bizarre issue of whether children's play parks ought to be open on Sundays.

In the Stormont General Election campaign of November 1965 one of the parliamentary strategists demonstrated his ability and the extent of the Party's willingness to confront Orange ideology by marching through the constituency at the head of a band playing Orange songs. His intention was to show Protestant electors that he was not 'soft' on the border. The Protestant electors reacted by throwing him out, reasoning, perhaps, that if they had to choose between two Unionists they might as well opt for the real one. The Party also lost the Victoria seat to the former disc-jockey and future cabinet minister Roy Bradford, reducing its parliamentary strength to two. Around the same time the Party supported, and Party members served on, a government-sponsored 'Economic Council'. (Members of the Communist Party also participated.)

The fact was that in the sixties the Labour leadership had no alternative to offer to the Unionist strategy for halting the decline in the economy. They supported it. On the political level Labour thus had very little to attack the Unionists about.

Labour in the South was a little more active. In November 1963 a group around Noel Browne, the National Progressive Democrats, dissolved into the Party. Increased urbanization and a growing militancy on the part of workers, resulting in part from the reduction in pressure to emigrate, gave the Party a firmer urban base. (In the mid-sixties Southern Ireland had the highest strike record in the world.) The second largest union in the state, the Workers' Union of Ireland, affiliated in 1964, and the largest union, the Irish Transport and General, followed in 1967. Membership increased rapidly, 'paper' branches came to life, and commentators wrote of 'a growing sense of purpose and urgency' (Rory Quinn in *Impact*, 1966, p. 21). In the 1965 General Election the Party increased its number of seats from 13 to 22, its best performance since 1927. Trade-union militants, disillusioned Republicans and 'left-wing' academics joined in impressive numbers. The Party voted to reinstate in its constitution a commitment to strive for a 'workers' Republic' and rejected the idea of ever again forming a coalition government with Fine Gael. The Party's self-confidence was expressed by Dr Conor Cruise O'Brien, now Minister for Posts and Telegraphs in the coalition government with Fine Gael, at the 1968 Conference: 'No coalition with Fine Gael! No coalition with Fianna Fail! No

227

support for a Fianna Fail or Fine Gael minority government!'

Yet in a sense none of these developments was of Labour's own making. It was thrust forward, almost despite itself, by developments over which it had no control. It, after all, had had little to do with the growth of the urban working class or of its militancy. That it was not going to strike out decisively to challenge the political set-up was demonstrated by its failure to enter a candidate against Mr de Valera and Mr O'Higgins of Fine Gael in the Presidential Election of June 1966. Nor, at any cost, did it intend to fight against the ideological hegemony of the Catholic church. Indeed it still contained within it parliamentarians such as Mr Coughlan of Limerick and Mr Murphy of Co. Kerry who believed that, if anything, the church was not a powerful enough force in the land. After the retirement of Mr Norton in March 1960 the Party was led by Mr Brendan Corish, whose own attitude to the Church in politics had been expressed some years previously: 'I am an Irishman second, I am a Catholic first . . . If the hierarchy gives me any direction with regard to Catholic social teaching or Catholic moral teaching, I accept without qualifications and in all respects the teaching of the hierarchy' (Dail Debates, 1953, Vol. 138).

Mr Corish's expressions of subservience to the church, like everybody else's, became progressively less crude during the sixties. But there was never any doubt that he was a sound man, and Labour a sound Party.

II

Freedom from any threat of disruption from the left smoothed the way for the ascendant classes, North and South, finally to settle their differences.

The shifting set of relationships between them, and between the parties and interest groups associated with them, ought in the end to have produced a situation of which the Northern Catholics would be immediate beneficiaries. Discrimination ought to have ended. 'Normal' democracy ought to have been instituted. And these benefits ought to have accrued most substantially to Catholics in the western part of Northern Ireland. Not only was it economically the worst-off part of the state, but the Catholics' majority position therein had required a more obtrusive presence and a more ingenious operation of the Orange machine than was needed elsewhere. If Protestant hegemony was to end and the Northern Catholics' situation thus to improve, it was in places like Derry that the improvement would most sharply be experienced, and it was there, as a result, that it was most eagerly anticipated.

In 1951 Birmingham Sound Reproducers, the family firm of Dr Robert McDonald, received 175,000 square feet of free factory to set up a branch in Derry. BSR was the sixty-eighth business to be attracted to Northern Ireland by the post-war Development Acts, but the first to come to Derry, despite the fact that we had the biggest unemployment problem in the land. Derry's second factory arrived in 1953, the third in 1960.

The BSR factory was in the Bogside, and most of the men who worked there – over a thousand at the height of the operation – were men from our area. In 1957 an industrial estate was opened at Maydown, four miles outside the city. In 1960 Du Pont (UK) Ltd began production of neoprene on the estate. Du Pont was followed by the British Oxygen Company and Molins Machines Ltd. By 1965 £20m. had been invested in Maydown and an industrial training centre established on the site. The new industries did not end unemployment; the rate never dipped below 10 per cent. But those who did get work in the new plants did not experience the pinpricking humiliations and the barriers to promotion which would have attended work in the 'traditional' industries.

By March 1966 there were seven new factories in the Derry district. But smaller Protestant towns to the east, all of whose unemployment figures were derisory by Derry standards, had done better. Coleraine had nine, Bangor ten and Lurgan thirteen post-war projects. It was the job of Stormont ministers and their civil servants to process applications from manufacturers for factory facilities and to help direct investment to particular areas. Derry being disadvantaged anyway by its geographic position, Stormont would have had to intervene decisively to offset the inequality. Obviously that was not happening. The unemployment figures were a little better, certainly, and some people in the Bogside were better-off than they could have hoped to be in the past; but it was still not fair.

In the early sixties the Stormont government had commissioned a series of reports on future development to ensure that the modification of the economy proceeded in orderly fashion. When the reports began to appear after 1964 it was clear that, taken together, their effect would not be to redress the imbalance between the western and eastern parts of the state but actually to increase it. Almost certainly it was no part of the authors' conscious intention to discriminate against Catholic areas; what they had done was to accept, codify and make recommendations for the efficient organization of tendencies already inherent in the economy. Ministers' and civil servants' ready acceptance of the reports may have been based as much on aversion to direct state intervention against the free flow of capital as on determination to perpetuate Catholic privation. But no matter. What gradually came through to the Bogside was that Catholic Derry was being done down again.

In 1964 the Benson Report on the railways recommended the closure of the city's two rail links with Belfast by September 1966. Once there had been four rail termini in the city. Now there was to be none. Protest from Derry and from other towns along the line forced the government to retain the Midland line through Coleraine and Ballymena – temporarily at least. But the Great Northern, through Strabane and Omagh, closed down.

Around the same time the Matthew Plan selected the Lurgan–Portadown area in Co. Armagh as the major centre for new urban development. A new city of 100,000 people – 'Craigavon' – was to be built, thus creating another powerful economic magnet pulling investment away from the west and towards the Lagan Valley.

The Lockwood Committee on Higher Education in Northern Ireland recommended the building of a second university – in Coleraine. Not only was Derry the second largest city in Northern Ireland, it already had, in Magee University College, the nucleus of a new university. There were protest meetings and a car-cavalcade to Stormont, but the plan went ahead. Inch by inch Derry was being pushed beyond the pale, while politicians grew passionate about the new era which was at hand.

Suspicion that the Orange machine was controlling events was reinforced – proven absolutely as far as the Bogside was concerned – when it was revealed later that a seven-man deputation from the local Unionist hierarchy had travelled to Belfast to plead that the new university be established anywhere but Derry.

At the beginning of 1967 the unemployment problem suddenly became worse. Under the terms of the Development Acts, when BSR set up shop in 1951 it had been given seven years to establish itself, during which it was substantially free from tax and rate commitments. At the end of seven years Dr McDonald closed the factory. He then re-opened it as 'Monarch Electric Ltd'. Monarch Electric began *its* period of financial support. Just before Christmas 1966 half the workers were paid off because of 'trading difficulties'. It was generally believed that the difficulties were temporary. One morning in January 1967 the remaining workers were told not to come back in the afternoon.

231

Monarch Electric was closed. There were some who wanted to smash the machinery up, but calmer councils and full-time officialdom prevailed.

In March 1966 the unemployment figure in Derry had been 10·1 per cent, the lowest since the war. Comparative figures for March 1967 were:

Great Britain	2·6%
North of England	3·9%
Scotland	4·1%
Wales	4·2%
Northern Ireland	8·1%
Derry City	20·1%

Normality once again.

And the housing situation was getting no better. The Corporation had run out of land in the Catholic South Ward. The Unionists could not afford to house Catholics in any other ward. So they stopped building houses. In 1967 Derry Corporation built no houses at all. In the same year it refused to extend the city boundary to take in new building land lest this disrupt the delicately-drawn ward boundaries. And it refused a local housing association permission to build an estate in the North Ward in case this upset the sectarian arithmetic. Government planning consultants estimated that in 1967 there were five thousand houses in Derry 'in one way or another sub-standard' – that is, two fifths of the dwellings of the city.

To change this we would have had to change the Corporation. But that was impossible. The 1966 revision of electoral rolls showed that there were 20,102 Catholic voters and 10,274 Protestant voters in the city. At the May 1967 Municipal Election there were eight Nationalists and twelve Unionists returned.

There was still not a single Catholic working in Derry Guildhall. The new Corporation proceeded to elect its committees and sub-committees, on each of which there was, again, a Unionist majority. Four Unionists and two Nationalists were elected to the Derry Port and Sanitary Board. The Derry Port and Sanitary Board had not met for fifteen years. If the 'new spirit' which was alleged to be abroad meant anything it would have been safe enough, surely, to toss that one to the Nationalists. But: 'We are the front-line Unionists' proclaimed Councillor Albert Anderson.

Thus, stalemate. Post-war factors had not enabled the Bogside to break down local Orange power. What they had done was to make the Bogside more articulate and self-confident, more sensitive to the existence of discrimination and less willing to accept it any longer. Captain O'Neill could mince around and drawl about democracy and shake nuns' hands to his heart's content; and so what?

St Columb's made contact with its local Protestant equivalent, Foyle College, by inviting the President of the Foyle College Old Boys' association to the annual dinner of the St Columb's Past Pupils' Union. The Mayor of Belfast visited the Mayor of Galway and was accorded 'a warm reception'. Ulsterbus tours were extended into the Republic. Captain O'Neill and Mr Faulkner were invited to the Swilly (Co. Donegal) Sea Angling Club's annual festival. Etc.

Those were the 'changes'. As far as we could see, those were all. By the time Captain O'Neill's never-ending non-sectarian gestures had led many Protestants to regard him as a potential traitor he was seen in the Bogside as a proven trickster. At the beginning of 1968 Mr McAteer issued a New Year message to his constituents. 'The sky', he began, 'is still heavily shadowed by perplexities...' And in McClenaghan's house at the bottom of Wellington Street Dermie was saying that we would have to get the people out on the bloody street.

Part 5

Obviously, the idea put about in August 1969 that the army had come because British cabinet ministers were upset by the prospect of innocent people being slaughtered in considerable numbers is nonsense. The British army came because British interests in Ireland were threatened. When the slaughter of innocents had not threatened British interests – in the twenties and thirties for example – there had been no intervention.

British interests were threatened by the apparent inability of the existing political structures – shaken by the adjustments and attempted adjustments of the previous decade – to assimilate and articulate the emotions now being aroused. This was true in the South as well as in the North. There were tens of thousands of people on the streets of Dublin and other Southern cities demanding that Mr Lynch's government move to protect the Northern Catholics from what looked like an impending pogrom. Demands were voiced that British property be taken over and held in ransom for the safety of Northern Catholics. Workers at many factories struck. It subsequently emerged that at least two members of Mr Lynch's cabinet had been in favour of sending the army across the border. Some officers of the army were momentarily more than enthusiastic about doing just that. Had a stop not been put to what was happening in Belfast and Derry it might well have proved impossible for Mr Lynch to 'hold the line' against the gut-Republicanism suddenly surging again, not least in his own party.

The situation in the North was such that it threatened the stability of *both* Irish states. The Army arrived to restore stability and to supervise and insist on reforms – now unmistakably overdue – which would take cognizance of the new pattern of economic relationships. The 'Downing Street Declaration', issued on 19 August 1969 over the names of Wilson and Chichester-Clark but penned by Wilson alone, spelled it out. It 'reaffirmed that in all legislation and executive decisions of Government every citizen of Northern Ireland is entitled to the same equality of treatment and freedom from discrimination as obtains in the rest of the United Kingdom, irrespective of political view or religion'.

What this had to mean – if it was to mean anything – was that the power of the Orange machine was to be broken. Initially there were indications that the Labour government was indeed intent on doing that. The disarming of the RUC and the disbandment of the B Specials were interpreted by both Catholics and Protestants as earnest of a determination to render the machine incapable of reimposing itself. However Mr Wilson's government, never characterized by the whole-heartedness of its commitments, did little to follow through this initiative. Sir Arthur Young was brought from London to replace the Inspector-General of the RUC, Anthony Peacocke. But none of the senior police officers responsible for the thuggery of the previous twelve months was dismissed. Some were promoted. Oliver Wright, formerly British Ambassador in Copenhagen, was installed in an office in Stormont Castle to keep an eye on Chichester-Clark and his government. But there were no enforced changes in governmental personnel, no shake-up of the civil service, no interference with the local government administration. In other words Wilson's government did not pursue with any semblance of determination even the very limited, non-revolutionary objective it had set itself and which the majority of Catholics at that stage might have been prepared to accept.

It began gradually to dawn on the Catholics that when Callaghan talked about 'new structures' what he meant was that two Englishmen would be given supervisory positions at the top of the old structures. That was all; and because it was all, the 'reform programme' was doomed.

It is comparatively easy to put reforms on to the statute book. All one needs is a parliamentary majority. To put the reforms into effect, however, requires much more. One needs a police force, a magistracy and an army of officials: an administrative apparatus capable of putting them into effect and willing to do so. The administrative apparatus of which Stormont was the lynch-pin was simply not available for that task.

For example: when, in July 1970, Chichester-Clarke's government, with the connivance of all Catholic MPs, simultaneously passed the Criminal Justice (Temporary Provisions) Act and the Incitement to Religious Hatred Act it probably seemed to British ministers exactly the type of legislative package which was required. The Criminal Justice Act, providing for mandatory prison sentences for rioters, was clearly aimed at the 'hooligan element' constantly disrupting the peace of the Catholic ghettoes. Equally clearly, the Incitement to Religious Hatred Act was intended to deal with the various demagogues who were stirring it up in the Protestant ghettoes. One law against the Catholic trouble-makers and one against the Protestant trouble-makers. 'Firm but fair government,' commentators kept calling it.

By the end of 1970 109 persons had been brought before the courts charged with offences under the Criminal Justice Act. 105 went to prison. Only one prosecution was brought under the Incitement to Religious Hatred Act, that of Mr John McKeague for the publication and distribution of a book of songs of which the following verse is a fair example:

> If guns were made for shooting
> Then skulls were made to crack
> You've never seen a better Taig
> Than with a bullet in his back.

Mr McKeague was found not guilty.

The law against the Catholic trouble-makers worked. The law against the Protestant trouble-makers did not.

The arrests of those jailed under the Criminal Justice Act were, of course, effected by the British army. The instinct of the Bogside rioters in 1970 that 'the Orangemen are still in power' was soundly based. The power-structure which the British army was defending was not, in any essential, different from that of which the RUC had traditionally been the repressive arm. The pusillanimity of the Wilson government had made it certain that its army would become part of the apparatus of Orangeism. Once that happened the emergence of the Provisional IRA was inevitable.

Much has been written about the emergence of the Provos, almost all of it silly moralizing. The Provisional IRA was not created by a section of the Fianna Fail Party, although some money from Fianna Fail sources did ensure that it was better financed at the outset than would otherwise have been the case. Nor was it the creation of a few blood-lusting Catholic Nationalists in the North. Nor, despite the paranoiac ramblings of churchmen and contributors to the *Daily Telegraph*, is it part of an international terrorist conspiracy to destroy civilization as we know it.

The machinery of government could not operate democratically. It was not designed for the job. So the fight for a democratic Northern Ireland was always likely to become a fight against the state itself. The 'national issue' was going to be posed. The only question left open was: by whom and in what form?

When, in January 1969, Johnnie McMenamin saw a crowd of men in his street in the middle of the night smashing up houses and beating up his neighbours and rushed to the telephone to dial 999 he was reacting as any working-class person in an 'ordinary' society would to such a spectacle. But what does one do when it is the police themselves who are doing the marauding? Who then does one call in?

237

A few months later that question would have been answered in the Bogside with: 'the British army'. And when the army begins to behave exactly as the police had done, what then?

One turns to oneself, there being no one else, and tries to put together an organization as capable as possible of repelling the assaults. In the short term the politics of the defence group is irrelevant. It is irrelevant whether it has any politics at all. The long term is different. On a day-to-day basis defence groups can prevent random arrests, assaults and worse in an area simply by refusing admission to forces so intentioned. But tiny enclaves cannot exist in isolation for ever.

In 1970 the poster most frequently to be seen in windows and on gable walls in the Bogside and the Falls depicted a clenched fist and the words: 'Never Again!' Never again were mobs, whether in uniform or not, going to be allowed to rampage through the streets shooting and petrol bombing. The logic of that demanded that an offensive military campaign be launched against the state. When it is the state itself which threatens to destroy you it is necessary to attack the state, not just to defend oneself against *its* attacks, to try to ensure that there will be no repetition.

The trajectory of events led inevitably to a military campaign against the existence of Northern Ireland. The responsibility for the launching of the campaign rests entirely with those who created the situation which made that inevitable; that is, with the British ruling class and its agents in Ireland. That said, one can analyse why the campaign took the form that it did, how the politics of the activists involved developed and what, in the light of that, ought now to be done.

In 1968 and 1969 the left and the right, the 'militants' and the 'moderates' in the civil rights movement, were united on one point: that partition was irrelevant. No meeting was complete without at least one speaker declaring that we wished to make it clear that we were not setting out to unite Ireland, rather to achieve change within Northern Ireland – the extent of the change desired varying according to the tendency to which the speaker adhered. This was in line with the general drift of Catholic politics for the previous decade.

The left was, if anything, even more determined than other anti-Unionist groups to 'keep partition out of it'; and for reasons which were not ignoble. The partition issue had for so long been the 'property' of what we regarded as contending Tory factions that the mere mention of it smacked of jingoism. The result was that when, in 1969–70, Catholics in Belfast and Derry were, in the literal sense of the word, forced to raise partition there was no existing organization for them to turn to naturally. So they created one. The Provisional IRA – notwithstanding allegations to the contrary from various 'leftists' in Ireland and Britain – did not 'bring partition into it'. The Provisional IRA exists because partition was going to come into it whether or not the right, the left, or anyone else thought this advisable.

The one organization which might have been expected to have preserved its anti-partitionist credentials in the period before 1969 was the Republican movement, which traditionally had offered little other than a '32-County Republic' as a remedy for all Irish ills. After the débâcle of the 1956–62 border campaign, however, the Republican leadership had turned away from their traditional politics – or lack of them. Realizing that their emphasis on purely military activity had played no small part in rendering them politically irrelevant, they sought to make an analysis which would enable them to build a firm political base for the future. Assisted by products of the British Communist Party such as Dr Roy Johnston – the Number One Republican ideologue of the middle and late sixties – they finally adopted a crudely updated version of Joseph Stalin's 'Stages Theory of Revolution'. This laid down that there were predetermined stages through which 'the Revolution' must pass, that it was not possible to skip stages, and that therefore it would be a tactical mistake to make demands designed to achieve, say, stage three before stage two had been reached. As Dr Johnston explained it to us in Derry in 1969, stage one in the Irish Revolution would be the winning of 'bourgeois democracy' in the North; stage two would be the achievement of an 'independent capitalist Ireland'; stage three would be 'socialism in Ireland'. In an effort to achieve stage one the Republicans had helped to found the Northern Ireland Civil Rights Association and had directed the energies of its members in the North towards the building of the NICRA as a 'broad-based movement for reform'.

Stated briefly the theory sounds crazy; and indeed it is. Still, in the mid-sixties it represented a genuine attempt by the leadership and the remaining rank and file of the Republican movement to escape from the narrow nationalism and gun-fetishism of the past and to lay the basis for a socialist republican organization. One of the effects of the adoption of the theory was that in 1968 and 1969 some Republicans were among those most vehemently opposed to mention of partition (that had to wait for stage two) and equally strongly opposed to attempts to argue socialist politics from civil rights platforms (that was stage three).

When after 1969 Northern Catholics began to raise the question of partition without waiting for the culmination of stage one the Republican perspective became irrelevant.

The non-Republican left failed to understand the importance of the national question because it had no coherent analysis of the situation. The Republican left failed to understand it because its coherent analysis turned out to be wrong. Moreover, the left as a whole had not managed by August 1969 clearly to demonstrate the difference which *did* exist between itself and the 'moderates'. And it was largely as a result of *that* failure that when the national question was posed anyway it was posed in stark and increasingly sectarian, for-or-against-partition terms.

Lacking any clear, common programme the original detonating group in Derry all but disappeared into the Citizens Action Committee. After that, left-wingers directed attention and hopes towards the People's Democracy. But while maintaining a separate existence the PD too was for a long time effectively submerged in the mainstream of civil rights agitation, establishing itself not as an organization with a programme qualitatively different from that of the 'moderates', but as a lively and aggressive ginger-group within the same broad movement. To the mass of the people it was clear that the PD in Belfast and White, Finbar Doherty, myself, and others in Derry were more militant than the NICRA or the Derry Citizens Action Committee. But it was not clear what we were being militant about. This meant that Unionist spokesmen were able plausibly to suggest that the difference was this: that the moderates were anti-Protestant – and the militants even more anti-Protestant.

This was plausible because it contained a tiny kernel of truth. There was one sense in which the civil rights movement was 'anti-Protestant'. The movement was demanding an end to discrimination. Its leading moderate spokesmen, such as John Hume and Gerry Fitt, insisted endlessly that this was all they were demanding. In a situation in which Protestant workers had more than their 'fair' share of jobs, houses and voting power the demand for an end to discrimination was a demand that Catholics should get more jobs, houses and voting power than they had at present – *and Protestants less*. This simple calculation seemed to occur to very few leading civil rights 'moderates', but five minutes talk with a Paisleyite counter-demonstrator in 1968 or 1969 would have left one in no doubt that it was not missed by the Protestant working class. There never was the slightest possibility of a movement demanding 'fair play' in Northern Ireland engaging the support, or even securing the neutrality, of Protestant workers. In terms of strict economics the only programme with any potential to undercut sectarianism would have been one which linked the demand for fair distribution of the relevant commodities to demands designed to increase absolutely the number of jobs and houses available for distribution. This would have involved campaigning for an end to the system of grants and inducements to private industry, a ban on the export of profits from Northern Ireland, direct state investment in areas of high unemployment. With regard to housing it would have meant demanding the cessation of repayments and interest payments by the Housing Trust and the local authorities to the London banks – payments which were and are crippling the housing programme in the North. In a phrase, it would have involved the elaboration of a comprehensive anti-capitalist, not just anti-Unionist, programme.

If any group had fought consistently – from within or without the civil rights movement – or both – for such a programme, the all-class Catholic alliance, which is what the civil rights movement became, could not have held together. And such a programme, hardly the normal stuff of Northern Irish politics, would not have attracted immediate mass support; but it might have enabled those of us in Derry at least to go on *talking* to Protestants in the Fountain in 1969. At any rate the matter was never put to the test. No such group existed or emerged.

By the middle of 1969 'the left' was established as those who were most impatient and most willing to run risks, who wanted to go along the same road as the moderates, but further, faster. It was not at all established that the left wanted to go along a different road. Thus, when the explosion came in August we were still imprisoned within the sectarian strait-jacket, forced to operate almost exclusively within the Catholic community but quite unable in doing so to give any clear lead to the Catholic masses. When the raging bitterness of Catholics in Belfast and Derry swamped Fitt and Hume and carried the partition issue on to the centre of the political stage, support did not pass over into the socialist camp. There was no socialist camp there to receive it. The politics of the Provisionals was predetermined by that fact, and it is bottomless hypocrisy for 'leftists' in Ireland, including and especially those who held leadership positions in the Official Republican movement before 1969, now to attribute the reactionary social attitudes of a part of the Provisional movement to the malign influence of agents of Fianna Fáil or some other suggested *diabolus ex machina*. The primary reason why the Provisionals *exist* is that 'socialism' as we presented it was shown to be irrelevant. The Provisionals are the inrush which filled the vacuum left by the *absence* of a socialist option.

That the national question was going to be posed in non-socialist terms, that it was going to be posed as a straight, sectarian choice between the maintenance of the border and the incorporation of the Six into the 26 Counties, was further guaranteed by the fact that the 'struggle' had been confined to the North. Since 1922 the majority of Protestants had understood and had been encouraged by their leaders to understand that any attack on Unionism was an attempt to extend the rule of the Dublin government of the day over them. For very sound reasons the Protestants were against that. Every self-respecting left-winger was against it too. At all times we were opposed to the low wages, the bad housing, the pathetic level of welfare benefits and Rome-rule in the schools in the South, and we were never done saying so. (In the period before August 1969 this indeed was one of the reasons why we were against raising partition at all – that Dublin had nothing to offer.) Thereafter, when we found that we *had* to deal with partition, we continued to make it clear that in supporting a fight to end the Northern state we were not advocating its absorption into the South as it stood.

But these unimpeachable sentiments had no convincing practical expression. We were not part of a fight *in* the South against the set-up there, and one cannot expect acceptance as an opponent of bourgeois nationalism if one is not seen to be part of a struggle against that section of the national bourgeoisie which is actually in power.

The point was illustrated by one early elaborate attempt to 'extend the fight to the South'. In April 1969 the People's Democracy organized a march from Belfast to Dublin. The marchers swung into O'Connell Street after four days on the road chanting, pithily enough, 'Lynch Lynch, lynch O'Neill'. What we meant was that Lynch and O'Neill represented two equally oppressive Tory régimes and that the working class in each area ought to rise up and eject them from power. There was a difference, however. We had been involved in a well-publicized campaign to bring O'Neill down. We had not been involved in any similar movement against Lynch. So what the people standing in O'Connell Street understood us to mean was that O'Neill, as a Unionist, would have to go, and that Lynch would have to go because he was insufficiently militant in pursuing this same objective. The difference between Fianna Fail and the revolutionary left was seen, not in terms of the social content of the societies they aimed at, but almost exclusively in terms of the intensity with which they were willing to attack the régime in the North.

That is how the Protestants in the North saw it: not that we were opposed to Catholic bourgeois-nationalist rule in any part of Ireland, but that we were in favour of its extension to every part of Ireland – even more strongly than the bourgeois-nationalists. And that was some difference.

All this resulted in confusion so total as almost to defy description. At one of our meetings at the bottom of Westland Street in the summer of 1969 I recall making a ten-minute speech which included the following two points: (1) that Lynch was a traitor because he had not sent his troops over the border when we needed them, and (2) that if he had sent them we would have opened up a 'second front' to drive them out again. Looking back, I find it difficult to know what the listeners can have made of this.

The absence of a movement in the South allowed the establishment there much room for manoeuvre, and they certainly needed it. And it gave the Provos, with their lack of any analysis of the South and therefore of any basis on which they *could* oppose it, an almost clear field in the North. It was they and their politics which began to dictate the course of events. What most significantly they dictated was the final destruction of the Orange machine as a ruling institution.

By the time the Provo campaign got into gear all tenuous links between Catholic radicals and Protestant workers had been broken. The mass of the Protestant population reacted to the campaign by demanding ever more stringent measures to smash the culprits down and made no distinction between Provos and Officials once the Officials joined in. That, after all, was the way such affairs had always been managed in the past. For a long time the British government tried to accede to the demand. The British strategy from mid-1970 until March 1972 was militarily to defeat the IRA and to hope that the Protestant population would be so cheered by this victory that they might readily accept a reformed Stormont. The Catholics, suitably demoralized by the IRA's defeat, would thankfully accept the reforms and wait quietly for them to have some effect. That is what the Falls curfew, the 'arms searches', the murder of Cusack and Beattie and internment were all about. It failed totally. The reason why it failed was that the Catholic guerrilla forces were not defeated. As long as they held out the strategy could not work. Bloody Sunday was the last desperate effort to make it work, and it was the most disastrous failure to date. Catholic intransigence increased tenfold. Once that became apparent, Stormont was doomed and the stage set for direct rule.

Direct rule presaged a new British strategy. But it did not connote any change in the overall British objective. Britain was still seeking to achieve a reformed 'democratic' Northern Ireland. That had been the central thrust of British

245

policy in Ireland for a decade. Direct rule meant merely that Heath's government had realized that buying off the Protestants by publicly brutalizing the Catholics was not going to achieve it.

When Stormont was prorogued a shudder went through the Orange machine of such violence that it began to fall apart. Unionism had always meant two things: Protestant power and the link with Britain. Direct rule made it dramatically clear that the Unionists now could choose one or the other – but not both. And they could only choose the former *in opposition* to Britain.

That had always been on the cards. That is what the Downing Street Declaration had meant, although Wilson was too cowardly a bourgeois leader to face up to it.

While the strategy of repressing the Catholics had been open and unashamed it had been possible for Unionist leaders to maintain or to pretend that the choice need never be made. Not any longer. What has happened to the Unionist Party since March 1972 is that the various elements within it have made their choice – always excepting Mr Faulkner, who has never been a one for making choices while there remains a sliver of a chance of having it both ways. Mr Faulkner has been impaled for so long on the fence that he could be torn neatly in half along the perforations.

Those, like Mr Craig, whose political careers had been entirely within the Orange-Unionist complex and who represented, objectively, small local business threatened by the expanding operations of outside monopolies, went so far as to contemplate cutting the link with Britain if that was the price to be paid for clamping the machine back on to the state. More sensitive to the overall needs of big business were men such as Roy Bradford who had achieved political eminence other than by threading their way up through the various Orange and Unionist institutions. They had no real commitment to Orangeism and in the year after direct rule they scuttled out of it, most of them issuing press statements drawing attention to that passionate commitment to common decency which had always characterized their public lives. Some of them joined the 'moderate' Alliance Party; others waited, refusing to place bets until the likely winner emerged more clearly.

Dr Paisley was the one significant Protestant leader who had been outside the apparatus from the start. He was a member neither of the Unionist Party nor of the Orange Order. It was for that reason that immediately after direct rule he plumped more quickly and decisively than any official Unionist for the maintenance of the British link. UDI, which Mr Craig was wont to canvass in his more flamboyant moments – that is, the machine back in place as the effective state apparatus and this time with no 'outside' supervision – would have denied Dr Paisley, as surely as his erstwhile enemies Bradford and Faulkner, any position in the power structure. For a time Dr Paisley therefore advocated the total integration of Northern Ireland into the United Kingdom and began to adopt the required 'British' attitudes to Southern Ireland, community relations, and so on. British commentators, rather charmingly, attributed Dr Paisley's new moderation to the civilizing effects of membership of the Westminster Parliament.

Direct rule lifted racks of Catholic politicians off the hooks on which they had been dangling. Mr Lynch, for example, had not had an easy time. Each British outrage against the Northern Catholic community had sent a gust of Republicanism across the border, and he had spent the previous three years frantically trimming his sails to suit the prevailing wind, all the time hampered by the fact that some of his crew were intent on making the craft capsize. Every time the British army killed a Catholic he would essay a Republican phrase. A few days after the funeral he would make the point that of course he and his government were firmly committed to a moderate course. After Bloody Sunday he sent a car-load of cabinet ministers to the requiem mass. A fortnight later, the furore having slightly calmed, his Minister of Justice, Donagh O'Malley, announced the introduction, 'if necessary', of 'military or special courts' to deal with Republicans. With Stormont gone Mr Lynch was able to make much less erratic progress towards an Anglo-Irish consensus. With only an occasional judicious genuflexion towards a Republican past, he was able gradually to tighten the screw of repression.

Direct rule forced the Protestant workers to realize that Britain cared little for them and their 'loyalty'. At the same time Catholic workers were being made to see that the South cared just as little for them and their 'Republicanism'.

This realization drained from the Catholic ghettoes some of the fierce passion for a united Ireland which twelve months previously had provided an emotional dynamic seeming to carry the community forward towards the achievement of the old goal. Coupled with the welcome given anyway to the end of Stormont and the fragmenting effect of incidents like the Best killing, it created in the Bogside and like places emotional and political confusion which led in turn to a degree of passivity. By the end of 1972 the Bogside was more ready than it had been for two years to accept whatever package the British government wrapped up in its White Paper. The fact that Catholic acceptance was not certain, the fact that there remains considerable doubt whether the collection of plastic conventionalities issued on 20 March 1973 will work at all in the long run, is attributable in large part to the factor which had removed Stormont in the first place – the dogged refusal of the Provos to give up.

If the Provos had heeded the chorus of advice to call a halt when Stormont was prorogued, support in the Catholic ghettoes would have flowed rapidly to the SDLP. The Provos did not have a *political* base from which they could have counteracted this swing. The Nationalist Party was withering away. The Officials and other leftists had solidified their organizations in some places but did not wield decisive influence in the crucial areas, Belfast and Derry.

Once established as the sole authentic voice of the Catholic masses the SDLP's team of quick-change artists – perhaps with an occasional dissenting voice from within – would have worked energetically to deliver their constituents up to the settlement Whitelaw was attempting to dictate, and, being proficient in such things, they might well have succeeded.

At first sight the SDLP is a curious party. Of the six members of the Stormont Parliament who came together to form it in the summer of 1970 three had been elected as Independents, one as a member of the Republican Labour Party, one as a Nationalist and one as a member of the Northern Ireland Labour Party. Mr Gerry Fitt was selected as leader because he was, on aggregate, the least unacceptable to all the others. Mr Fitt is one of those people whose personalities seem to create a particular atmosphere, no matter where they be.

Since it was formed by the coming-together of six individuals elected on four different platforms, each of whom had his own local power-base, the SDLP was riven with contradictions. But underlying all the contradictions there has been a basic consistency, the significance of which far outweighs that of various internal squabbles. In the period after August 1969 it was, from the British point of view, necessary to have an organization which could speak plausibly for the Catholic community in the North, which would be willing to accept, and capable of leading the community as a whole to accept, a reformist solution in the British interest. No such organization existed. The SDLP emerged to take on the role, and it is not without significance that members of the Labour Party front bench at Westminster were active in promoting its formation.

Since then it has striven manfully to coax the Catholics towards acceptance of the British objective. It has not been easy. The SDLP has not always been helped by the means the British government has used to attain its objective. Military assaults tended to stiffen the resistance and boost the

Republicanism of Catholic areas and on occasion this carried the SDLP, conscious of the necessity not to lose contact with its base, outside the pale of consensus politics – for example after the murder of Cusack and Beattie. In the six months after internment, particularly in the period immediately after Bloody Sunday when it appeared that Catholic rage might not be assuaged by any British reforms, a few of them took the precaution of hedging their bets – driving Provo leaders around for all to see or trying to break into the gelignite-trafficking business. But always the overriding aim was to find a way back into the bourgeois consensus. Mr Fitt never lost sight of this. During the period when the SDLP was pledging daily that it would not ever, under any possible circumstances, etc. talk to British ministers while a single man remained 'behind the wire', Mr Fitt's chatter was such as to lead a junior minister in Whitelaw's administration to lament to a political correspondent on a weekly paper: 'If this is what he is like when he is refusing to talk to us, God help our eardrums when he changes his mind.' As change his mind he did, of course.

At the beginning of 1973, as Whitelaw prepared to announce the Tory blueprint for the future, Provo persistence remained the single most formidable stumbling-block: because whether or not the Catholic community as a whole now adjudged attacks on the army to serve any worthwhile purpose, the mere fact that the attacks continued forced Catholics to take sides. And when it came to the sticking point there was still no doubt which side most of them would take.

Whitelaw's White Paper and the Bills based on it set out the framework within which British capitalism wanted Irish politics to be conducted. What, in summary, they said was this: the contradictions between the two sections of Irish capitalism have all but disappeared. A new relationship between the political representatives of these interests must therefore be found. At present this requires political office to be shared between the Catholic and Protestant middle classes. Under an executive so constituted Catholic workers will not and must not be exploited more than Protestant workers. Once an assembly is elected we shall look at its composition. If it appears likely to be able to work towards such a situation it will be allowed powers to do so. If it appears unlikely to be able, or willing, to achieve this, we will intervene directly to impose the structure we wish to see.

The White Paper was issued to the accompaniment of a massive propaganda effort. On the Sunday before its publication Cardinal Conway delivered a 'sermon' in Armagh Cathedral which came close to suggesting that it would be a sin to reject it. (It is to be noted that in the nineteenth century Catholic prelates in Ireland retained a certain regard for public decency and a modicum of self-respect; they waited until British governments had actually announced their plans for Ireland before issuing endorsements.)

In the months before and after the publication of the White Paper other stratagems, less public and innocent than the employment of pliant clerics, were used to maximize its chances of popular acceptance. British Army murder squads were sent out in Belfast to shoot up Catholic areas, hoping so to terrorize the inhabitants that they would accept whatever was offered. It was very difficult to distinguish between the activities of these units, who operated in civilian clothes from unmarked cars, and the parallel activities of right-wing Protestant assassins. Probably it will never be known what percentage of the 'unexplained' murders in Belfast since mid-1972 each can claim.

In the 26 Counties at the same time British agents were at work petrol-bombing police stations, suborning members of the Irish security services and, almost certainly, planting bombs and killing people. There was later to be some dispute between two of these agents, Kenneth and Keith Littlejohn, and British ministers about whether the Littlejohns had been in breach of orders when they robbed a Dublin bank; what was not in dispute was that the British government was sending criminals into the 26 Counties to make mayhem, in the hope of engendering a law-and-order atmosphere conducive to an anti-IRA crackdown. The most dramatic piece of such mayhem occurred on 1 December 1972, when two bombs exploded in Dublin while the Dail was debating the Offences against the State (Amendment) Bill. This lays down that if a senior police officer says that you did it, you did it.

The Bill was opposed by the opposition parties, Fine Gael and Labour, not because they were hostile to law-and-order, but because they saw no reason to help Mr Lynch out of difficulties which, they reckoned, were of his own making. Some dissident members of Mr Lynch's own party were also pledged to oppose the measure. It seemed certain, therefore, to be defeated. Then the bombs exploded outside, killing two and injuring more than a hundred. With the dead and the maimed strewn all around, concern for civil liberty quickly disappeared. A few Labour Party mavericks did hold on to the stubborn belief that to send a man to jail on the unsupported say-so of a policeman was going a bit far. But the main Party spokesman on such matters was Dr O'Brien.

The fact that some members of Mr Lynch's party were not enthusiastic about the bill – or about law-and-order generally – had much to do with the defeat of Fianna Fail in the General Election of February 1973 and its replacement by the coalition of former fascists and reformed radicals led by Messrs Cosgrave, Corish, Fitzgerald and O'Brien.

With both the Protestant and the Catholic communities in the North divided and confused, with a more-than-friendly government in the South and a blank-cheque endorsement from the leader of the Catholic Church, hopes for the success of the White Paper plan were high indeed. Elections for the 'Northern Ireland Assembly' were held in June. On the Catholic side, only the SDLP offered candidates in all constituencies and they swept the board. (The Provisionals, as an illegal organization, could not of course put candidates forward.) Before the election Mr Craig, having despaired of taking the Orange machine with him in a piece, had left to form the 'Vanguard Unionist Progressive Party' from as many of the components as he could get. He made an electoral alliance with Dr Paisley and they, together with various other dissident loyalists, won rather more Protestant votes than Mr Faulkner's Official Unionists. The Alliance Party did poorly, the Northern Ireland Labour Party disastrously.

After the election a protracted period of wheeling and dealing between these parties commenced in an attempt to form a 'power-sharing' executive. How far, if at all, the RUC should be reformed, and what powers, if any, a Council of Ireland should possess were notable stumbling-blocks. Formulas and counter-formulas were produced. Mr Whitelaw held meeting after meeting with representatives of the various parties. In August Mr Heath went to Belfast to express irritation that more rapid progress was not being made. In the same month the Provos started bombing Britain.

Since the publication of the White Paper, and presumably in order to assist in its implementation, claims that the Provisionals had finally been smashed multiplied. Such claims were compounded of – in about equal measures – fact, wishful thinking and misunderstanding.

The British tactic of directing both open and covert military operations, not at the Provisionals as such, but more generally at any community which might be tempted to give the Provos support, had met some success. It had made things very difficult for Provo activists; it had not made them impossible. In Belfast, where the pressure was strongest, the campaign continued, albeit at a reduced level. In Derry there was a bombing or a shooting weekly. Activity in the countryside was stepped up. In South Armagh particularly, Provo units fought and seemed to win a series of set-piece battles.

The decision to launch a campaign in Britain was taken

after much heartsearching. The fact that the British had taken the war to the people in the North removed any quasi-moral inhibition Republicans felt about involving British civilians. The new campaign was directly in support of what had become the Provos' central, short-term demand – that the British set a time-limit for the withdrawal of their troops.

Support for withdrawal among British people had been growing for some time. It had manifested itself in a 'bring the boys home' campaign among service families, in the speeches of various Labour politicians and in a general weariness with the whole question of Ireland. Mr Heath was quite explicit that the bombing campaign would not lead to the growth of this movement, nor would it direct the thinking of any British government along such lines. Rather would it stiffen the will of the British people to see the Northern Ireland operation through. Editorials in all major British newspapers made the same point. Time will tell. And, contrary to the assertion that the Provos are on the verge of defeat, time is something they believe they have in abundance.

The Provisionals are very young. Most of them were at school when the 'troubles' began on 5 October 1968. Since then, trouble is the only life they have known. They are very, very determined. If the Irish conflict could be settled by determination, by unconcern for personal aggrandizement, by an ability and a willingness to fight on against overwhelming disadvantageous odds, the Republicans would be assured of victory. On their own, however, such qualities are not decisive.

The Provos, in the North especially, are almost entirely working-class; but for the reasons outlined earlier many of them have little understanding of the need for working-class politics. At leadership level they are shot through with Catholic Nationalism. Their ideologists tend frequently towards a mystical conception of Nationhood and are, therefore, sometimes more concerned to re-enact scenarios from the past than to deal with present reality. Between 1971 and 1973, as the Provos developed into the most effective urban guerrilla army of the twentieth century, they managed marvellously to frustrate the designs of British governments. But finally to frustrate such designs it is necessary to have a coherent, class-based programme. Thus far, the only detailed programme the Provisionals have produced is the document *Eire Nua*, the centrepiece of which is a hare-brained scheme for four regional parliaments in Ireland. (This idea was first mooted by Brian ua Dubhghaill in the columns of *An Phoblacht* in 1934.) As an alternative to British plans it is quite unreal and despite energetic promotion it has excited little interest, much less gathered support.

Only the revolutionary left could offer the programme which is needed. If it is to do that it must quickly learn the lessons of the last five years. The left failed in Ireland. There is nothing to despair about in that. Even Trotsky made mistakes. Mistakes are disastrous only when one fails or refuses to recognize that they were mistakes and fails thereby to learn from them.

We have learned that mass 'influence' or prominent involvement in mass agitation is, despite sometime appearances to the contrary, meaningless and fruitless unless one is in the process of forging the political instrument necessary to lead such agitation to victory over the opposing force. We have learned that it is impossible to do that if one is not forearmed with a coherent class analysis of the situation and a clear programme based on it.

We need a movement without illusions in any section of the bourgeois class, which understands that the interests of all sections of the ruling class in Ireland, Orange, Green and pastel-pink, are now identical and that to attempt to ally with one section against another is to become the plaything of the enemy.

We need a movement which will deal with sectarianism by fighting all its manifestations. That means, among other things, confronting the power of the Catholic church in the South.

We need a movement which understands the continuing importance of the national question – that it cannot be avoided; and which will seek to show to those, like the Provos, who are tempted therefore to concentrate on it exclusively that to demand a 'united Ireland' in the 1970s without reference to its social content is to demand something which imperialism, in the long term, has no essential interest in denying and which a large section of the working class in the short term, has no essential interest in achieving.

In a phrase, we need to build a mass, revolutionary Marxist party. The opportunity to do it will present itself. In the Catholic community in the North, particularly among the rank and file of both Republican movements, there are many who seek for an analysis which will enable them to carry the struggle on to a new phase.

The apparatus of discrimination, the mechanism whereby Protestant workers had been given an illusory sense of privilege, has been wrecked beyond repair. Placed in the same social situation as their Catholic counterparts many Protestant workers will react – as they have done – by moving to the right. Others will recognize that the ferocious loyalty they gave to Orange leaders was never really reciprocated. They will recognize more quickly their identity of interest with Catholic workers if there emerges an organization with roots in the Catholic working class which is seen to be opposing the conservatism and clericalism which has shrouded that community for so long.

Either British imperialism or the Irish working class will win. There is no other social force in Ireland with a potential for power. In the end, the only thing which can prevent William Whitelaw putting his priorities into operation is the revolutionary overthrow of his parasite class. The future in Ireland lies with the small, but at last steadily growing, forces of Marxism. To make the revolution we need a revolutionary party. This book is intended as a contribution to discussion of how best to build it.